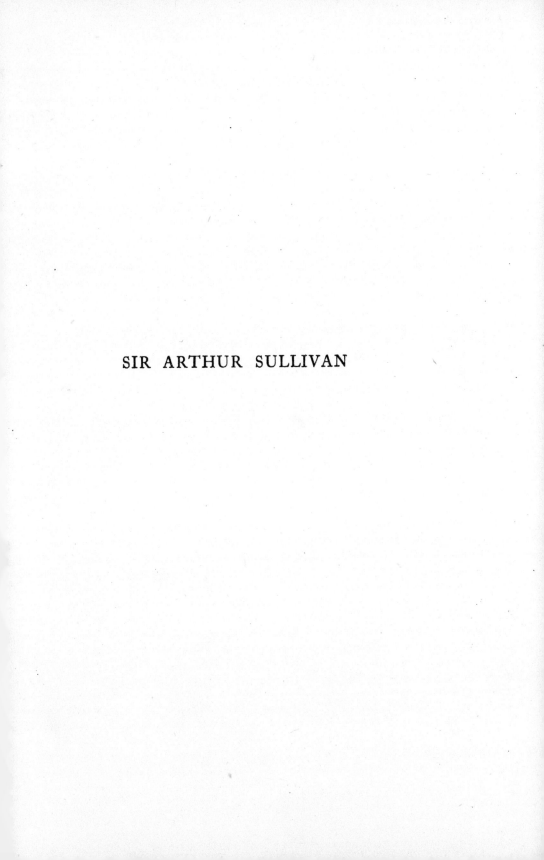

SIR ARTHUR SULLIVAN

Arthur Sullivan, at the time when the Savoy operas were at the height
of their success

SIR ARTHUR SULLIVAN

HIS LIFE, LETTERS & DIARIES

BY

HERBERT SULLIVAN

AND

NEWMAN FLOWER

SIX HALF-TONE PLATES

CASSELL & COMPANY, LTD.

LONDON · TORONTO · MELBOURNE · SYDNEY
& WELLINGTON

First Edition 1927
Second Edition 1950

Printed in Great Britain by Butler & Tanner Ltd., Frome and London

950

To
LADY GILBERT

CONTENTS

BOYHOOD

CHAP.   PAGE
I   OF BOLWELL TERRACE AND THE SULLIVANS   I

II   THE CHORISTER   8

YOUTH

III   LEIPZIG   21

IV   "THE TEMPEST" AND AFTERWARDS   34

MANHOOD

V   FOUR YEARS (1863–1867)   44

VI   THE SCHUBERT DISCOVERIES   52

VII   FIRST DAYS IN LIGHT OPERA   63

VIII   THE PARTNERSHIP BEGINS   75

IX   "H.M.S. PINAFORE"   90

X   A BALTIC JOURNEY AND "PATIENCE"   109

XI   "IOLANTHE" AND "PRINCESS IDA"   124

XII   "THE MIKADO"   138

XIII   MORE ADVENTURES IN AMERICA AND "THE GOLDEN LEGEND".   150

XIV   "THE YEOMEN OF THE GUARD" AND "MACBETH" .   .   167

XV   STORM—AND "THE GONDOLIERS"   .   .   .   184

XVI   THE RIFT IN THE LUTE   199

XVII   "IVANHOE"   204

Contents

CHAP.   PAGE

XVIII   ILLNESS AND "HADDON HALL" 214

XIX   THE END OF THE PARTNERSHIP 220

XX   ROYAL MEETINGS AND WAGNERIAN NIGHTS . . . 236

XXI   THE FINAL OPERAS 245

XXII   THE LAST PHASE 256

LIST OF WORKS 268

INDEX 285

ILLUSTRATIONS

Arthur Sullivan, at the time when the Savoy operas were at the height
of their success . . . . . . *Frontispiece*

FACING
PAGE

Arthur Sullivan, when he was a chorister at the Chapel Royal, St. James's 16

A letter from Arthur Sullivan, aged 15, to his mother 32

A page from Arthur Sullivan's notebook which he used in Vienna at the
time of the Schubert discoveries 64

The entry in Sullivan's diary after the first night of "The Mikado" . 144

Portion of a letter from Gilbert to Sullivan 144

A cartoon of Arthur Sullivan drawn by Linley Sambourne for *Punch* . 240

SIR ARTHUR SULLIVAN

BOYHOOD

CHAPTER I

Of Bolwell Terrace and the Sullivans

IF the pedestrian wandering through South London chanced
to go along the Kennington Road he might---if some
ulterior motive did not direct his footsteps otherwise—pass
up Lambeth Walk until he came to a quiet thoroughfare
known as Bolwell Street. Here, probably, he would pause
and wonder awhile at the solitude of the place. All the
clamour of London's outgoing and incoming traffic would
be to him a subdued and distant rumble. For Bolwell Street
appears like a small oasis, secret and obscure, between two
highroads from a mighty city.

In Bolwell Street little happens nowadays, but the dignity
of the Street and its Terrace remains. The austerity and
simplicity of the houses suggest that they once possessed an
importance which Time in its passing has stolen away. They
are severe, they are graceless. The tiled roofs have sunk
in places, and now seem to melt into each other with queer
and grotesque familiarity. They crouch lovingly together,
these houses, appearing to droop, as if for protection against
the ravages of the elements, like weary comrades into each
other's arms. The smart bricks from which they were builded
have become smutted and dulled by the fog and soot, or by
the sudden baking heats of nearly a hundred London years.

Happily, all changing life has left little marked impression upon Bolwell Terrace. The Victorian architect conceived the Terrace as a structure that would remain after the later builders of adventurous fashion and decoration should sleep with their fathers. So the curious little basements to the houses, the five steps up to each front door—those very dignified front doors—and the double handrails, which somebody in 1838 thought so necessary, remain, and are a part of the character of Bolwell Terrace.

Not that Bolwell Terrace has hidden the secret which is its pride. It carries on one of its walls—above the windows of Number 8—as if it were an escutcheon, a tablet which records why the Terrace should be remembered. The thoroughfares of London may change, the press and beat of the City's life may force new and wider arteries, now here, now there, but the tablet above the windows of Number 8 will probably stay the hand of one who would sweep the Terrace away to raise from its stones new buildings. For on this tablet is inscribed the following legend:

In this house was born, 1842, Sir Arthur Sullivan, musician.
Died 1900, and buried in St. Paul's Cathedral.

When Bolwell Terrace was first opened in 1838, an Irish musician named Thomas Sullivan, then aged 33, entered into the occupation of Number 8, and paid a rental of twenty pounds a year for the privilege of what was a modern and desirable dwelling-place. But, if the rent was small, it was the dragon of his expenditure, for he was in receipt of only a guinea a week in salary for playing the clarionette at the Surrey Theatre, where grand opera was then being performed. He had no means of supplementing his income apart from copying music and teaching. After the curtain had fallen on the last act at the theatre, he would sit long into the night at his work, just as the son who was to be born in that house was destined to do in the years that followed.

In Thomas Sullivan was a knowledge of music which slumbered because opportunity had passed his door. He worked ceaselessly, not because the guinea a week was the substance of life to him, but because he loved work. His understanding of musical instruments—especially the clarionette—and of

musical effeds was profound. His chances were small at the
Surrey Theatre, and he was not intended for obscurity.
Opportunity—real opportunity—may have swept by him,
but he passed on those talents that were his to his son.

In spite of the gloom that hung over his future, Thomas
Sullivan married. It was a love marriage; till the end of
his days it was a happy marriage, in spite of the new difficulties
which it provoked. The accord lay deeper than the marriage
bond. His wife, Maria Clementina Coghlan, had music in
her blood, for she had come from the Italian family of Righi
which, in its day, had been well known in artistic circles. A
Righi had been one of Michelangelo's principal assistants.
The Sullivans spent their honeymoon at Number 8, the bride-
groom going to the theatre as usual at the end of the day which
had seen the most adventurous episode of his life. And at
Number 8 they settled down. The furniture was indifferent,
there were no prospects beyond the guinea a week, but such
marriages are both wonderful and accommodating in the
little they demand when, in the mere pronouncement of
the marriage vows, comes completion.

On the second Christmas Day after their marriage, the first
of a remarkable pair of sons was born to them. But the
coming of Frederic Sullivan into the household at Number 8
sharpened the bitterness of adversity. The guinea a week
refused to expand. The music-copying dragged its painful
way through longer hours of the night. Number 8, after
Frederic arrived, held more romance than the stage of the
old Surrey ever knew. But, in spite of it, the three could not
live together; the family exchequer would not permit it. The
extra burden on the breaking string produced catastrophe.
Mrs. Sullivan, therefore, departed from the home and became a
governess, and the baby Frederic Sullivan was put out to nurse.

The disaster—if it was ever a disaster—did not separate
them. The letters of these two all through the worst days
of penury were constant, and revealed a fidelity beyond
reproach. Under the fierce hammering of ill-chance, they
saw the promise of better times shining in the courage of
each other's letters.

Ultimately circumstances began to improve somewhat.

Sullivan secured more pupils, and the music-copying increased. Although there was no release from anxiety, they snatched at this opportunity of coming together again. Once more the family of three was united at Bolwell Terrace, and on May 13th, 1842, Maria Clementina Sullivan, now 31 years of age, gave birth to a second son. They decided to call him Arthur Sullivan, but for some reason they changed the name to Arthur Seymour Sullivan when in June they took him to his baptism, and thus he was christened.

Thomas Sullivan rejoiced in the possession of these two sons; he wanted two boys and he had been given them. He was undemonstrative, but his placidity concealed a wealth of affection. His tastes were simple. If money had not been his good fortune, if the future promised him nothing at all, poverty did not spoil the enjoyment of life for him. He was supremely content with these two boys, and, with the fervour of one who obtains what he desires, he thanked God for them.

Although music had yielded him so little, except complete satisfaction in his work, he had secret hopes, even in those days, that one, if not both, of his children, would adopt the same calling. The ultimate discovery of the gift of music in Frederic, and, at a later stage, and in a more pronounced form, in the younger son, opened up for him the revelation of life. Frederic eventually forsook music for drawing. As the years passed Sullivan nurtured the love of music in the younger boy as some tender thing, encouraged it, and ultimately strove and fought at great personal sacrifice to make the road to music easier for his feet.

He did not know that in the fullness of Time the musical genius of that son was to bear him to his place in St. Paul's Cathedral.

*   *   *   *   *

In 1845, eight years after Thomas Sullivan went to Bolwell Terrace, a transformation took place. He was appointed bandmaster at the Royal Military College.

"The change," he wrote in a later letter, "drew me out of the awful life of sameness. It was like the coming of a new day."

4

Of Bolwell Terrace and the Sullivans

The appointment gave him a certain independence, an outlet for initiative. He found immediate success, so that promotion was not long withheld.

"Sullivan," his colonel wrote, "is one of the most remarkable people we have ever had here. He is what we have lacked—a real musician."

The association with military affairs was appropriate, since many years previously Thomas Sullivan's father, in a very unequal conflict with a recruiting sergeant in Ireland, had taken the King's Shilling. He had been drafted out to the war in the Peninsula, raw, his Army training very incomplete. He was a tough Irishman, and the Army needed tough men. He grew up with the Army; he smelt its powder and took its medals. The Army, that had at first crushed the strong adventurous spirit in him, proved his salvation. It chastened him into a fine soldier. Eventually, when the Napoleonic *débâcle* changed the face of the world, Sergeant Sullivan was sent to St. Helena to assist in guarding the monarch who for so many years had kept Europe in disorder and turmoil.

He preserved many memories of the Emperor in exile. He recalled how, on the day when his wife was to bear their youngest son, John Sullivan—brother of Thomas Sullivan, and uncle of the composer—a British soldier had been sentenced to the "cat" for rudeness to the Emperor. Napoleon in captivity was still a great man. He approached the British officer in charge and begged the man off, so that Mrs. Sullivan should bear her child undisturbed by the cries of the victim. The request, from one who had never considered suffering in his days of activity, was granted, and John Sullivan was safely ushered into the world.

This John Sullivan, who became a printer by trade, lived to a great age, and did, in fact, outlive his nephew Arthur. He was a kind of Methuselah of the Sullivan family, and his memories were as extensive as his years.

"Your father's sister, Elizabeth,[1]" he wrote once of his own sister to Arthur Sullivan, "used to receive sweets and cakes every morning from the hands of Napoleon, in conjunc-

---

[1] She eventually died Mother Superior of a Convent at Bruges.

Sir Arthur Sullivan

tion with another little girl, a daughter of Countess Montholon, whose husband was in exile also."

In the same letter he referred to a young Irish soldier from Cork who had been engaged with his father to guard the body of Napoleon whilst it was in process of being embalmed at Longwood House. Sullivan was sergeant of the guard in charge, and one night, while on duty with a comrade, Napoleon's heart, which had been taken from his body, was carried off by rats, and was only recovered by the two Irishmen just as it was being dragged under the wainscoting of the chamber.

John Sullivan always recalled vividly the return of the family from St. Helena, and on one occasion he wrote to his nephew:

"When the vessel that brought them home arrived at Portsmouth, there were several men in uniform on the landing-stage, and, seeing mother with a beautiful parrot in a cage, one of them shouted out: 'Come along, my good woman, we're waiting for that parrot.' The mater, thinking they were Revenue Officers who meant to confiscate the bird, said: 'If you want it, you'll have to come aboard for it.' Then darting down into the cabin she put the parrot in her pocket, and so escaped with it. I sold it for a good sum of money shortly afterwards. . . . Before she went out to St. Helena, the news came that father was dead. Of course she put on widow's weeds, and she wore them for five weeks when, one day, to her utter astonishment, he marched in and demanded his dinner!"

The veteran lived for many years yet, but not to see his son, Thomas Sullivan, become bandmaster at the Royal Military College. He would have rejoiced in the appointment, for the blood of the Army was now abroad in his veins. Nor did he live to see the Army marching to the music composed by his grandson. He became one of the honoured pensioners at Chelsea Hospital, and his widow was the first matron of the Duke of York's School.

The weft of character in Arthur Sullivan found its pattern in these forbears. The tough Irish spirit of his grandfather, which never wilted under adversity, was the certain heritage to the future musician from the soldier of St. Helena.

6

Of Bolwell Terrace and the Sullivans

His father, though he toiled assiduously through a difficult life, was a man in whom lay the best instincts of music. To some extent he was a dreamer, and generous to the strictest self-denial for those he loved, but his musical abilities were beyond question. From his mother Arthur Sullivan inherited much of his ability and imagination, and hers was the influence that helped to light the lamp of genius in him.

Twelve years after his father had been made bandmaster at the Royal Military College, Kneller Hall was opened as a training centre for military musicians, and Thomas Sullivan was at once attached to its staff. Much of the success of Kneller Hall in its first years was directly attributable to Sullivan's knowledge of instrumental organization. Albeit, the Army Paymaster rewarded him with a wage so meagre that it was often exceedingly difficult for the family of four to live. Musicians were cheap in the Army of those days, just as soldiers were cheap.

The exigencies of military life, and the greater exigencies of family finance, temporarily swept away Sullivan's desire that his sons should adopt Music as a profession. The future, he decided, must look after itself. But the genius of music was stirring in the second son before the parent was aware of it, and at the age of eight Arthur Sullivan was familiar with every instrument in his father's band.

The problem had solved itself. Whilst coaching the child in the first musical rudiments during these tender years Thomas Sullivan had shaped his son's career.

CHAPTER II

The Chorister

AT the age of eight Arthur Sullivan composed his first
anthem, *By the Waters of Babylon*, which clearly
indicated what was passing, as yet unformed and nebulous,
across his mind. Thomas Sullivan thereupon resolved to
send the boy to a private school, and let his destiny shape
itself. The school was situated in Bayswater, and was kept
by a Mr. William Plees, to whose credit be it said that he
quickly saw the musical talent in young Sullivan, and did his
utmost to encourage it whilst the boy remained under his roof.

Arthur Sullivan's letters home, filled as they were with the
commonplaces of youth, often referred to the music that was
beginning to absorb him. Delightful letters of ingenuous
boyhood. "I say," he wrote at the age of ten to his mother,
"I want to speak to you. One of our boys, Higham, has
taken a great fancy to my knife. He has a little gold pencil-
case which I have taken a great fancy to. He asked me
whether, if he gives me the pencil and a two-bladed knife,
will I give him mine. I have submitted this to your discretion. Mr. Plees has a lodger, Miss Matthews, who has a
nice piano, and I often go up to her room and play."

Later on he wrote that he had heard that he could get
a piano by paying 15*s*. 6*d*. down, which "I think is rather
dear." However, the fifteen-and-sixpenny piano did not
mature, and the dream to possess it drifted away when some
one told him that the strings would not wear.

He loved singing: he loved the music of choral singing, and
it gave birth to the dream which followed that to buy a piano
for 15*s*. 6*d*. He wanted to join the Chapel Royal. He
wrote letters home about it, but, believing that the musical

8

demands of the Chapel Royal would interfere with the boy's education, Thomas Sullivan was at first adamant in his refusal. More letters arrived at the Sullivan home—letters insistent in their demand for two things, the glory of being a chorister at the Chapel Royal, and the possession of a small chemical set containing "50 boxes like pill-boxes, 12 little bottles, a glass measuring cup and a little book containing 100 experiments sold at a shop in the Edgware Road for 5s. 6d." His father sent the stamps for the chemical set and a refusal for the Chapel Royal. But he had not heard the end of the matter. Had he not brought this upon himself by teaching the boy music? Letters, pleading to be allowed to go to the Chapel Royal, poured into the Sullivan home like shots from a gun. "It means everything to me," the boy wrote, as if he had suddenly visioned the whole plan of his life laid out before him. Thomas Sullivan pondered over the problem —then he gave way.

So, in 1854, Mr. Plees of Bayswater might have been seen going up Great Portland Street with a boy of twelve trudging along by his side—a boy in whom every nerve responded to excitement. The object of the pilgrimage was to see Sir George Smart, the composer, and organist of the Chapel Royal. The boy described the visit in a letter to his father:

"I went to Sir G. Smart yesterday afternoon. He is a funny old gentleman. He read your letter, patted me on the head, and told me that I must go to Mr. Helmore of Onslow Square, Brompton. I and Mr. Plees went there, and found that he had gone to live in Cheyne Row. When we got there he was not in and would not be back till 7, so Mr. Plees took me into a coffee shop and [we had] a cup of coffee and a roll each. Then we went back to Mr. H's. He tried my voice and said it was very clear. Asked me some of the Catechism. He seemed very pleased with me."

His surmise was accurate, for the same day Mr. Helmore wrote to Mr. Percy Smith who had been the first of young Sullivan's schoolmasters: "Little Sullivan has called here this evening. I like his appearance and manner. His voice is good, and if arrangements can be made to obviate the difficulty of his age being greater than that of the probationers in general, I shall be glad to give him a trial. I shall speak about A. S. to the Sub-Dean to-morrow, and, if he approves of his admission, I will write early next week to his father."

The stars in their courses were set for Arthur Sullivan. Although Mr. Helmore had a rule that no boy should be admitted to the Chapel Royal after the age of nine, he made a ready exception in Sullivan's case. In a later day Helmore frankly admitted that the boy impressed him at their first meeting, not so much because of his enthusiasm and the beauty of his voice, but because of the musical knowledge so unusual in one of his age. He saw promise in the boy at this interview, and he foresaw genius in him before he had been in his hands a year.

Arthur Sullivan was admitted to the Chapel Royal in Easter week, and, a couple of days after his admission, he was singing the solo in Nares's *Blessed Is He*. The youth with his wonderful voice had achieved his ambition. The red coat with gold braid of the Chapel Royal chorister, the solemn and beauteous music sung by picked voices—his own voice could reach with rich purity to A or B Flat—the note of religious melody which coloured his own composing in later years, and often stole, as if unaware, into his operas, gave him now all that his clamouring youth demanded.

Twice every Sunday and on each Saint's Day he had to walk in his heavy scarlet and gold coat to St. James's Palace and back, a total distance of over ten miles, but it failed to break his ardour. On one occasion the Duke of Wellington came up to him after a service, chatted with him awhile, then gave him half a sovereign. He was serenely happy. The tattle common to boyhood passed out of his letters; the little chemical set was forgotten; the riotous excitement of forbidden fireworks was a dead emotion. His thoughts followed only the paths of music with a certainty which Youth and ultimate success share together. Who shall say what memories of those first days in the Chapel Royal strayed into his mind when, thirty-four years later, he composed his superb song *The Chorister* in the space of six hours!

"I went to St. Mark's College to a concert on St. Mark's

day," he wrote to his father shortly after his admission to the Chapel Royal. "I had to sing a lot of 'Recits,' and the air 'Rejoice Greatly' in the 'Messiah.' Yesterday I had to sing a long solo in the Chapel Royal. The Duchess of Sutherland, Lord Hardinge, Lord Ernest Bruce (the Vice-Chamberlain) and Lord Wilton [1] were present. Watch *The Times* every day and most likely you will see all about it, for there was a reporter from there, and he took down my name and a good deal else. I had to pay 7*d.* for my trunk, and that broke into the money I was saving up for my chemical chest, so that I have only got 2*s.* odd left."

Helmore understood the soul of a chorister. He sent the picked voices from place to place. "Experience," he said to young Sullivan; "it will teach you more than I can hammer into you."

When the Duke of Albany was christened, Sullivan was one of the choristers chosen to sing the Anthem which Michael Costa had composed for the occasion [2]—a setting of the words: "Suffer Little Children to Come Unto Me." Costa rehearsed the boys himself. One day after Sullivan had sung the solo, he exclaimed: "Vell done, Soolivan, very vell done. But you must make your accent as clear as your words. Now listen to me," and Costa sang: "Soofer leetle cheeldren to come unto me, and forbeed them not, and forbeed them not, for of sooch is the Kengdom of Haven." [3] One can conjecture what would have happened if Sullivan had sung the words as the composer sang them. But the Prince Consort congratulated him on his singing, which, he said, had greatly pleased the Queen, and he then gave him a present of ten shillings.

"We went to Battersea to do *Judas*," young Sullivan wrote to his father after one of these occasions. "I sang all the solos. After it was over, Captain Claxton proposed three cheers for the young gentlemen, especially the one with the

---

[1] The father of a great friend in his later life.

[2] He was present also at the Duke of Albany's wedding and played by Queen Victoria's command.

[3] Chris. V. Bridgman, a fellow-chorister of Sullivan's. *Musical Times*, March, 1901.

black hair. Wasn't that a compliment?" Little more than a year later he sang in the Chorus at the first Handel Festival at the Crystal Palace, and his brother Frederic played the violoncello in the orchestra.

The boy had fallen into strict hands, and probably his father at Kneller Hall was glad of it. Though conscious of Arthur Sullivan's qualities, Thomas Helmore was prepared to give him no special treatment. Helmore with his John Bull countenance, his clean-shaven face and side whiskers, was a remarkable man. He painted admirably and exhibited at the Royal Academy; he also wrote a standard work on Gregorian music. The Chapel Royal Choir was his whole life. Groups of choristers came and passed, and he watched them go out like boats bent on discovering the secret kingdoms of music or failing in the quest. He never ceased to watch them, though they had long since passed from him. His hair greyed, became white, the stern mouth softened, the expression of severity mellowed. But he never really changed. He was Victorian in all he did, and thorough to the backbone. Arthur Sullivan's letters home reflected the iron hand of the master. "We have had the Gospel to write out ten times for not knowing it," he said in one letter. In another he said that "M" had been thrashed for not knowing the meaning of *fortissimo.* Then he wrote of his brother: "What is Fred doing cutting capers down in Suffolk, while I am getting cuts for not knowing this and that?"

And yet, in spite of his iron discipline, Thomas Helmore had a flaw in his armour. He revealed it when he wrote to Mrs. Sullivan a few months after her son's admission to the Chapel Royal: "Arthur sang a very elaborate solo in Church to-day, with a good many diversions in it, requiring flexibility of voice, very nicely. His expression was beautiful, it brought the tears very near my eyes (although the music itself was rubbish), but as I was immediately to enter the pulpit, I was obliged to restrain myself." One can see the phlegmatic Helmore shrugging his shoulders, marching with stately and rather pompous tread to the pulpit, too proud to let the boy know how his singing had moved him!

Helmore was like that, and, withal, the perfect master of

the Chapel Royal. When young Sullivan sat aloof and apart, dreaming over his music, his youthful compositions, Helmore became soulless and drove him back to the *Pons Asinorum.* "What sort of a figure do you think you're going to cut without general education!" he declared, and floundered the boy in Latin. He smothered him with many things it was never necessary for him to know, but he did not kill the soul of music in him. In later years Arthur Sullivan declared that Thomas Helmore was the greatest teacher of his youth. He was. And others, who never sang as sweetly as Sullivan, could have said the same.

With the passage of months, Helmore's confidence in young Sullivan increased. He pushed, he cajoled, he drove. He wrote letters to Mrs. Sullivan. "Arthur should try and get on in his Latin and other lessons," he said, "so that he may take rank in the school more proportionate to his excellence in music." Not content with plying the whip on one side, he then plied it on the other. "He should do every week about twelve exercises and compose a little something, a song or a sanctus, or an anthem, etc., of his own. This is the practical way of testing his industry."

The boy went on unperturbed. When he reached Devonshire to enjoy his summer holidays with a fellow-chorister, C. V. Bridgman, he spent almost the entire time in singing, and so engaged was he with his compositions that it was difficult to persuade him even to join a picnic party.[1] The letters home did not vary, save that there crept into these epistles certain musical opinions which showed the trend of his thoughts. "The cake is all gone, and *I shall soon be in want of another.* I like Mr. Goss's [2] new anthem very much; it is very fine. It opens with a fine chorus 'Praise the Lord, O My Soul.' *Very Fine.*"

Or again, Mr. Helmore had stopped the Fifth of November fireworks because he was in a temper, and he (Arthur) enjoyed everything at the Philharmonic concert except the playing of Rubinstein who "had a lot of clap-trap about him, whose own composition, lacking in even two bars of harmony or melody,

[1] C. V. Bridgman. *Musical Times,* March 1st, 1901.
[2] Afterwards Sir John Goss.

is a disgrace to the Philharmonic." So the letters went on—
the frank letters of a boy who wrote home everything, big or
little, that was alive in his thoughts.

Very soon Thomas Sullivan at Kneller Hall received fresh
proof of his son's brilliance. The boy had been taken to hear
Frederick Ouseley's work, *The Martyrdom of St. Polycarp*,
which Ouseley had composed for the purpose of his qualifi-
cation of Doctor of Music. The composition impressed
Sullivan deeply, and he wrote immediately to his father to
inform him that it contained a march admirable for military
purposes and suggested that it should be introduced to Kneller
Hall. "It is," he wrote, "the very march for a band." His
father replied that it was impossible to form any opinion of
the march because it was not in print. Arthur Sullivan
immediately cleared the difficulty away; he wrote out the
march with band parts *from memory*, and sent them to his
father.

Of the boys at the Chapel Royal at this period, only few
gave their lives to music. One was Arthur Sullivan, another
Alfred Cellier, and in later days they were destined to come
together in Sullivan's operas. Youth offers so many flickering
flames that are too easily snuffed out in the first draught of
life. Most of the boys in that choir had music in them, but
they drifted out to other callings and ultimately disappeared.
There were seven particular colleagues, and of these, apart
from Cellier, one became a wood-carver, another went into
a stockbroker's office, two migrated abroad, one qualified as a
chemist, another lost touch altogether, and the last re-appeared
from nowhere and ate a dinner with Arthur Sullivan a few
nights after the production of *The Gondoliers*.

His thirteenth birthday came and passed. Now his letters
home were filled with little else save music—his music and
demands for the musical scribblings which he had left at
home over the holidays; comments on the music he was
interested in, criticisms of performers and orchestras to which
he had had an opportunity to listen. If Thomas Sullivan had
ever held any doubt as to the career towards which the boy
was speeding, he could have held this doubt no longer.

The Mendelssohn Scholarship, which had been established

to the memory of the composer, was thrown open for competition in London, and the boy, who two years before had dreamed of the Chapel Royal as a medium for his musical ambitions, now looked higher. The Mendelssohn Scholarship, if it could be won, would open the gates of music so that he might pass through. But his chances of winning the Scholarship were small. At the final there were seventeen competitors, each one older than himself. He certainly did not believe that the Fates would be kind to him, for he wrote home that although his chances were meagre he was going "to make a fight for it."

Six weeks after Sullivan reached his fourteenth birthday— in 1856—the competition was held in London, and to his intense surprise he tied with the oldest competitor—Joseph Barnby, a boy of seventeen who, in later days, was to be one of the firmest friends of his musical life. A second contest to decide the winner was quickly arranged, and Sullivan won it. Shortly afterwards, on July 4th, 1856, he received the following letter:

"I have much gratification in informing you, by order of the Committee of the Mendelssohn Scholarship Fund, that you have been elected a Mendelssohn Scholar. The Scholarship you are to hold for one year, commencing as the 21st September next at the Royal Academy of Music. I am, etc.—

"C. KLINGEMANN.
Hon. Sec. Mendelssohn Committee."

Ecstatic letters home followed the announcement. It was not the achievement that pleased him so much as the prospect of the great musical training that now lay open to him. "I have chosen music, and I shall go on," he wrote, "because nothing in the world would ever interest me so much. I may not make a lot of money, but I shall have music, and that will make up if I don't."

To his father there came what was possibly the greater joy. Maybe he saw in his son's achievement a reward for all the care and thought he had put into his letters to the boy, for the saving and self-denial he had exercised for him. When he received the Mendelssohn Committee's letter he forwarded it to his wife and wrote:

"Can you not picture my very great pleasure when I read the enclosed this morning? I could not suppress the tears that accompanied my prayer to the Almighty for his goodness. You will, I hope, call on Mr. Helmore and arrange about Arthur. . . . Bring the darling little fellow down with you if you can for a day or two. I long to embrace him. Kiss him a thousand times for me."

The Committee's letter gave Thomas Sullivan the happiest day of his life. Never afterwards, though he watched the boy climb, and was his most severe critic, did he experience the same emotion, for the winning of the Mendelssohn Scholarship was the first fruits of his prayers.

Although he was still a chorister at the Chapel Royal, Sullivan now attended the Royal Academy regularly. After his first visit he wrote to his mother: "I went to the Academy this morning at 10 o'clock, and learnt that I was to have a lesson a week from Professor Bennett [1] on the pianoforte, and one from his preparatory master Mr. O'Leary. I am also under Mr. Goss for harmony. Mr. Geinson asked me if I played any orchestral instrument, and I said 'No.' He then asked me what I should like to learn, and I responded 'the violin.' He said he would see me about it. I am also going to try and learn Italian."

The extra duties which the Royal Academy brought to him left him little leisure, but, in such spare time as he had, he ran an unorthodox orchestra. On wet half-holidays he would persuade his fellow-choristers to stand round the pianoforte at which he presided, and each boy had a comb covered with paper. He would take a comic song and turn it into a Psalm tune. He was brilliant at fugue. Sometimes he would exclaim to a colleague, "Now, like a good chap, sing or whistle me something." Whereupon he would sit down at the piano and make an excellent fugue of the subject given him. [2]

"Every time I have made up my mind to sit down and write to you," he said in a letter home, " some fellow or another is

[1] Afterwards Sir William Sterndale Bennett.
[2] C. V. Bridgman. *Musical Times*, March 1st, 1901.

From the painting in possession of Herbert Sullivan, Esq.

Arthur Sullivan, when he was a chorister at the Chapel Royal, St. James's

sure to turn me away from it by asking me to come and lead our band, which, by the bye, consists of two 'French Squeakers,' which, by singing through them, produce a twangy sound like an oboe, 2 combs, a cover of a book for a drum; I am organist and go on composing something for it. By the bye, I have sold 22s. worth of my songs to different gentlemen. This is very good, but I've only got 26 here. You've got 23, have you sold any yet?" His letters, unfortunately, do not record what the songs were. He was, however, composing continuously at this period, and a bishop gave him a sovereign when he discovered that the piece Sullivan had sung was of his own composing.[1]

At the end of his first year at the Academy he had no idea that the Scholarship would be renewed. He believed that he would now be thrown on his own resources, and that his parents would by some means or other provide for him. But he took the Mendelssohn Examination again, and then wrote to his mother: "At the Mendelssohn examination on Thursday they made me sing one of my own songs. When I had done, Sir George Smart said I was not to sing another note, or else I should have no voice at all afterwards, because it was breaking. He is going to speak to Mr. Helmore to-morrow about it, for this short notice has taken me quite *aback* as the sailors say. If I am to leave next week, what am I to do for *board*, *lodging*, and *washing*? Do write as soon as you can, or perhaps I shall have to go to the *Union* for relief." But he might have spared himself anxiety, for he was re-elected Mendelssohn Scholar for the second year in consideration of the progress he had shown.

---

[1] Although this is the first recorded instance of Sullivan receiving a gratuity for his composition, he shortly afterwards mentioned a second occasion, for writing home the day after his thirteenth birthday, May 14th, 1855, he had said: "When I had composed my anthem I showed it to Sir George Smart, who told me it did me great credit, and also told me to get the band parts copied out and he would see what he could do with it. So I copied them out and he desired the Sub-Dean to sing it, so it was sung. The Dean was there in the evening and he called me up to him and said it was very clever, and that perhaps I should be writing an oratorio some day. Thereupon he shook hands with me with a half-sovereign." The Dean's kindness would seem to have been excelled only by the accuracy of his prophecy.

During these two years he was closely watched by Sir George Smart, who was in truth his musical sponsor. Perhaps he recalled the day when Mr. Plees had come up to his house with the dark-eyed boy of twelve who, eager-faced and shy, had asked for a place in the Choir of the Chapel Royal. Perhaps he recalled his first impressions of the latent talent in the boy, and he was not a man who made many mistakes. Pedantic, sometimes a little self-important he may have been, but, behind a very thin veneer of pose, was concealed a big heart and a most lovable nature. So many who had attained the musical honours that were his would have let the youngsters choose their paths and pass on forgotten. But this was not his habit. He constantly called for Sullivan and put him through a brief examination to determine whether music was really holding him, or if the little chemical set, the rides through London which delighted the child, were pleading more successfully the claims of youth. After each examination came a little grunt from the great musician, a brief, a very brief word of praise or none at all. But he knew, and the boy knew, that he was satisfied.

The simplicity of Sullivan, the affection for his parents remained undiminished. He loved his home and all the trivial things that mean so much to boyhood. In November 1857 after cogitating with his brother, he wrote thus to his mother on her birthday: "Fred and I have been ruminating for the last half-hour what to say to you on this happy occasion. May God bless you and keep you to see many more brighter and happier years than this has been. We have no presents to offer you, but as a small token of affection, if you like to keep that 30s. you owe us for singing money you are quite at liberty to lay it out in whatever way you like."

During the second year of the Scholarship, Sullivan's progress became so pronounced that the Committee resolved to send him to Leipzig. He was openly talked about as the most promising pupil at the Academy. He climbed as if with ease, where others floundered and laboured. What was the task of a week to those about him, was frequently a matter of only a few hours to the boy who used to sit on the stairs and dream about the singers to whom he had listened. This

18

transition to Leipzig was assured, and, almost a year before it took place, Sir George Smart wrote to him: "After you left us on Friday, we were discussing the importance which a good knowledge of the German language would be of to you, and Mrs. Klingemann[1] most kindly said, if you would come to her house, she would with pleasure give you lessons gratuitously twice a week, of course at such hours as shall suit her convenience. Now this very advantageous offer demands your ready acceptance."

The offer was accepted. With counterpoint and harmony, German became his intellectual food. "I frankly hate the language," he wrote home, "but it is so expressive, and one cannot hate that which expresses what one feels, for that, after all, is the essence of music."

In the following July Mr. Klingemann wrote to him again: "You have been re-elected a Mendelssohn Scholar for another year in order to enable you to pursue your studies in the Conservatoire at Leipzig during the course beginning Michaelmas next."

It was a rule at the Chapel Royal that every chorister on leaving should receive a present of sixty pounds from the Queen, and a Bible and a Prayer Book from the Bishop of London, provided that the cause of his leaving was the breaking of his voice. But Sullivan's voice had not actually broken when he left to go to Leipzig. What was to be done? The rule had been inviolate. The Queen must be assured that the boy's voice had actually broken before the sixty pounds were forthcoming. The Bishop must also have assurance of the broken voice before the stock Bible was taken out of the personal cupboard in the Palace. But Sullivan's voice refused to break completely. There was only one thing to be done. He had been a great singer; he was still a great singer. The Privy Purse allowed him the sixty pounds; the Bishop produced the Bible and the Prayer Book, and so, between them, they made the boy the only exception in a law as inviolate as that of the Medes and Persians.

Very cautiously Sir George and Mr. Klingemann still watched him. Just before he was to leave for Leipzig they

[1] Wife of the Honorary Secretary of the Mendelssohn Committee.

decided to put him through his notes for the last time, as if to be sure that he had not failed them. Sir George Smart sent for him to come down to his house at Chertsey. He instructed him to bring with him the Overture which he had composed, and which had been performed at the last concert of the Academy, together with some of his other compositions. Sullivan had no consciousness of being one still under observation. He wrote home [1] extolling this great white palace, its lawns, its fruit gardens, its conservatories, "and *such* grapes." Those grapes held a greater importance in his mind than the detail later recorded in the letter, which really meant so much more. "I played my sketches to them, and then they said I had very much improved and Sir George made me read from sight, score, etc., which pleased them much."

Sir George and Klingemann had put him through his last drilling and he was unconscious of it. They nodded their wise old heads one to the other.

"He'll be all right," said one of them.

But the boy was still thinking about the grapes! Leipzig belonged to to-morrow, but the grapes were part of to-day.

Such were the thoughts of a boy.

[1] September 15th, 1857.

CHAPTER III

Leipzig

WHEN Arthur Sullivan reached Leipzig in September, 1858, the musical reputation of the City had reached its zenith. The Gewandhaus Concerts were the talk of Europe. Mendelssohn, who had founded the Conservatoire with the sum of 20,000 thalers—which sum he had persuaded the King of Saxony to devote to the cause from a bequest —had been dead eleven years.

The influence of Mendelssohn and his music had begun to wane. A fresh trend of musical thought was stealing like a new current through Leipzig, indeed through all Germany, whilst in London concert halls and drawing-rooms Mendelssohn remained the one sweet singer beloved of the British people.

The Leipzig Conservatoire, when Sullivan reached it, was governed by Ignez Moscheles. Moscheles was an amazing figure. He had once walked with Beethoven. He had taught Mendelssohn harmony when the future composer was but fifteen. He dominated European music in his day, not so much on account of his compositions, which never reached a great height, but because of the spirit he kept alive in music. He wandered from country to country, the standard-bearer in a great campaign for music. His concerts were superb ; his following greater than that of any musician of his day. He adored Mendelssohn and Schumann, possibly their intimate friendship helped this adoration; and he grieved over the "sugary" compositions of Chopin as unmanly. He dined at royal tables, and was the best friend of any young musician of talent.

Once during the Mendelssohn rule at the Conservatoire he had passed through Leipzig. Mendelssohn immediately organized a great musical reception for him. The best musicians from all German and Austrian cities were drawn to the reception; the finest music ever heard in Leipzig on any occasion was given in honour of this man. Mendelssohn was crafty in the honour he paid to Moscheles, for he sought the advantage of the occasion to persuade him to become a professor of the pianoforte—the instrument of which he was a master—at the Conservatoire. Moscheles, possibly overcome by the reception, agreed, then vanished across Europe again. He swept through Holland, so that there came to Leipzig echoes of the most resplendent concerts given at Amsterdam. In Paris he caused a furore in a single night. He appeared in London, created a sensation with his concerts and his conducting of Beethoven's 9th Symphony; moved on to Edinburgh, and other provincial cities for single performances of extreme brilliance. Then he disappeared as quickly as he had come, and suddenly and unexpectedly reappeared at Leipzig to take up his post. In spite of the luxurious manner in which he had been entertained, and the extravagance poured out upon him by Society, he was frugal almost to meanness in his mode of living. But he would work twelve hours a day at Leipzig, and then still longer if he could help a young musician to success by private lessons at his house.

This was the man into whose hands Arthur Sullivan passed in 1858. Just before the boy came out, Moscheles had written a letter concerning him to Mr. Klingemann, a letter of some importance since it reveals the mode of tuition which young Sullivan was to know. He wrote : [1] "Sullivan's excellent talent and the manifold instruction he got from his former masters gives him a rank among the young musicians, which claims the highest interest, and cannot but be flattering to our Conservatoire which he is to enter. The Conservatoire founded by Mendelssohn is still administered after his inten-

[1] August 26th, 1858.

tion. Pianoforte and violin players have to learn the truly beautiful in the classics. You know who are the teachers. Hauptmann for counterpoint, Richter for organ, Rietz for instrumentation and composition.[1] Although Leipzig only *tolerates* the music of the future, the taste here is not for being so rigid as *only* to like the music of Sebastian Bach's deep learning and antiquated manner. We like our young composers to find a *juste milieu*, and develop elements fit for every school of Art. Our weekly evening conversations in presence of teachers, pupils and some dilettanti, give the pupil an opportunity to practise in chamber music, piano, violin, violoncello and singing, and even to produce their own compositions. If in rehearsal a composition proves good, it is included in the programme of a public examination concert which commands a full orchestra. As you tell me Sullivan has a peculiar talent for composition, it stands to reason that his chief time will be devoted to this branch.''

It is quite certain that when Arthur Sullivan went to Leipzig he had no belief that he would ultimately earn his living by composition. He desired above all things to become a master of the pianoforte, and this in spite of the success which had so far attended his composing. The pianoforte was the instrument he loved, and he believed that he would ultimately excel any player in London at this period. Certainly when he came into the hands of Moscheles and Plaidy his knowledge of the instrument was already far in advance of that of any other student at the Conservatoire. Moscheles openly said so.

Exactly when he changed his mind finds no record in his letters. Even when the change was made, his future as a composer did not foreshadow itself to him, for he decided to become a conductor. It may have been the influence of Ferdinand David, who was his instructor in orchestral work and conducting, which was responsible for this determination. David was without equal as a conductor in Central Europe, and he had the additional gift of being able to inspire a pupil,

[1] Two of these, together with David who was also at Leipzig, and Moscheles himself, were four of the Committee of six appointed by Madame Mendelssohn to select which of Mendelssohn's manuscripts should be published after his death.

B

however backward, with his enthusiasm. Like Moscheles,
he spared himself nothing in helping his charges. Tired
out with his work at the Conservatoire, he would sit up half
the night with a pupil, giving him private instruction without hope of any other reward than could be found in bringing the backward one into line with his fellow-students. Not
for nothing had Mendelssohn written of David: "He is
sympathetic, straightforward, and as honest a man as ever
was, a first-rate artist, and one of the few who love Art for its
own sake, come what may."

Though he worked assiduously at the pianoforte, this obsess-
ing desire to become a conductor before all things remained
with Sullivan for at least a year; certainly it did not entirely
leave him for many years. David had fired his enthusiasm.
He took long walks with the Professor, discussing, as he said
in one of his letters, nothing else but orchestral work and
orchestral effect. He even wrote to Sir George Smart about
it, but the latter had perceived perhaps that genius for an
even greater art lay in the youth he had sent to Leipzig,
for he threw cold water on the project when he replied:
"I am glad you are devoting your attention to pianoforte
playing, for that will be of the greatest importance in your
musical progress. As to your becoming a conductor, that
office is not so lucrative in this country as it was in former years,
for there are now so many conductors that some of them are
non-conductors."

Few of the students at the Conservatoire were well off, and
Sullivan, unquestionably, had less money than most. He
kept a very careful record of all his expenditure and sent the
account, properly balanced, to his father once a month. He
knew, no one better, that every unnecessary thaler spent meant
an additional burden on the parent who was compelled out of
his meagre income to finance his son's living expenses. The
boy's strenuous efforts towards Spartan economy are indicative
of the deep affection which was part of his nature, and which
never left him.

"I am now living in the same house with Taylor [1] of whom
I have written you sometimes," he remarked in one of his

[1] John Franklin Taylor.

first letters home. "I have a very nice room with a little sleeping apartment attached to it for which I pay *five* thalers a month. For breakfast *four* thalers a month. I dine at a Restauration with Wright, Taylor, etc., for 6½ thalers a month, and a very excellent dinner it is at the price. I mean to be very careful, and not spend a groschen more than I can help. I began fires to-day for the first time. I did without them as long as I could, but it is so very cold now that I thought it right to have one, for I cannot work in the cold, and I am working very hard now. By my living with Taylor we shall both be able to save a good deal. In the evening when I am at home we write together, and therefore only burn one fire and one light. Supper costs me very little. One evening at Moscheles', one at David's, Barnett's, Oldenbourg's, etc."

He went everywhere and saw everything, provided no expenditure was necessary to do it, and would often walk miles to avoid paying a few groschen for a public conveyance. Only at Christmas, when in honour bound he was compelled to give presents to a host of acquaintances who had befriended him, was the monthly account hard to balance, though he had stinted himself for weeks beforehand in order to be able the better to meet the extra call.

In spite of the fact that he was one of the hardest worked students at the Conservatoire—since there were many sides to his musical talents to be explored and developed—this ceaseless battle with expense continued, nor had it the smallest effect upon his high spirits. It was almost in a spirit of reluctance that he wrote to his brother Frederic about a new coat. "Ask Father if I ought to have a new coat, for having worn this one a whole year, almost every day, the nap has all worn off, and if I want to go for a walk with the Moscheles' or Davids I am obliged to put on my dress-suit, which of course, besides wearing out, looks so absurd in the afternoon."

But the swing of the economic pendulum was bound to occur. He and another English student, named Payne, pooled their resources and went off in a spirit of mad adventure for a brief holiday to Schandau during the hot weather. At the end of the first week it occurred to Payne that it would be wise to call for their hotel bills, since their common purse had distinct limitations. When the bill arrived, Sullivan found that he would, after the bill was discharged, possess exactly one thaler, and Payne five. They had insufficient money to pay their fares back to Leipzig. But whilst looking at the Royal Palace Sullivan received a smart blow on the back, and turned to see an acquaintance from whom he promptly borrowed two thalers. The problem of the railway fares was solved. "Well, we got back to Leipzig at last," he wrote, "after having bullied all the porters, guards and railway officials on the line, who naturally thought us young 'Milords' with hundreds of pounds in our pockets instead of a few groschens."

At the end of his first year at Leipzig the Mendelssohn Committee renewed his scholarship for a year longer. He worked harder than ever. His letters, written to his parents and the friends who had helped him, were full of keen enthusiasm. Then, by way of showing his gratitude, he composed an anthem and dedicated it to Sir George Smart who, as head of the Committee, had been the most staunch friend of all. Sir George replied (February 22nd, 1860):

"DEAR SULLIVAN,

"Your letter dated the 4th of last month, also the MS. of your Anthem *We Have Heard With Our Ears* were left (*not by post*) at my house on the 11th inst. I sincerely thank you for the Dedication, and beg you to believe that I fully appreciate your kind intention by this compliment. According to your request I sent the copy to Mr. Helmore; in answer to my note he writes: 'I am very much pleased with its general character, although I have not yet had time to fully examine the general excellencies.' "

A couple of months later Julius Rietz, who had been Sullivan's Professor for composition, left Leipzig to take up a post at Dresden. To the student this blow was severe. It was unquestionably Rietz who had turned his thoughts more seriously to composition, and Rietz who, with no honeyed words, rejected his compositions when he believed the young student could do better. Rietz, too, was responsible for the works of which he approved being produced. Rietz, silent,

26

phlegmatic—a stolid figure in whom emotion seldom showed, and then only as the wind might ripple the surface of a still pool and pass—had a great affection for Sullivan, and possibly greater belief in him than any other professor at Leipzig.

"Poor Rietz, I'm sorry he's gone," Sullivan wrote to his father the day after the great man had shaken the dust of Leipzig off his feet and departed, "he was a splendid master and very kind to me. There were no end of grand doings to honour him before he went. We got up a celebration in the Conservatorium, giving first a small musical performance consisting of nothing but his works, and which I had to conduct (in a white tie; I come in for all the conducting now) and then presenting him with a dozen magnificent silver knives and forks in an elegant case. The scene in the concert last night when he retired was something tremendous. The cheering, the bouquets thrown, his desk covered with wreaths, and a splendid silver *bâton* laid on it—a present from some of the subscribers to the Concerts—made the whole affair most brilliant and exciting. In the last rehearsal when the orchestra and he took leave of each other, there was scarcely a dry eye. We brought him to the station last night, as he went to Dresden directly after the Concert, and sang him a farewell serenade."

Sullivan was now composing incessantly. He was nearly eighteen, and his outlook would seem to have changed somewhat. Rietz's influence, his disapproval when work was poor, his flicker of a smile when it was good, led Sullivan towards his future. Not till many years later did he realize how this influence had moulded him and borne him towards the place he was to occupy in British music. And yet very few of these compositions made under Rietz still exist, for many were given as presents to mark birthdays or the coming of Christmas. His interest in the pianoforte was as keen, his love of conducting as warm—"Mr. David says I shall make a capital conductor," he wrote home—but the lure of composition was growing. It was beginning to control him as the real means of expressing all that was waking in his brain. Even his brother Frederic sent him some words of his own to set, and they were promptly spurned in so cutting a fashion that the Muse in his brother must have died a wretched and rapid death.

"Those words of Fred's [1] are very neat I must confess. They inspired me with a brilliant idea directly; all good words do; something of the following classical style came into my head.   Don't you admire it?

Tell Jack that if he wishes me to set any words to music they must be proper ones, not such rubbish as that, where sense, rhythm etc. are all wrong and confused."

But this spirit of banter between the brothers was ever alive.   Shortly after the above episode, Fred Sullivan wrote to his brother a criticism of *Messiah*, and received the usual chastening retort from Leipzig: "The slighting manner in which you speak of Handel's 'Messiah' is an insult to Sacred Music—and besides it is no fault [of his] if it is not exactly lively.   Perhaps you would have liked him to have interpolated a few Comic songs in each Act."

The flood of Youth was carrying him along with joyous exhilaration.   He composed; he conducted.   The only luxuries which he never denied himself were good concerts and the opera.   In the cheapest seats at the Opera the boy with music dreaming in his soul would sit accompanied by a couple of companions, criticizing with that unfearing frankness which is Youth.   Music was almost the food on which he lived, until, like one who has gorged too well, he turned against that on which he fed.   "I get horribly disgusted with music," he wrote to his mother only a few days after he had sent his Anthem to Sir George Smart, "one hears a little too much of it here.   I miss Handel and the Sacred Harmonic

[1] The two brothers always called each other "Jack," and this is one of the few allusions to Frederic in Arthur Sullivan's letters in which the proper name is used.

Society very much. It will be indeed a treat to hear all that again.".

But it was only a mood—a mood perhaps of home-sickness. The letters that followed were as enthusiastic as ever. He had seriously come to the conclusion that only music ever held everything for him, he said. He had begun a new composition; he detailed all that this meant to him, how it enthralled him. A little later—in June, 1860—came a birthday letter to his father recording the production of this work that had held him so long.

"I enclose you a programme of our last *Prüfung*," he wrote. "You will doubtless on looking over it recognize one of the names. Translated the thing stands as follows: 'Overture to T. Moore's Poem *"The Feast of Roses"* from *Lallah Rooke* (E Major), composed by A.S.S. from London (conducted by the Composer).' *The Feast of Roses* is the German name for *The Light of the Harem*. It was such fun standing up there and conducting that large orchestra! I can fancy Mother saying now 'Bless his little heart! how it must have beaten!' But his little heart did not beat at all. I wasn't the least nervous, only in one part where the drum *would* come in wrong at the rehearsal in the morning, but he did it all right in the evening. I was called forward *three* times at the end, and most enthusiastically cheered. I shot the bird, as Mr. Schlemitz said, *i.e.* had the greatest success in the whole *Prüfung*."

He was now preparing to return to England in the autumn. There was little more that Leipzig could teach him. The hot summer of 1860 had made Leipzig an inferno. He yearned for the sea, even for the hustle of London—that London which he believed to be so indolent in its musical creeds. He blamed London for its apathy towards Schumann—this new star that had blazed across his horizon. He smote London hip and thigh because it had not acclaimed Schumann; London still faithful to the choruses of Handel. London still wrapped up in the softness and dainty luxury of Mendelssohn, the sensuous lure of Chopin, and yet a London with its circumspect musical life to which he longed to return. Writing of Schumann to his father some months later, he said:

Sir Arthur Sullivan

"I cannot understand the reason why the Critics, and in consequence, musicians themselves, should be so prejudiced against that unfortunate composer; at the very name of Schumann an English musician draws back alarmed, shrugs his shoulders, and mutters a few words about Zukunftsmusik, Weimar, etc., and, doubtless with fine judgment, will point out the marked difference between Schumann and Handel! And yet if you ask that man to tell you conscientiously if he ever heard a note of Schumann's music, he will probably be obliged to answer—No. I am called away suddenly. Joachim and Clara Schumann are going to give a little private *matinée* in the Conservatorium for the benefit of Masters and Students only."

The interest in his letters at this period does not lie in music alone. He was conscious of all the colour and movement of a German city, and he recorded it in these letters. The German Christmas was to him a feast of reverence—the humanity and selflessness of it stirred a kindred chord in him.

The stormy politics of War in which Germany was involved passed as some airy cloud above his head which he was almost too engaged to watch. Columns of marching soldiers impressed him with the silliness of it all, and he turned again to his music as if the column of soldiers had marched out of his memory. The heat and the sullen indolence of politicians seemed to create an atmosphere of unrest and discomfort.

Then came the great storm [1]—the worst ever recorded in Germany—and he described it vividly in a letter:

"If you have not heard ahead of the fearful storm, I must tell you something about it. At about six o'clock Monday evening, the clouds began to blacken, the air became hot and oppressive, and 'a thick darkness' came over the town. Then came the long distant moans of the wind, a few thick large raindrops, and finally the whole storm broke out with wild fury, such as the oldest inhabitant declared never to have seen the like of. We were in the Grunma Street, and had to rush for our lives for the hailstones would have killed us had we been exposed to them too long. We soon took shelter under an archway, and here we had the opportunity of observ-

[1] August, 1860.

30

ing the whole scene. And terrific it was. Chimney-pots were falling, tiles rolling down, windows smashing. Women and children screaming. Horses taking fright and running away. In fact, everybody imagining that the Last Day had come. Every window that looked towards the West was smashed, the average size of the hailstones being that of a *hen's egg* without· exaggeration. It only lasted about ten minutes, but it was perfectly melancholy to see the state of the town. Trees were torn up by the roots. Of the 80 front windows of the Post Office not a pane was left. The streets were covered with tiles and broken glass and heaps of conglomerated hailstones. The large Augustus Platz looked like a huge sea of ice. When I got to my house I found it flooded, half my music spoiled, the piano, bed and sofa, together with my boots and clothes wet through and full of bits of glass. I was driven out of the house for two days. Although glaziers have been telegraphed for from Dresden and other towns, I see no probability of my windows being ready before another week. The damage done is calculated at 700,000 thalers, or £105,000 sterling. Three horses were struck dead by lightning, and three or four children by hailstones, besides numerous ·people being injured."

Sullivan intended to return to London in the autumn, when the extra year granted to him by the Mendelssohn Committee would expire. That he would be given the opportunity of remaining longer did not occur to him; certainly he knew now that he could expect no further extension of the Scholarship from the Committee. A letter which he wrote to his father in July reveals what took place.

"My dear Father,—

"I should not have delayed writing so long, but I have been waiting for a letter from Sir George Smart which I expected and which came yesterday. I enclose it in order that you may read it, and will at the same time explain what he is referring to. I wrote to him to tell him that my masters, especially Mr. Moscheles and Mr. Plaidy, wished me to stay here until Easter, as my execution would by that time be much improved, and I should also probably play in the Grand Public Examination, besides deriving divers other benefits therefrom. Now read his letter before you go any further. Now, you see, to stay here half a year longer would cost, I have calculated, 40 pounds, from which, subtracting Sir George's kind offer of 5, would leave you the sum of 35 to pay, and which you are in about as good a position to give as I am to fly. Therefore, dear Father, we must give up the Easter plan, and look forward to meeting each other in 3 months in that miniature Paris, Brussels. Polish up your French, and hurrah! for the beefsteaks and porter! Of course, if one of those mysterious friends that one reads of in novels should turn up and send me 50 or 100 pounds anonymously, I have no objection to take it. I would nevertheless though, if I were you, write and thank Sir George for his kind offer which you cannot accept."

Two months passed; the last weeks at Leipzig seemed to rush rapidly to a close. The little German parties, the comrades of the Conservatoire, the professors, old Moscheles and David—these things, these people had become so great a part of Sullivan's life that he feared to see them pass. The prospect of London and its reunions pleased him, but Leipzig and its friendships had yielded him so much.

His father meanwhile had secured employment at Broadwoods, the pianoforte makers, thus supplementing his small income at Kneller Hall. "I go four nights a week, having four classes to instruct," he wrote to the son at Leipzig, "and what with preparing lessons for each, and my duties at the Hall, the task is almost too much for me. I have 48 in all at Broadwoods, and what they have done already is the wonder of everyone."

Although his elder son Frederic was engaged in an architect's office, the parental purse was still woefully insufficient. But by some means or another, he raised the money necessary to keep Arthur at Leipzig till Easter.

The surprise of the boy was only surpassed by his gratitude. "How can I thank you sufficiently, my dearest Father," he replied, "for the opportunity you have given me of continuing

32

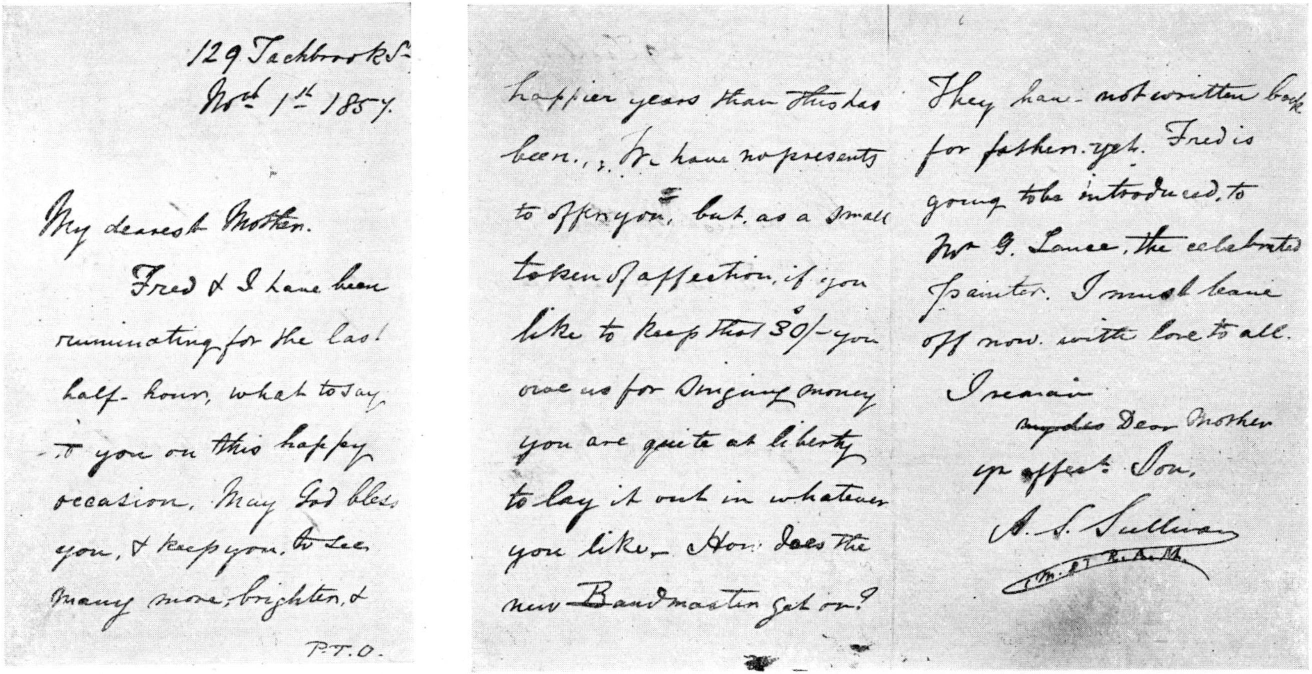

129 Tachbrook St
Nov. 1st 1857.

My dearest Mother.

Fred & I have been ruminating for the last half-hour, what to say to you on this happy occasion. May God bless you, & keep you to see many more, brighter, &

P.T.O.

happier years than this has been.. We have no presents to offer you, but, as a small token of affection, if you like to keep that 30/- you owe us for Singing money you are quite at liberty to lay it out in whatever you like. How does the new Bandmaster get on?

They have not written back for father yet. Fred is going to be introduced to Mr G. Lance, the celebrated painter. I must leave off now with love to all.

I remain
Dear Mother
yr affect. Son,
A. S. Sullivan
S.M. R.A.M.

A letter from Arthur Sullivan, aged 15, to his mother

my studies here. I am indeed very grateful and will work very hard in order that you may soon see that all your sacrifices (which I know you make) have not been to no purpose, and I will try to make the end of your days happy and comfortable. I had given up all idea of staying longer, and indeed was making preparations for my journey home, therefore the surprise was greater for me."

The Conservatoire Directorate also showed its appreciation of the young student by an act of grace which made him write home a few days later: "Mr. Schlemitz, the Director, has exempted me from paying for the Conservatorium during the six months I am going to stay here. When I went up to thank him for it, he said to me: 'O, yes, we will let that be entirely. You are a splendid fellow (*prächtiger kerl*) and very useful. We all like you so much that we can't let you go!' So, you see, that is 40 Thalers (£6) less in the expenses."

A couple of months later Sullivan began to score his music to *The Tempest*. Of so little significance was the work to him at the outset that he first mentioned it only in a postscript to a letter! "I am writing music to *The Tempest*." But as this work progressed and took form it absorbed him. It absorbed his letters. The music might sound harsh, he wrote, but it was different, and when his father became accustomed to it he might like it very much indeed. And in the following April (1861) it was performed. On the way home through Berlin he wrote from the Capital concerning it: "*The Tempest* was performed in the *Prüfung* last Saturday, and was most successful. I was called forward three times afterwards."

He reached home with the manuscript in his bag. The student days were over; the Chapel Royal and Leipzig mere chapters now in a youth that was passing. He had no means with which to face the serious business of life. But he had Youth and his Art, and—the manuscript in his bag.

CHAPTER IV

" The Tempest " and Afterwards

WHEN Sullivan returned to London he found that its music had changed but little during his absence of two and a half years. Mendelssohn was still the unchallenged god of every musical *salon* and suburban drawing-room. None other had arrived to displace him. London had sought none other. It had become customary to find one's way to musical understanding through Mendelssohn. One learned to play by means of his simpler melodies; one sang him as the only true interpreter of that spirit of docile domesticity and lavender love-affairs which had emanated from the throne and percolated into the English character. The old songs, with their blatant vulgarity and suggestion, had decayed slowly as the Victorian age progressed. The pendulum swung full circle. Now the songs in favour carried a sickly sentimentality which was sometimes an insult to one's intellect, as were the accompaniments to the instrument that was compelled to be used for their utterance.

Schubert was scarcely known, and seldom played. Not that this was entirely the fault of London, for only a small range of his works could be obtained at the music-sellers'. As for Schumann, few knew his name, and fewer still had ever heard a note of his composing. Sullivan glowed with an ardent fervour for both of them. He talked Schumann with such enthusiasm, that those who had known him before the Leipzig days were quite certain that he had returned with a bee in his bonnet.

The youth went straight to his old haunts—the Chapel Royal, the Royal Academy of Music. The latter was now in the hands of Cipriani Potter whom Sullivan afterwards

34

described as "a dear old man, with beetling eyebrows and high stuck-up collars, a fine musician who had known Beethoven very well." Sullivan did not hide his creed; he expounded Schumann with a wealth of detail. The old man shook his head. "I'm very sorry about Sullivan," he said to a mutual acquaintance afterwards; "going to Germany has ruined him."

Sullivan stuck to his opinions.

"But, Mr. Potter," he said one day when the Schumann argument waxed strong, "have you ever heard any of this music that you are condemning?"

The head of the Royal Academy confessed that he had not, whereupon Sullivan said:

"Will you play over some of Schumann's Symphonies with me? I have them arranged for four hands."

It meant conversion—ready conversion. Night after night Sullivan played the Schumann Symphonies with him, until, at the end of three months, Potter was the warmest advocate of Schumann in England. He drew in other apostles. George Grove, then Secretary of the Crystal Palace, was one of them, and the friendship between Grove and Sullivan (which began over a Schumann symphony) developed into what was almost the greatest friendship in the life of either.

The meeting of Sullivan and George Grove occurred in the gallery of St. James's Hall during a concert. Grove observed some one staring at him through the glass panel of the gallery door, and inquired of his companion the name of "the engaging young man" who watched him, to which his friend replied, "Oh, that's Sullivan; he's just come back from Leipzig." [1]

The introduction which took place in the gallery of the concert hall led to a Schumann discussion. Grove had heard of Schumann, but was unfamiliar with his work. But he had the open mind of a great man, for Grove was a great man. When Sullivan on a later evening showed him Schumann's First Symphony in "B Flat," Grove was so struck with it that he put it down for immediate performance at the Crystal Palace.

[1] "Life of Sir George Grove": C. L. Graves, p. 92.

Sir Arthur Sullivan

That chance meeting between two musicians laid the foundation of the Schumann cult in England. Item by item Schumann's music began to appear in London concert programmes. At first London thought him advanced; comment was cold. Sullivan and Grove nevertheless held to their opinions, and the latter performed Schumann as often as he could, while the former "preached" him into that circle of young musicians who were endeavouring to stir the musical thought of London from its lethargy

Meanwhile, Sullivan was working away at the manuscript which he had brought home in his bag. He re-scored more than half of it. *The Tempest* as it was performed at the Leipzig *Prüfung* was not *The Tempest* the Crystal Palace was to hear at Easter 1862. Not that Sullivan's fervour for Schumann involved the destruction of the Mendelssohn creed. He loved the music of Mendelssohn up to the end of his days—his *Tempest* bears the distinct influence of Mendelssohn—but his object at this time was to beat down that barrier which had been created by London opinion against any new thought in music.

London was not really musical in the sixties; it knew very little about music. Probably in all its history London had never known less. And it refused to be informed that music, other than that which it knew, could ever be music. It dreamed Mendelssohn and blared a Handel chorus, and called such a performance the beginning and end of all musical Art. The fact that Queen Victoria played Mendelssohn, loved him as no other British monarch had ever loved or even deigned to notice a composer—if one excepts the official acknowledgment of Handel by George II—was, in England, a sufficiency that made Mendelssohn—and held him—a fashion. Queen Victoria never played the piano well. Beethoven would have flustered her fingers, and have conveyed to her mind a conglomeration of arithmetic. But she loved a melody—slow and sweet. And were not Mendelssohn's music, his profile and his life alike beautiful? On Sunday evenings at Windsor she played him, gave him the laurels, and conveyed her approval of all he did. So had the Mendelssohn cult been spread.

'The Tempest" and Afterwards

Sullivan, at this stage, was entirely cosmopolitan in his musical beliefs. Apart from Schubert and Schumann, for both of whom he stood as the true apostle, he adored Beethoven, Handel, Mozart, Mendelssohn and Weber.

He found Weber reproduced in some of the melodies that were drifting into London, and commented on the rank plagiarism of phrases from him. A few months after his return Sir George Smart wrote to him a letter about Weber, in the course of which he said: "On March 5th, 1826, C. M. von Weber came on a visit to my house, No. 103, Great Portland Street, in which he was found dead in his bed early in the morning of June 5th, 1826; he had locked his bedroom door, therefore I had to break it open."

Sullivan had begun to love Weber in the Leipzig days, and he never broke his faith in the later years when Weber became no better than a pleasing orchestral turn at a theatre, and almost completely disappeared for a couple of decades from the concert programmes.

The problem now before Sullivan was that of earning a living, but several means contrived to that end. Thomas Helmore gave him a post to teach the Chapel Royal boys— not music, but the ordinary curriculum. He also gave music lessons; George Grove made him professor of Pianoforte and Ballad singing at the Crystal Palace School of Art. Dull work that could lead nowhere. Balfe and Wallace were now at the end of their day, and, in the belief that he could be their successor, Sullivan worked into the small hours on his *Tempest*.

A meeting with Jenny Lind at this time began a friendship that was only terminated by death. She possessed what he always declared to be the most beautiful voice which he had ever heard. Even in his Chapel Royal days her singing had aroused in him almost the fervour of worship. She had enslaved London, and become one of London's few justifiable crazes. Ladies bought "Jenny Lind stockings"; they slavishly copied her dress; and every garment she wore brought articles in the papers that dictated fashion. She now took Sullivan to task for overworking. "I am sorry to hear that you have not been well," she wrote to him. "Do you give too many lessons, together with too much—sleep (oh!) and too much indigestible food? (Oh! oh!) You don't doubt but that only the desire of seeing you shake off all that does not belong to a gifted nature dictates these *seemingly* harsh words from your true friend Jenny Goldschmidt."

The Tempest was finished and sent at once to George Grove. Doubtless Sullivan hoped that Grove would have the work produced at the Crystal Palace, but, since the work of only the greatest musicians was then being performed at the Palace, it was a bold adventure he sought. Grove, however, had the courage of his convictions. The music impressed him, and, after discussing it with August Manns, who was then in control of the Palace music, they decided to perform *The Tempest* at Easter, 1862, on Saturday, April 5th.

"This was the great day of my life," Sullivan wrote many years later. "It is no exaggeration to say that I woke up the next morning and found myself famous. The papers, one and all, gave me most favourable notices, and the success was so great that *The Tempest* music was repeated on the following Saturday. All musical London went down to the Crystal Palace to hear this second performance. After it was over Charles Dickens, who had gone with Chorley [1] to hear it, met me as I came out of the Artists' room. He seized my hand with his iron grip and said: 'I don't pretend to know much about music, but I do know I have been listening to a very great work.'"

The success of *The Tempest* music settled Sullivan's future. The changing moods he had known at Leipzig—the desire to be a maestro of the pianoforte—the desire to conduct the best orchestras he could get together — these things were forgotten as if they had been the chrysalis shell from which the active life had departed. He dedicated *The Tempest* music to Sir George Smart, sat himself seriously down to the work of composition, and secured the post of organist at St. Michael's, Chester Square, in order to derive the means to live while he composed. The Rev. the Hon. Francis Byng, afterwards Lord Strafford, was then Vicar of St. Michael's. Meanwhile Sullivan gave up teaching. "I hated teaching,"

[1] Musical critic of *The Times*.

he said, "and nothing on earth would ever have made me a
good teacher. The first guineas that I gave up for the work
that I wanted to do were those that came from giving lessons."

The choir at St. Michael's provided him with work that
he loved, and he rapidly made it one of the best in the West
End. His later composing of Church music proved how
full was his understanding of religious thought in music.
He once said that his music was really intended for the
Church. Lying somewhere in his brain was an inexhaustible
store of melody upon which he drew to express religion as no
contemporary composer could express it, except perhaps
Stainer and Gounod.

He was proud of his choir, ardent and never failing in his
duties towards it. "We were well off for soprani and con-
tralti," he wrote at a later date, "but at first I was at my wits'
end for tenors and basses. However, close by St. Michael's
Church was Cottage Row Police-Station, and here I completed
my choir. The Chief Superintendent threw himself heartily
into my scheme, and from the police I gathered six tenors,
and six basses, with a small reserve. And capital fellows they
were. However tired they might be when they came off
duty, they never missed a practice. I used to think of them
sometimes when I was composing the music for 'The Pirates
of Penzance.'"

The *Tempest* success had carried him at once into the best
musical circles in London. New friends came in plenty,
but he cultivated only a few. Grove, Sir George Smart,
old Helmore ageing and, with the years, growing prouder of
his late pupil; Otto Goldschmidt and his wife, Jenny Lind,
with whom Sullivan spent the Christmas of 1862. "Come
down on Christmas Eve," Goldschmidt had written, "and
help to light the tree. We have been playing your *Tempest*,
and Mrs. Goldschmidt has been repeatedly singing the pretty
song and duet. She likes the work *very much*."

And there was Frederic Clay, a genial, wandering soul,
and a slave to music. He was two years older than Sullivan,
and he had studied with Hauptmann at Leipzig in the days
after Sullivan had passed under the same professor. In the
Leipzig room in which Bach had composed some of his

greatest fugues, Hauptmann taught them both. Clay afterwards composed *I'll Sing Thee Songs of Araby* and sold the copyright for five pounds. True, the publishers gave him a bonus of twenty pounds when the song had percolated into nearly every home in England, but £25 was all he ever made out of it. Fred Clay, whose brothers were Ernest Clay Ker Seymour, and Cecil Clay, was the son of James Clay, the great whist player and a member of Parliament. Fred Clay held a clerkship at the Treasury, but on the death of his father he relinquished it and lived a life for music. He was a great bohemian, and introduced his friend Sullivan into a social circle which was entirely new to him. He composed *The Sands of Dee* and *She Wandered Down the Mountain Side* (the latter he sold for five pounds), both big selling songs in their day.

It was Fred Clay who eventually introduced Sullivan to Gilbert and thereby brought about the great Savoy partnership.

In the same year that Sullivan made his début at the Crystal Palace with his *Tempest*, Clay appeared at Covent Garden with *Court and Cottage*, a setting of a libretto by Tom Taylor. The production failed. Clay smiled, as he always smiled in good times and bad. He appeared in the Clubs with his spirit as joyous, his *bonhomie* unimpaired. He had only just begun to work, he said, and he went back to his songs. He would sell a song as soon as he composed it, without regard to its qualities. He lived for what was going to happen; indeed, to him, to-morrow was always that tremendous mystery so rich in promise ere it comes.

Sullivan had the satisfaction of having his *Tempest* music performed repeatedly at the Crystal Palace before the end of the year. In one of his letters to Mrs. Frederic Lehmann (the Lehmanns were his intimate friends for over a quarter of a century, and with them he constantly travelled abroad) he said: "Joachim [1] is very low-spirited at our being all together in perfect enjoyment without his being able to join

---

[1] The great violinist who began to play the violin at the age of five, and afterwards went to Leipzig under Mendelssohn in 1843, when Arthur Sullivan was a year old. He eventually became leader at the Ducal Court of Weimar under Liszt.

us. He asked most affectionately after you and Miss Dickens.[1] Is he smitten? I see a great deal of him. They did a little *Tempest* at the C. Palace concert yesterday, and he, Clay, and myself dined at Grove's afterwards, and spent the pleasantest of evenings playing Bach's sonatas for viol and piano, Salon Stücke of Spohr's (very slow), talking no end of pleasant nonsensical small-talk, and finally all coming home together smoking gorgeous cigars, running down Meyerbeer and praising Auber."

The success of *The Tempest* urged Sullivan to set six Shaksperian songs, and he sold the copyrights of them all for five guineas apiece. His famous song *Orpheus With His Lute* followed, and, in spite of the fact that it was one of the popular songs of its day, he received no more than ten guineas for it. *O Mistress Mine*, *If Doughty Deeds* and *The Willow Song* were all composed at the same time, and brought him but ten guineas apiece. He found publishers willing enough to take his songs, but not so eager to pay even a living wage to the man who composed them. Not that he was greedy for money, for he was now able to keep himself. It was George Grove who pointed out to him at last that the terms he was receiving for songs that were selling most profitably for their publisher were ludicrous.

"I was getting on," Sullivan said, "but by this time I had come to the conclusion that it was a pity for the publishers to have all the profit. My next song *Will He Come?* went to Messrs. Boosey, on the understanding that I was to have a royalty on every copy sold. And oh! the difference to me! I did very well with *Will He Come?* and never sold a song outright afterwards."

Once the royalty was assured, the flood of songs continued. Some of the most popular songs of the Sixties, *Sweethearts*, *Looking Back*, *Once Again*, *Let Me Dream Again* were written in the space of a few hours. He worked with amazing rapidity, and, before one song was finished, the melody of another had formed and was complete in his brain. He was then staying a good deal with George Grove at Sydenham, and the urge of his friend was largely responsible for the flood

[1] The daughter of Charles Dickens.

of songs which continued for eighteen months, and now began to bring him in something of an income.

"I have worked like a horse this laſt week," he wrote to his mother at the end of 1862, "and have got over a great deal of ground. Mr. Grove and I write on till two every morning, and then have a cigarette and go to bed. I thought to have seen you perhaps on Thursday. I was at the Church (St. Michael's), and gave the Police a long grind."

The friendship with Charles Dickens ripened; the noveliſt declared that young Sullivan was a genius, and some day London would discover the faſt for itself. At the end of the year, Dickens and Sullivan, accompanied by the Lehmanns and Chorley (who was then writing a libretto for Sullivan to set), went off to Paris. The noveliſt was in his gayeſt mood, and the simplicity of the man left a lifelong impression upon Sullivan. "I was never so conscious of the greatness of that man as I was during that Paris visit," he said of Dickens in later years.

They hurried from point to point in Paris, with Dickens as a guide; visited all the operas, dined at small and very excellent reſtaurants which Dickens in some mysterious way had discovered or been told about, called on the principal musicians of the day—Madame Viardot, Rossini—Dickens arguing with the cabmen in bad French—and talking, talking all the time, as voluble and intereſting as his books.

Rossini, the ageing, kindly man, with his white hair and little black skull-cap, fascinated Sullivan. They played duets from *The Tempeſt* music together, and Rossini would after-wards sit crouched in a low arm-chair, his face as white as his hair in the half-light of the ill-lit chamber. There he expounded in his subdued melancholy voice all that was happening in the world of music, as if he were a returned ghoſt, who had the power to look down and forecaſt the changes that music was to know. He gave brilliant recep-tions; musicians, poets, painters crowded his Art-ſtrewn room. The babel of conversation would suddenly hush—the maeſtro was going to play. He would creep to the piano rather painfully with his rheumaticky knee-joints, run his fingers over the keys, and drop into a minuet, or improvise something of quaint delicacy that was lost ere the instrument was dumb.

One short note Sullivan made on December 10th about Rossini is of particular interest:

"Went with Courtenay to see Rossini at 3½. He was out. Went back in half an hour and were admitted to his bedroom *à la Française*. The old gentleman was very kind and affable; asked me if I sang, as every composer for the voice ought to be able to sing. Invited me to his reception the same evening. I found Carl Rosa [1] there playing a new violin sonata by a young German. Rossini introduced us: 'M. Sullivan—M. Rosa.' We looked at each other and burst out laughing. The idea of being introduced to each other by Rossini was too droll. I went again in the evening with Courtenay, saw a lot of blue and red ribbons—Delle, Sedie, Lacource, and his wife, etc.—accompanied Courtenay in Fred Clay's 'Point du Jour,' and slipped away unseen. Thursday at 9½ a.m. I was at Rossini's house and found him alone, composing a little pianoforte piece for his dog! He played us a new minuet, very pretty and quaint."

The year 1862 came to its close—the year that had made Sullivan the most discussed among the younger musicians. During the year Frederic had married Charlotte Lacy, and his brother was best man.

Sullivan was not earning a large income, but at least he was living by his Art, and not many musicians have subsisted by music when their years were but twenty. The battle was hardly begun; he must still struggle for his place, for his opinions. He came back to composing, the passion for work blazing in him. For the first three weeks after his return he slaved through the night, and dawn, glimmering into his room, found him bent over his paper untired.

[1] Carl Rosa had been at Leipzig with Sullivan.

MANHOOD

CHAPTER V

Four Years (1863–1867)

DURING the Leipzig years, Sullivan had wavered as to the form of his career—he had wished in turn to be a pianist, a conductor, a composer. This indecision, due to the talent he possessed for each method of musical expression, had definitely solved itself with the composition of his *Tempest* music. With his mother and father he was now living at Claverton Terrace, Pimlico. He still played for long stretches on the piano daily, he studied pianoforte technique with the old enthusiasm, he conducted, he hustled his policemen and others at St. Michael's into greater choral efficiency, but composition had now become the purpose of his life.

This certainty brought with it a new problem, a new uncertainty. He had not yet assured himself as to the form his composition would take. The stream of songs continued to pour from him because they brought him a livelihood, but, during the four years that followed his return from Paris with Dickens, he also composed a suite of ballet music, a symphony, a musical comedy (never performed) his *Kenilworth* music, and, finally, *In Memoriam*.

The ballet music, named *L'Île Enchantée*, was more or less the result of an accident. Shortly after *The Tempest* was produced, Sullivan told his friend Michael Costa, who then controlled the fortunes of Covent Garden, that he wished to study grand opera. He spent endless hours at Covent Garden watching rehearsals and the business of putting on an opera. Ultimately Costa offered him the post of organist in the theatre, and a little later he asked him to compose a work specially for Covent Garden. *L'Île Enchantée* was the result. It hindered rather than helped Sullivan's progress. He was hampered by stage limitations so imperative in ballet. "It means to me," he declared, "that I've got to do a carpenter's job. When I do get into my stride I am reined in with brutal suddenness because·what I have laboured on, in order to give the best that is in me, is going to ruin the show. I am a musical carpenter, and I like the trade so well that I am going to get out of it."

He did get out of it very quickly. In spite of the fact that *L'Île Enchantée* contained some gems of melody, Covent Garden saw him no more. He went back to his songs. His reputation as a song writer was now fully established, and "words" of songs poured in upon him by almost every post. "If I were to set all the verses of good quality I receive," he wrote to his mother, "I should work twenty-four hours a day, and then half the songs would not have the credit—or discredit —of my notes."

Robert Browning sent a poetical friend to him with this letter of introduction:

"DEAR MR. SULLIVAN,—

"I venture to take this way of introducing to you a friend of mine, a countryman of yours, and a benefactor to us all, the poet, Allingham, to wit. He knows and admires your music; if you know his poetry the business of 'introduction' will not be a long one. What concerns you particularly is, that I don't believe anyone could write a better, nor so good a lyric opera with a view to the requirements of music as well as of poetry—and one day you may want such a poet, as, I hope, now he wants a musician.

"Ever Yours faithfully,
"ROBERT BROWNING."

A journey to Ireland in the late summer of 1863 had set Sullivan's thoughts running in a new direction. He wrote to his mother from Belfast: "It is true I am not working much, but I shall feel the practical results when I return to London. My life is a lazy one, as I do little else but lie on the grass (if it is fine), or lie in the drawing-room, reading and playing, but already I feel my ideas assuming a newer and fresher colour. I shall be able to work like a horse on my return. Why, the other night as I was jolting home from Holywood through the wind and rain on an open jaunting car, the whole first movement of a symphony came into my head with a real fresh flavour about it—besides scraps of the other movements."

This was the origin of his first symphony. It was produced eventually at the Crystal Palace, but it was not called the Irish Symphony till many years later, nor was it printed until after his death.

Meanwhile Chorley had completed the libretto of an opera —a work begun before the Paris journey—and he handed it over to Sullivan for setting. It was a wretched confusion, utterly lacking in all knowledge of stage-craft and quite unsuitable for any music. But Sullivan struggled with *The Sapphire Necklace*, as it was named, for the sake of his friend. Chorley was all enthusiasm—"Chorley talks the opera most of the time," Sullivan had written from Paris. The setting of the work was nearing completion when Sullivan returned from Ireland, for he wrote to his mother: "The Finale is the thing I stick at, as there is another storm to make in it, and having done one already, it is hard to make another which shall be quite different."

The Sapphire Necklace was never produced, and the greater part of its music was subsequently used in other works. The libretto killed any chance it might have had, but Chorley was sufficiently conscious of the defects to admit them. The pair sat in conclave. The promoters of the Birmingham Festival had asked Sullivan to compose a work for production at the Festival. Sullivan hesitated; he had no libretto suitable for a composition of this kind, so Chorley stepped into the breach. In a few days he produced the libretto of the *Kenilworth* Cantata, and Sullivan accepted the Birmingham invitation and sat down to the work of composing. He worked at feverish speed all day, all night. "This is the fourth day that I have worked all night (Irish!)" he wrote. "Last evening I even forgot my supper, and was painfully reminded of the oversight when my watch conveyed the intelligence that it was 4 a.m."

Chorley's libretto was bad; it was unquestionably one of the worst Sullivan ever set. In later years he admitted that no libretto in his life had ever tried him so much. But he smothered its defects with a great piece of composing. He gave to it the same ardour he had devoted to *The Tempest*, believing that he would be judged, and his progress or his falling away from grace assessed, on the comparison of the new work with *The Tempest*. When the work was in rehearsal at Birmingham, he was well satisfied with it. The midnight oil had not been burned in vain, nor did the defective Chorley ever seem to matter so little.

Of all his judges and his critics, he held but one in high esteem, almost in awe, and that was his father. Full of content with *Kenilworth*, he wrote from Birmingham during the last days of rehearsal, and urged his father to come.

"DEAR FATHER,—

"I wish so much that I could persuade you to run down to-morrow by the 2.45. You could return the same night, or I would find you a bed somewhere. You see, 1st: You will never have another opportunity of hearing the work performed in such a magnificent style again; 2nd: It is a great event in my career, and one which I should like you to witness. Do come (with Fred), there's a dear.

"Yr. affec. Son,
"ARTHUR."

Such an appeal was irresistible to the parent. Moreover, this was one of the few first performances of his son's work that Thomas Sullivan was to hear. *Kenilworth* made a deep impression and the echo of its success rippled through London. Some critics, after *The Tempest*, had regarded Sullivan as a youth with cleverness in him, who, like some swift unformed comet, had flashed for an instant and would disappear as quickly in the murk of musical uncertainty. They now began to wonder. Possibly this young song writer, now so firmly established, had better stuff in him than they had foreseen. Even the musical press began to take more serious notice of him; its former hesitating paragraphs changed to articles definite in their assurance as regards Sullivan's talents.

He was shaping his place in music, and it was a new place. He collided with nobody; he set up no controversies as an improver upon any master's style. He might even compose an opera one day! Some critics doubted if any Englishman or Irishman could produce an opera of lasting value, and they openly declared that no Scotsman could, for had not the waning Wallace been born in Waterford! To these worshippers at the shrines of foreign genius it seemed a schism to suppose that the realms of Victoria—in spite of the little spasms of musical enthusiasm from the throne, and the secret compositions of the Prince Consort—could produce its great composer. Purcell had been a freak, Handel borrowed from another country; indeed London bought its composers. So they said.

Sullivan's Symphony in "E" Flat, produced at the Crystal Palace in 1866, completed the conversion of those who had doubted him. The concert in question consisted mainly of excerpts from his own works, with the Symphony as the new attraction. Jenny Lind appeared on the platform and drew the town to the Palace, so that more than 3,000 listened to this, the first Sullivan Concert of any importance.

Applause is sweet to the ears of Youth, but the concert produced what was sweeter still to Sullivan, and that was a letter of warm appreciation from his old master John Goss. Since the Chapel Royal days when, after listening to Goss's new anthem, Sullivan had written home that it was "fine," Goss had been an influence in his musical life. True he had given the boy so much homework at fourteen that he had no time to devote to the recreations for which Youth was clamouring, but Sullivan's adoration of the craftsmanship of Goss remained unimpaired. Perhaps John Goss, too, realized, better than anyone else at the Crystal Palace Concert, what its success meant to the young composer, for had he not been a Chapel Royal chorister in the days of the Regent? After the concert he wrote to Sullivan:

"I rejoice that I was at your concert, and that I can heartily congratulate you on all points. It was a great triumph, and

Four Years (1863–1867)

that Madame Goldschmidt should have given her help crowned it to perfection! Her you can never repay, except in the way she, the greatest of artists, would heartily desire! I mean, by going on—on—on—on until (as I hope) you may prove a worthy peer of the greatest symphonists. Enough now that I congratulate you and I joy with you—for you have attained a great success. Go on, my dear boy, and prosper."

Shortly after the production of the Symphony, Sullivan proceeded to Manchester, whence a proposal had come to him to write the incidental music to a theatrical production on an elaborate scale which was to be made at a local theatre during Christmas week. The journey proved fruitless, but it gave him an experience which he constantly related against himself. He arrived at Manchester on an evening of drizzling rain, and drove at once to the theatre. He asked to see the libretto for which his music was required; it had not been written. Then, he insisted, he must get into immediate touch with the author. This individual, so Sullivan to his surprise was informed, was an amateur of considerable merit, and a lodge-keeper at the local cemetery! A keeper of graves as a collaborator! This was either romance or an absurdity, but the insistence of the theatre people assured him that he had not been brought from London on an errand of madness. So he would go and see.

He hired a cab and drove for miles in search of the cemetery. Rain was now coming down in torrents, and the roads were a flood. It was late at night when he reached the cemetery lodge, and there seemed to be no other house for miles. Neither were there any lights in the lodge windows; everyone was in bed. He scrambled out of the cab, groped to the lodge door in the dark, knocked and waited. After an eternity, a candle appeared at the bedroom window, and an aged man, wearing a nightcap, put his head out and volubly cursed Sullivan with well chosen oaths. Then he came down and unbolted the door.

Sullivan, wet and not too pleasantly disposed, went inside. The old man, wearing a short coat over his nightshirt, and holding up a fluttering candle, asked him brusquely what he

49

required. In a few words Sullivan explained that he wanted
to know something about the plot of the Christmas piece, for it
was important that he should return to London in the morning.
The cemetery keeper listened, his jaw fell; in a few moments
he was quite sure that he had been called out of bed by an
imbecile. Had the intruding fellow driven here in the middle
of the night about a "plot" or a grave? In vain did Sullivan
try to push into a seemingly addled brain that he had come
about a "plot"—the plot of a theatrical piece. They jabbered
at each other in terms which neither understood, then Sullivan
went out and left him with his candle and nightshirt, and the
melancholy return to Manchester began.

It was not until the next morning that Sullivan discovered
that the cab-driver had driven him to the wrong cemetery!

The discovery only increased Sullivan's chagrin. He had
finished with Manchester. The next day he returned to
London to find awaiting him an invitation from the Committee
of the Norwich Festival to write a new work for production
at the Festival in October. He accepted it, but, as the weeks
passed, the idea for what he wished to be a master work seemed
ever elusive. He began composing; in the morning he tore
up what he had composed, only to go through the same false
start again on the night following. He walked the streets
for hours, but the melody that appeared to wait round the
next corner had slipped away among the chimney-pots before
he reached that corner. The passage of the days became
an obsession that terrified him. August slipped away;
September found him still brooding.

Some of Sullivan's best music came from sorrow. He was
so sensitive a creature, his affections so deep, that feeling forced
itself to expression only through his notes. By the middle
of September the work that was to be produced at Norwich
at the end of October had not been begun. Themes, as they
occurred to him, were still being discarded. Then at the end
of September his father died suddenly after a few days' illness.

The blow that came to the two youths Thomas Sullivan
left behind was unspeakable. They could not imagine him
stealing out like this—the beloved figure—the man who had
stinted and fretted to make the paths straight for their feet.

Four Years (1863–1867)

All remembrance of the Norwich Festival passed out of Arthur Sullivan's mind beneath the burden of grief. The solace of friends yielded him little at all. But it was a sentence in a letter from George Grove—that unfailing friend—which brought him back to the reality of things. "It was a great thing for him," Grove wrote, "to have lived to see your triumph. If he had died last year, or even in February of this year, before your Symphony was due, it would have been quite a different thing to him, and he could not have felt such a satisfaction in your music as he did."

These words had their effect. Less than one week after the passing of his father, Sullivan began the scoring of his *In Memoriam*. He worked at it night and day, ceaselessly, as if it were the link that held him to the beloved figure. In the grandeur of its theme, in its simplicity, was all the majesty of Death's farewell. *In Memoriam* is the cry of a man in sorrow translated into Art and beauty as the best votive offering.

The Overture was produced at the Norwich Festival on October 30th, 1866. This new work from the young composer drew enormous crowds, and Sullivan was even compelled to pay for the tickets for his friends, though conducting his own Overture. He was immediately acclaimed as one of the finest composers of his time, and the few doubting critics who had clung to their dogmatic creeds like old leaves to a tree scurried away defeated.

The triumph of the work pleased its maker. But what pleased him more was the ultimate realization that no finer monument would ever be put up to the memory of his father.

CHAPTER VI

The Schubert Discoveries

THE cult of Schubert and Schumann which followed the enthusiasm of Sullivan and Grove for these composers had become definite in London in the year 1867. Grove had given Schubert continuously at the Crystal Palace, and his enthusiasm was spreading fast to the amateur musical Societies. Even Mendelssohn, the great approved, seemed now to show the first signs of losing the passionate popularity he enjoyed with the Victorians. Could there be another who sang as sweetly as he? This Schubert, whose work was so little known because there was so little of it in print, was, they argued, a Viennese importation of small account; he would fade and pass.

The details of Schubert's life were so complete that it was obvious to Sullivan and Grove that, somewhere or other, much of Schubert's lost music must still exist. Grove's great ambition was to complete the *Rosamunde* music, the beauty of which was impaired by so much of it being lost or missing. They wrote to Herr Spina, the music-publisher of Vienna, on the subject. Then, acting on an impulse of musical enthusiasm, they set off together for Vienna on Thursday evening, September 26th, 1867.

Frederic Sullivan accompanied them as far as Paris, then the two musicians passed on to Baden where they broke the journey in order to visit Madame Schumann and Madame Viardot Garcia. "We walked to the Schumann's," Grove wrote,[1] "and were very well received and saw the album which R.S. and she kept full of the most interesting letters and

---

[1] "Life of Sir George Grove": C. L. Graves, p. 145.

portraits and locks of hair of every composer and poet and painter from Jubal and David downwards." These hair-collecting enthusiasts! Had not Rossini once declared to Sullivan that his admirers would have shorn him!

Then Munich—Salzburg and the memories of Mozart. Sullivan and Grove followed Mozart's footsteps through the city, ardent in their reverence.

"We went and saw the house Mozart was born and lived in," Sullivan wrote to his mother, "and the Mozartium where all relics of him are preserved. Both his harpsichords, various portraits and many letters and manuscripts are here. When we wrote our names in the Visitors' Book the librarian asked me if I was the composer of whom he had often read in the 'Signale' and other musical papers. I modestly owned that I did occasionally write a little music, and we bowed and complimented each other. Grove and I left Salzburg the same night and tried to sleep in the train, but for two giants, Chang and Anak, who sat opposite, and took up so much room that we could not even cross our knees, but sat upright like Egyptian statues."

Spina welcomed them with open arms. If there were discoveries to be made, all the manuscripts he had were at the disposal of the visitors. "Spina produces a pile of MS. music about as big as a portmanteau and says 'Here is all I have that you wish to see. You shall go into my room with it and do what you like,'" Grove wrote.[1]

Spina plied the pair with cigars, and compliments as sincere as the cigars were good. "Mr. Spina has behaved quite nobly to us, anything kinder it would be quite impossible to conceive," Sullivan recorded in a letter on October 9th. "He gave up his rooms to us to-day, with all the MSS. carefully arranged, plenty of cigars on the table and pens, ink and paper, and nothing to disturb us. We selected a heap of things, and he is going to have them copied at once and sent after us, to keep for ourselves, and to perform when and where we like. He gave us a letter of introduction to Dr. Schneider (a relative of Schubert's) from whom we

[1] "Life of Sir George Grove": C. L. Graves, p. 143.

succeeded in getting two Symphonies and an Overture! [1]
O Joy!"

A glorious week passed. They dug in dusty parcels.
Forgotten musicians, whose work was as forgotten as they,
could have watched—if the power to see had been yielded to
them again—their old compositions being turned over from
this reverence of dust, in the hope that the work of one
who was greater than they should lie with theirs in honour.
The whole of Spina's shop with its quantities of music was
ransacked. And the most interesting thing in the shop was
Spina's ancient clerk—a lame and fading fellow—named
Döppler, who wore an old skull-cap and limped after them
like the surviving crony of a dead age.

Döppler had known Beethoven; he remembered his
coming frequently to the shop, he had sold him music.
Moreover, he had been at Schubert's christening. The luck
of the fellow! The two musicians from England, as they
looked at his weather-beaten face, knew that they had discovered one who had walked with the immortals. Yet he
still slaved behind the counter, ill-dressed, hobbling from
point to point, very quiet, seemingly without an opinion on
anything. Sullivan kept a careful book of notes throughout
this journey, and the material which he obtained from Döppler
is of the greatest interest.

"An old clerk, V. Döppler, in the shop of C. A. Spina,
who had known Beethoven and Schubert well, told us many
little things about them," he wrote. "Beethoven wore a green
and Polish coat with frogs on it—and when in the shop
generally leant against a wooden pillar by the counter, whilst
Czerny, v. Siegfried and Stradler sat on a leather sofa. They
wrote down their conversation on a slate as B. was stone deaf.

"Döppler corroborated the story told by Jahn in his
Aufsätze of Beethoven composing under a tree at Heiligen-
stadt. He it was who was told by the peasant. Döppler
also said that the portrait by Kriehuher is the most like of all
the portraits of Beethoven.

[1] "From Dr. Schneider: Simfonie in 'C' Major. Simfonie in 'C' Minor
(Sogenannte 'Tragisit'). Overture in 'D' 'Die Freunde von Salamanca'."—
Arthur Sullivan's notebook used in Vienna.

The Schubert Discoveries

"Pointing to the 'Missa Solonelle in "D" ' which is in B's hand in the engraving, he said: 'Ah! he sketched some of that in a storm, for he was lying under a tree writing when it began to rain. He was, however, so engrossed in his work, that he took no notice of the rain, and it was not until his paper was wet, and his pen had gone through it, that he left off.'

"He told us that Beethoven was very absent, and that, for instance, he would often order his beer, pay for it, and never drink it.

"I said: 'Did you know Schubert?' "

" 'Know him?' said he. 'Why, I was at his christening, and a pupil of his father's. Beethoven recognized and acknowledged Schubert's genius. Schubert naturally had a great reverence for Beethoven.' "

Interesting as had been the Schubert discoveries already made, the lost *Rosamunde* music was still elusive. There was no trace of it. Spina had turned out his last drawer, had withdrawn from the limbo of forgotten things the most obscure parcel. He could conceive no other means of finding the lost treasures, but his time and his cigars were at the disposal of his visitors. Dr. Schneider, too, had taken out of a dark mysterious cupboard all parcels that were likely to yield the missing music. The search seemed hopeless, and the two Englishmen resolved to leave for Prague. Obviously, as Grove said, *Rosamunde* could never have been completed. The music had been entirely lost. Perhaps Schubert himself had lost it.

On Thursday afternoon they returned to Dr. Schneider to bid him farewell before leaving for Prague on Saturday. Grove's story of what happened is dramatic.

"The doctor was civility itself; he again had recourse to the cupboard, and shewed us some treasures which had escaped us before. I again turned the conversation to the *Rosamunde* music; he believed that he had at one time possessed a copy of the sketch of it all. Might I go into the cupboard and look for myself? Certainly, if I had no objection to being smothered with dust. In I went; and after some search, during which my companion kept the doctor engaged in

55

conversation, I found, at the bottom of the cupboard, and in its farthest corner, a bundle of music-books two feet high, carefully tied round, and black with the undisturbed dust of nearly half a century. . . . These were the part books of the whole of the music in *Rosamunde*, tied up after the second performance in December 1823, and probably never disturbed since."[1]

So out of the dirt they dragged the divine *Rosamunde* like a recovered jewel from an ash-heap. The dust had given back that which belonged to the ages. Tense with excitement, Sullivan and Grove sat up till two in the morning copying the parts. They were worn out, but probably it was the faith of Schumann's "der einzige Schubert" which had stolen unawares into their blood as they worked, for, when the task was completed, and *Rosamunde* lay scattered in a mass of paper on the table in front of them—*Rosamunde* a mystery no more—Sullivan and Grove played leap-frog.[2]

With the discovery of *Rosamunde* nothing held them longer to Vienna. Their journey had been a triumph, and they packed into their trunks the pages of some of the best Schubert London was to know. On Saturday afternoon (October 12th) Sullivan left for Prague, and pushed on to Leipzig where Grove rejoined him five days later in time for Sullivan's concert at the Gewandhaus. Before leaving London, Sullivan had sent certain of his music to Moscheles, and it was in active rehearsal ere the Schubert researches at Vienna were complete.

Five years had passed since he had left Leipzig—and he wanted the Leipzig concert to be worthy of the return of the apprentice from his *Wanderjahre* as an acknowledged master. Moscheles, with the old warm affection, had written to him with enthusiasm about the music. He was proud of his old pupil, proud of his return. Moscheles was no longer the travelling firebrand, but was ageing, mellowing, loving his memories of those he had helped to their places in the world of music.

[1] "Life of Sir George Grove": C. L. Graves, p. 148.
[2] *Ibid.*, p. 148.

The Schubert Discoveries

The first concert was held on the Thursday after Sullivan left Vienna, and he made this entry in his notebook:

"*Leipzig*. My Overture *In Memoriam* was performed at the Gewandhaus Concert to-night, Thursday, October 17th, with great success. I was recalled. A very fair performance. Afterwards Rubinstein (who played his own 'D' Minor Concerto in this Concert), David Seuff (Publisher), Grove and myself went and had supper at Dähne's." (Had he forgotten, perhaps, his boyish rebuke of Rubinstein's "claptrap" at the Philharmonic!)

The next day he wrote to his mother:

"You will like to know about the Overture. It was a great success. I went to the Orchestra undaunted by the frigid audience, made my bow and began. It went splendidly—with great delicacy and great fire. I expected applause, but I got more—a hearty recall after I left the Orchestra. Everyone of note came and congratulated me, and I think it has laid a firm foundation to a good reputation in Germany. Next Monday the Symphony is to be tried, and then I leave for Paris. Grove arrived yesterday, and is happy, as the separation was telling on his health! * He sends his love; so do I.

"Yrs. A."

"*Bosh! Yours affectionately. G. Grove."

Sullivan spent a couple of days in the old Leipzig haunts, then he went to Dresden to see Dr. Rietz, the professor he had loved second only to David. He made a note in his book:

"*October* 20. Ran over to Dresden. Did not see Dr. Rietz, who was out, which was a great disappointment. Did see Wagner's *Rienzi* which was also a great disappointment—a mixture of Weber, Verdi, and a touch of Meyerbeer. The whole very commonplace, vulgar and uninteresting."

He went on to Paris, to the newly opened Exhibition, for the musical arrangements of which he had been partly responsible. Thither Grove had preceded him, and together they returned to London.

It was in this year (1867) that Sullivan made the acquaintance of Alfred Tennyson, and a collaboration was decided upon. It was ultimately arranged that Sullivan should set a cycle of songs which the Poet Laureate had written, and that Millais[1] should illustrate them. Tennyson at first seemed disinclined to fall in with the suggestion. With the accustomed splendour of his Victorian manner he held aloof. Sullivan wrote from Tennyson's house: "When I got here I had a cup of tea, and then went and smoked with Tennyson until dinner time. He read me all the songs (twelve in number), which are absolutely lovely, but I fear there will be a great difficulty in getting them from him. He thinks they are too light, and will damage his reputation, etc. All this I have been combatting."

Tennyson eventually did agree that Sullivan should set the songs, and he took the young composer closely into his friendship. He called constantly at the house in Claverton Terrace, Pimlico, to discuss the project, garbed in the dress of the man of poetry in which he loved to strut about London. Previous to one of his visits to dinner Sullivan warned the maid that the guest of the evening might seem to be a little eccentric, in which case she was to appear to observe nothing. But after the poet had gone, she came into her master's room and remarked:

"Well, Mr. Sullivan, he *do* wear clothes."

"Yes," said Sullivan. "All poets do. You forget he is the Poet Laureate."

"Lor'!" she responded. "What a queer uniform!"

After he had agreed to the project, and Sullivan was well advanced with his music, Tennyson began to repent. The scheme would injure his reputation; the time was not propitious. Excuses indeed were plentiful. He offered Sullivan five hundred pounds to let him cancel the arrangement, but Sullivan refused. Sullivan had spent infinite time on the work, and was not prepared to tear up that work to please a poet's caprice. The cavilling went on. Millais drew one picture—a beautiful pencil-sketch of a girl at a window—but Tennyson's dallying tired him out, and he ultimately dropped the work. "I am very sorry," he wrote to Sullivan, "as of course I should have liked to have carried out the original

[1] It was during this year—1867—that he was elected to the Garrick Club, where he first met Millais and a great friendship was begun.

idea. You muſt remember that I did keep the drawings for *months* before they were parted with. One line from him (Tennyson) at the time would have saved the trouble."

For over three years Tennyson argued that the publication of the songs should be dropped. At laſt he wrote to the publisher Strahan:

" 'He that sweareſt to his neighbour and disappointeth him not'—so I muſt consent to the publication of the songs, however much againſt my inclination and my judgment, and that I may meet your wishes as to the time of publication, I muſt also consent to their being published this Xmas, however much more againſt my inclination and judgment— provided, as I ſtated yeſterday that the faſt of their having been written four years ago, and of their being published by yourself, be mentioned in the preface, also that no one but Millais shall illuſtrate them.

"Yours very truly,

"A. Tennyson."

The introduſtion, upon which Tennyson insiſted, upset Sullivan. It was unnecessary; it seemed to be gratuitously unkind. It ran as follows:

"Four years ago Mr. Sullivan requeſted me to write a little Liederkreis, German fashion, for him to exercise his art upon.

"He had been very successful in setting such old songs as 'Orpheus with his lute made trees,' and I dreſt up for him a puppet in the old ſtyle, a mere motif for an air, indeed the verieſt nothing unless Mr. Sullivan can make it dance to his inſtruments.

"I am sorry that my four year old puppet should have to dance at all in the dark shadow of these days,[1] but the music is now completed, and I am bound by my promise.

"A. Tennyson."

In vain did Sullivan plead that the preface was a refleſtion upon himself. Tennyson withdrew into his shell; he refused for a long time to answer letters. He was suffering from a bad attack of poet's *malaise*. At long laſt he replied:

[1] The Franco-German War was then in progress.

59

Sir Arthur Sullivan

"DEAR MR. SULLIVAN,—

"I have been some time in answering your note because I have been asking several friends who had already seen my little preface to the Songs of the Wrens, what their impression of it was. They had all failed to see in it the slightest kind of unfriendly allusion to yourself, and only took it as an expression of my own regret at the unappropriateness of the time of publication, and even that my words were not worthy of your music.

"You may feel certain that there was and is no intention on my part to give the public any other impression; and you can, if you choose, let all your chaffing friends of the Club know that you have this under my hand and seal.

"A. TENNYSON."

It was the final word that turned away wrath. The songs, with the single illustration by Millais, did not appear until the beginning of 1871, but the friendship which had seemed in such jeopardy remained unbroken until Tennyson's death.

Throughout 1867 and 1868 Sullivan worked at a fierce pace. In those two years he produced no fewer than eleven songs—the most successful *O Fair Dove, O Fond Dove* which took the drawing-rooms by storm—thirteen Anthems and Part Songs, including *O, Hush Thee, my Babie* [1] and *The Long Day Closes*; seven hymns, and his overture *Marmion* produced at the Philharmonic. Now he had turned his composing at a tangent to an Oratorio, *The Prodigal Son*, the first themes of which had come to him during his brief visit to Leipzig on his way back from Vienna. He had also composed a comic opera, *The Contrabandista*, and a comic operetta, *Cox and Box*. Moreover, he founded the Civil Service Orchestral Society of which he was appointed conductor, and he was given the first keyless watch on his retirement. Mr. Gladstone, an enthusiastic amateur musician, sang bass at a number of the early performances.

The Prodigal Son was Sullivan's first challenge in oratorio. It was composed with amazing speed; the music rushed from him, and the work was completed from beginning to end in a little over three weeks.

[1] Written for his nephew, Herbert Sullivan, August, 1868.

The Schubert Discoveries

He had returned from a hurried visit to Paris, where he had met Balfe. The object of the journey was to get his work performed before a French audience, and Pasdeloup of the Cirque Napoleon had made a tentative promise to produce *In Memoriam*.

"The concert at the Cirque Napoleon startled me," Sullivan wrote. "It takes place in a great circus, capable of holding more than 4,000 people, and yesterday, as at all his concerts, it was crowded. I never saw such a sight. The people sit in tiers, rising from the floor, half-way up to the roof, and everyone can see everyone else. If the people like the things, they applaud vociferously; if they don't, they hiss with equal energy." That night Sullivan sat up till dawn making parts of *In Memoriam* because Pasdeloup's strings were so numerous, and he could not get a copyist.

The same energy and restlessness urged him forward with his new oratorio. "I seemed to work without fatigue," he said, "through the day, through the night again, and then well into the next day till my hand grew shaky with fatigue which I did not otherwise feel."

Jenny Lind wrote to him:

"I have just received your note, and hasten to say how *very* sorry I am not to be able to come to your 'Prodigal Son' to-morrow. Saturdays are my reception days, and I cannot possibly be absent! All my neighbours generally flock in to see me on these days, and you will find that I must not disappoint them. I wish you a good performance in every respect. I should indeed have been happy to have found out the good points in your work, as I shall always, if only for Auld Lang Syne's sake, take interest in your welfare.

"Your old friend,
"JENNY L. GOLDSCHMIDT."

But when *The Prodigal Son* was produced at the Worcester Festival in December 1869, the performance was spoiled by the absence of two of his best principals, Mdlle. Titiens and Sims Reeves. True, Madame Trebelli and Santley were present, but Sims Reeves, who was to sing in *The Prodigal Son* so frequently afterwards, had confused his dates, and was engaged at another concert on the evening of the first performance. The manager refused to release him. "Let the Prodigal Son go to his Father. Keep your engagement with me at any cost," the manager telegraphed Sims Reeves, and the singer had to obey. The substitute proved to be a poor one. His words failed to reach the gallery; people strained their ears in vain to hear what the prodigal son had to say. Only the music held them.

If *The Prodigal Son* was not Sullivan's greatest effort in oratorio, it was at least a brilliant first attempt. John Goss knew he was capable of greater things, and wrote critically to him after the production: "All you have done is most masterly. Your orchestration superb, and your efforts, many of them, original and first-rate. Some day you will I hope try at another oratorio, putting out all your strength—not the strength of a few weeks or months. Show yourself *the best man in Europe*! Don't do anything so pretentious as an oratorio or even a Symphony without *all your power*, which seldom comes in one fit. Handel's two or three weeks for the 'Messiah' may be a fact, but *he* was not always successful, and was not so young a chap as you."

Sullivan had no immediate intention of following *The Prodigal Son* with another work of the same type. Light opera had begun to attract him, and four years were to pass before he returned to oratorio again.

CHAPTER VII

First Days in Light Opera

A CHANCE meeting with F. C. Burnand turned Sullivan
definitely towards light opera. Burlesque was then
filling the Continental theatres; it stormed London and was
victorious. Theatres which had staged plays of merit turned
out these plays and put on burlesque. The music to these
burlesques, both at home and abroad, was, in the main,
blatant, dull and uninteresting. Even the comic songs, which
had disappeared with their innuendo and coarseness, returned
in a new and more virulent form. That which afterwards
became known as "Gilbert and Sullivan" was to throttle much
of the coarseness that had held London too long, and to prove
that, even in its laughter, London preferred Art and Beauty
before all else.

The meeting with Burnand was small in its importance at
the time. Some musical friends who ran an amateur theatrical
company were short of a piece. Burnand wanted to help
them out, and when he met Sullivan in the street he suggested
a collaboration. There was no money in it; he frankly said
so. This accident of chance, which led ultimately to the
Savoy triumphs, took place in 1866. Sullivan agreed to write
the music without fee since it was to be performed by friends,
and "F. C. B." set about making a burlesque of Morton's
"Box and Cox."

He reversed the names, and called the piece *Cox and Box.*
Sullivan began to work on the music, completed it in great
haste, and thought very little of it at the time. But after the
first private performance the merits of the piece were such
that it was decided to put it on at the Adelphi, on behalf of a
fund which was being organized by *Punch* for the relatives

63

of a deceased member of the staff of that journal. His friend, George du Maurier, the *Punch* artist and the future author of "Trilby," played the leading part; he had a charming high tenor voice and was a first-rate musician. Sullivan performed at the piano.

The public acclaimed the piece. It was transported to Manchester; then returned to London and looked like being a money-maker. The individual most astonished over the success of *Cox and Box* was Sullivan. At the moment when he was thinking of making oratorio his method of composition, at the very hour of his life when he thought more seriously about the higher form of music than at any other, the spirit of light music, like some fanciful Puck, tweaked his sleeve.

Cox and Box was of the flimsiest texture, but the gaiety of it had appeal. Here was burlesque worthy of Victorian traditions for decency. The collaborators followed it with a comic opera, *The Contrabandista*, and sought about for a producer.

At that time the German Reeds had begun their rapid rise to popularity with their humorous sketches at the Gallery of Illustration in Regent Street. The vulgarity of the average burlesque sent Mayfair and Balham to the Gallery because the fun there was sound and clean, and it was the wave of questionable entertainment in London which brought the German Reeds into prominence since they were the antidote. They made money; at times their box office turned away more money than it took. They made a triumph of legitimate comedy. The questionable joke, often slanderous in its allusion—so slanderous that the victim could not take action without heaping upon himself more slander by so doing— heard at each performance in most of the burlesques, was always absent at the Gallery.

The German Reeds emigrated to St. George's Hall to accommodate the demands of the box office. Their simple entertainment with a piano, the only instrument engaged, became more elaborate. It developed into comic opera, well staged, remarkably well sung, careful in chorus and detail. The Reeds became a power in theatrical London. Balfe had written an operetta for St. George's Hall, and when

f. Doppler said that the portrait by Kriehuber was the most like of all the portraits of Beethoven. Pointing to the "Missa Solennelle in D" which is in B's hand in the engraving he said "this he sketched some of that in a storm - for he was lying under a tree writing. when it began to rain - he was however so engrossed in his work, that he took no notice of the rain, + it was not until his paper was wet + his pen had gone through it, that he left off. —

He told us that Beethoven was very absent, + that, for instance, he would often order his beer, pay for it, + never drink it.

I said "did you know Schubert?" —
"Know him"! said he. "Why I was at his christening! and was a pupil of his father".

A page from Arthur Sullivan's notebook which he used in Vienna at the time of the Schubert discoveries

First Days in Light Opera

Sullivan composed *The Contrabandista* the only means of outlet seemed to be the German Reeds.

The opera was destined to fail. It started badly. German Reed had engaged some of the best singers, he had faith in Sullivan, and a friendship that never failed for Burnand. Just before the last rehearsals began, his *basso* withdrew. There was a frantic hunt for a new soprano. Anyone with a voice was tried.

"A Miss H—— sung to me the other day," Reed wrote to Sullivan. "She has a fine voice with rather a coarse Italian style of singing. Short and fat. Not pretty, but with paint and bismuth might be made to look decent."

Sullivan spent his days listening to singers. He spared no trouble, and German Reed spared no money. But when *The Contrabandista* was put on, it failed even to get applause, and was withdrawn immediately.

The failure filled Sullivan with disappointment. The libretto had been good, and he felt so sure of the quality of his music that he put it aside, and, in the years to come, used a great deal of it again in his opera *The Chieftain*. Like most musicians, he was a creature of temperament—one who felt elation from success, or despondency from failure more keenly than those who live less closely with their imagination. He was for awhile uncertain as to the direction he would follow. Although the ambition for serious music remained, he was hurt by the ill-starred fortune of a work to which he had given so much. He called on the Goldschmidts, to whom he always spoke frankly about his work. Jenny Lind was out; Otto Goldschmidt in Paris. But a letter which Sullivan received from her next morning reassured him, and recalled him from the gloom of a day of despondency.

"Mr. Goldschmidt is in Paris," she wrote, "but he will be glad to hear that you have called upon me, for he is indeed very fond of you, and we are both of us slow to think that there should be no feeling of reciprocity on your side. No, I on my part, have so deep a confidence in a *true musical* nature, that nothing can make *me* believe in our want of faithfulness where there is no reason for withdrawal. It will do Mr. Goldschmidt good to the heart if you will believe both him and me to be your friends, and treat us accordingly."

The first two adventures into light opera had yielded Sullivan little. He went back to serious music. Songs came from him with steady flow; church music and cantatas. He went up and down the country to conduct special performances of his serious work. The flame of music was burning in him so fiercely that every call from music was answered, every offering to music freely given. He bombarded his mother with letters recording erratic movements here and there at the demands of music.

The war of 1870 swept down on France. In accordance with British tradition a fund for the sufferers in Paris was opened at the Mansion House, and Sullivan was selected as a member of the Committee. He hurried off to Paris, he wandered along through streets of smoke-blackened ruins before the Prussian guns were dumb. The Opera seemed to have lost its wonder beneath the melancholy of those guns. The absurdity of it all filled him with amazement. These Germans he had known and loved thundering here with monsters of destruction. The memory of this havoc, of the Communist terror of '71, remained with him for years.

One of his warmest friends was Madame Conneau, a lady-in-waiting to the Empress Eugenie. When the Empress took refuge at Chislehurst after the flight from the Tuileries, he visited her often. "She was," he wrote of the Empress, "one of the most brilliant women I ever knew. Her conversation was amazing. Whatever the subject, she knew all about it. I could see this personality swaying an Empire." Not so with the Emperor Napoleon. "In his eyes is a distant stare, as if he saw the things that might have been."

Madame Conneau lost her son in the Great War; the Prince Imperial, whom Sullivan knew so well, went down to an earlier and lonelier grave in Zululand.

To his mother, who was trying to keep house for a son who disappeared and reappeared like a will-o'-the-wisp, he was a conundrum. He appeared suddenly in the best houses in the land, and wrote her ecstatic letters about these homes before she even knew he was there. Or, after conducting his Overture at Liverpool or Birmingham, he would write her a full description of the performance when she thought he was at the other end of the kingdom. He was to her a form of joyous and riotous upheaval. She loved these letters, the wonderful expectancy of their surprises. "I shall arrive at Paddington at 5.30. Please have a sole, and a steak and a half bottle of claret and a good fire." Or, "We went shooting yesterday—I am sending you six brace of pheasants." What was she to do with six brace of pheasants? Before the problem had solved itself in her mind, the next post brought a slip: "a brace for you *of course*. A brace for So-and-so," and the pheasants dropped into their intended homes.

"I've sent on in advance, a real French bow for your birthday. You've got to wear it," he wrote from Paris. He rushed her off her feet in a wealth of affection. He wrote letters to her ceaselessly when he was travelling, till she had to study the postmarks to discover his whereabouts. The excitement of him was, to a mother who rejoiced in her two sons, the savour of life.

For his health he cared nothing when music called. He worked through one night after another without apparent disorder. When alone, he lived on a few shillings a day. The fleshpots of success meant nothing to him. "It's time you came home," his mother ventured to remonstrate with him on one occasion, "if you are living on fifteen shillings a week." There was no need for the economy of fifteen shillings a week, but—to him—there was no need for the expenditure of any more. He went back to the sole and the steak and the blazing fire, and told her that she was the most wonderful mother in the world and believed it.

Frederic Clay had been composing music for the German Reeds at intervals, and more than once had collaborated with William Schwenck Gilbert. The town knew Gilbert's work well; its whimsicality and cleverness were never failing sources of delight. The genial merriment of Gilbert was infectious and lovable. Besides, had he not been kidnapped by a gang of Italian brigands at the age of two, and ransomed for twenty-five pounds? It was difficult to be taken seriously after that. Only on the few occasions when Gilbert wrote serious plays was he grievously annoyed if he were not taken seriously.

Clay was collaborating with Gilbert in a piece called *Ages Ago* after the failure of *La Contrabandista*, and he invited Sullivan round to watch a rehearsal. At that rehearsal Gilbert and Sullivan met for the first time. There seemed to be no portent in the meeting of a future collaboration which was to prove remarkable. No collaboration was suggested at that meeting; probably it never occurred to either of them. Gilbert was six years older than Sullivan; both of them had reached the first flush of success. That their paths were to incline and join, then ultimately break apart again was beyond their imagining that day. The meeting at Clay's rehearsal was to change the whole character of English light opera, and those responsible for this change left the hall unaware of that inflexion of interest which draws men together.

Because the twain met at a German Reed rehearsal it is usually believed that Reed started them on their career together. He certainly so endeavoured, but he failed to make them collaborators. He wrote to Sullivan, after Gilbert and Clay's piece called *Ages Ago* came to the end of its brief life:

"Gilbert is doing a comic one-act entertainment for me—soprano—contralto—tenor—baritone and bass. Would you like to compose the music? If so—on what terms? Reply at once, as I want to get the piece going without loss of time."

The terms were never arranged. German Reed had lost money over *The Contrabandista*, and was not prepared to take much risk for the glory of bringing Gilbert and Sullivan together. The episode passed; composer and librettist never even met to discuss it. It was John Hollingshead who made them collaborators for the first time. Gilbert showed him the libretto of an operatic Extravaganza *Thespis*, and Hollingshead forthwith sent it to Sullivan to set.

This two-act piece—the first joint product of the pair—ran for only a month. Two days after the first performance Sullivan wrote to his mother: "I have rarely seen anything so beautifully put upon the stage. The first night I had a great reception, but the music went badly, and the singer sang half a tone sharp, so that the enthusiasm of the audience did not sustain itself towards me. Last night I cut out the song, the music went very well, and consequently I had a hearty call before the curtain at the end of Act II."

Sullivan saved the best music from it, and afterwards converted a small portion of it into *The Pirates of Penzance*. Gilbert, too, was laying up a store of some of his best work in his failures, for he used a great deal of *Ages Ago*—with which he and Clay had failed—for *Ruddigore* in due season.

At the end of the month's adventure, Gilbert and Sullivan shook hands and parted. Gilbert returned to the work of burlesque. He parodied Tennyson's *Princess*. At the suggestion of Palgrave Simpson—a playwright who had recently known the hot sting of reverse—he prepared a version of *Le Palais de la Vérité*. Then he went on to *Pygmalion and Galatea*, and found success.

Although working apart, Sullivan met Gilbert frequently. The friendship, which future success was to bind, was being slowly and certainly made. Bohemian London acknowledged them as the two men in their separate spheres worth watching. One theatrical manager offered to put a thousand pounds into a piece which Gilbert and Sullivan wrote entirely together. Unhappily for the long-sighted fellow, he had no interest in *Trial by Jury*, which was the first piece produced under these conditions.

One evening during these months, Sullivan accompanied Byron the dramatist to Charles Matthews's house. Gilbert was there; also Palgrave Simpson, who was now sinking into that lethargy and superiority which is the prerogative of the failing dramatist whose powers have declined. He was a dilettante, an exotic. Among the entertainments provided for the guests on this occasion was a raffle for penny toys. A paper was drawn; if it bore a number, you chose a toy to your liking. Sullivan drew a blank. Gilbert drew a blank. Palgrave Simpson drew a number. "Dear me!" he exclaimed, surveying the row of toys spread out for selection. "What shall I choose among all these?"

Byron, with his rapier wit, picked up a penny sword and pulled it out of its sheath.

"Choose this, Palgrave," he exclaimed. "You need something that will draw!"

For the time being, Sullivan gave up light opera. Publishers were pressing for songs; musical societies in the provinces for serious works. Liverpool offered him the directorship of its music, but he refused because he could not go and live in that city. Society, with an interest in music, gave him unceasing invitations, and, acknowledging his Art, brought all the best in Art to meet him. He was scarcely thirty, but these attentions failed to spoil him. One letter to his mother reveals the man:

"DEAREST MUM,—

"I am coming home. I want quiet—and you. I want to work. The *Overture* last night was a great success; I was recalled, flowers, etc. But I am coming home to work. Better still, I am coming home for your birthday."

He had now moved, with his mother, to Albert Mansions, Victoria Street.

He went home and buried himself in his papers. For a short time he disappeared almost entirely from musical circles. A few close friends alone had access to his sanctum, although only a few really shared his thoughts at this time. But out of this quiet and seclusion came the first brilliant numbers of *The Light of the World*.

Between 1871 and 1874, Sullivan produced, in addition to major works, such as the music to the *Merry Wives of Windsor*, the Festival *Te Deum* (first performed at the Crystal Palace), and *The Light of the World*, no fewer than forty-seven additions to the Hymnal (of which he had been appointed editor) including the world's greatest marching hymn, *Onward, Christian Soldiers*, twenty songs, four choruses, and a fresh scoring of Handel's last oratorio *Jephtha*. In 1874 alone he composed and published twenty-four hymns. His versatility at this period really impeded the establishment of his place in music. Those who acclaimed him the saviour of British music, because of *The Tempest* and *In Memoriam*, had been shocked by his departure into light opera, and the failure of *Thespis* pleased them.

First Days in Light Opera

In 1869 Queen Victoria had written to him and asked him to send her a complete set of his works, an honour she had conferred on no musician before. Even her beloved Mendelssohn had sung in sweetness from Berlin without such a command from the English sovereign who adored him. Sullivan's friendship with the Duke of Edinburgh, a friendship woven in a common bondage to music, had been a friendship without royal condescension, the intimacy of two kindred souls.

And now another link bound the Queen to this musical genius of her Kingdom. The Prince Consort had employed his Sundays composing music—music full of religious and German fervour, crude, perhaps, in its technique, but work from which sincerity of purpose was not absent. Queen Victoria now sent this music to Sullivan with a request, worded not with queenly command but in the friendliness of musical enthusiasm, that he would correct it. Sullivan turned the crochets into quavers, he kept the Prince Consort's melodies complete, and returned to the Court the manuscript perfect for the printer—if ever a printer should be required—and ready for the Queen's fingers to play on her Broadwood piano.

Other interests coloured Sullivan's life at this period; perhaps they restrained him awhile from the thrall of light opera which he was so soon to know. When 1873 approached he had passed through two serious love affairs. He was now thirty, ripe with possibility, beloved and admired by those with whom he came in contact. To these two love affairs he gave all the fervour of his youth. His music dreamed around them, and they left tangible evidence in his songs. He wrote and received copious love letters—letters which, in their phrasing, were often as beautiful as his notes.

The first love affair passed because, like Handel before him and for the same reason, i.e. that he·was a musician, he was forbidden to be more than a friend to the woman he loved. Just before *The Prodigal Son* was produced the finality of his passion was revealed to him in a letter from the woman he had striven so hard to marry.

"It can have no other ending, even in the future," she wrote, "and your young life shall not be dimmed by the nurture of a hope which will never be fulfilled. . . . I hear you are changed and ill. God help you, and give you strength to bear it all. You have others to work for, and your beautiful genius to live for, and neither I, nor any other woman on God's earth is worth wasting one's life for. With all my heart I thank you for the past which has given a colour to my life."

Much of the emotion of these days passed into his work. His song *O Fond Dove* was one of many songs that caught their sweetness from these moods. Then, as so often happens, distraction produced an antidote for the hurt of his heart. He fell in love with a woman in Ireland. The old ardours returned, the depression which had entered his composing and caused him to cast the written pages away, departed with this new promise of fulfilment. He went to Ireland repeatedly. Alone with this woman the lilt of youth returned. Music—some of his best music—poured from him. And the success of these songs in printed form made the publishers clamour the louder.

The second passion, less turbulent and demanding, was partially responsible for his return to serious music. It inspired *The Light of the World,* for the *inamorata* in Ireland sought only to exploit in him his powers that he might share the lists with Mendelssohn and Handel. She told him in her letters that his genius must be given to adorn no other school. He worked with more concentration than he had ever done. The two passions became in their turn great friendships. He had passed through the fires, and he ultimately resigned himself to celibacy, a man more alive to the instincts of life because these love affairs had happened.

New moods of energy drove him, fresh fires blazed in him for the uplifting of the better things in music. For two years a serious onslaught on good music had been again made by legitimate as well as bastard burlesque. Good music was coming back once more into the concert halls in London, while the provinces were waking more surely to its necessity. Sullivan issued a long tirade against Mr. Forster's new educational schemes, which he declared were going to throttle all

First Days in Light Opera

music in schools. He came forth at the head of a crusade. Faced with the competitive attraction of burlesque, the Crystal Palace concerts, upholding as they did the righteous standard of music, were falling rapidly in popularity. The Crystal Palace—that splendid holiday haunt of 1851—was now judged to be too far from London for a concert, and people were ignoring the fine music there in favour of the counterfeit elsewhere.

In a speech filled with ardour and spleen, Sullivan delivered his rebuke to a fickle public. He said:

"I once asked Charles Matthews, the brilliant prince of English actors, 'How is your new piece going?'

" 'Oh,' he replied, 'splendidly. As a piece, it is one of the greatest successes I ever had, only—the public don't come to see it.'

"That's exactly our case," said Sullivan. "Look at the orchestra, commonly called the Band, it is one of the finest in the world, partly from the reason that the nucleus of it is always playing together every day under the same conductor —a man who was showing the world what fine orchestral playing was when most of the star conductors were boys at conservatoriums and academies. Then our solo artists—all the singers and players of the world are heard at one time or another at the C.P.—or rather, can be heard if people will come. But is all in vain? The truth is that musical performances are overdone. You will soon have to pay people, or give them some extraneous attraction, to go to a concert, a stall and a packet of White's bubbling soap for five shillings."

The veterans nodded their heads; this young man was right. They forgot *The Contrabandista* and *Thespis*; they acclaimed him as the standard-bearer. They wrote of him as the apostle of sound music. Even if he did break into light opera, it was only an expression of the exuberance of youth.

Less than a year after the failure of *Thespis*, he produced *The Light of the World* at Birmingham. The Duke of Edinburgh had travelled up for the performance, and, when Sullivan sank into a chair in the artists' room exhausted, he was the first to grip his hand. "A triumph!" he declared. And he

stood there repeating himself. "A triumph. A triumph."
They went from the hall together to a cab, the Duke still
declaring that it was a triumph.

The Light of the World had been hastily scored—the entire
work occupied Sullivan less than a month—and its religious
ardour and beauty attracted all England. The work rose
high above the quality of religious composing which the
country had known for many years. A little later Gounod
came to London to hear the oratorio, and declared it to be a
masterpiece. Queen Victoria expressed her admiration for a
composition "that was destined to uplift British music." *The
Light of the World* settled into its place among the accepted
oratorios of worth, and it placed its composer on a definite
plane.

With such success his course appeared clear. But his art
was whimsical in the versatility of its expression. A year
later he produced the incidental music to *The Merry Wives
of Windsor*. He composed his songs; he conducted his
concerts. He went from one town to another in an endless
round of music. He appeared in Society, jocund, talkative,
always interesting. And ere to-morrow's sun broke over the
chimney-pots of Mayfair he had rushed in the first train
towards the North to conduct a concert.

He was tireless. He composed in the train with the aid of
little note-books. He tramped through wet streets with the
melodies of future songs singing in his brain.

Less than two years after the production of *The Light of the
World* came his definite union with Gilbert. The greatest
partnership in light opera England had ever known, and
probably ever will know, was unheralded and unexpected.

It just happened.

CHAPTER VIII

The Partnership Begins

THE man who suggested the Gilbert and Sullivan partnership was Richard D'Oyly Carte. He was in every
way a remarkable man. His father had succeeded to the
family business of Rudolph Carte, musical instrument-makers
in London. The son was born in Soho, within a stone's-
throw of the theatre where forty-five years later he was to
produce Sullivan's *Ivanhoe*, and he was put into the musical
instrument business as soon as he left college.

But at an early age he strayed from the path that had been
shaped for his feet, and became associated with the theatre.
He produced light operas, and produced them well. He
composed operatic music which was not lacking in certain
qualities. He ran the best dramatic agency in London. He
had taken Mario on his farewell tour. He knew everybody
and had the value of every actor, musician and stage-writer
well and surely assessed in his mind. He achieved his ends
without making enemies, and was unquestionably one of the
most popular theatrical managers London has ever known.
When, with the years, success came to him, he remained
unspoiled.

D'Oyly Carte was managing the Royalty Theatre in Soho
in 1875 when the idea of the partnership occurred to him.
Chancing to meet Gilbert in the street he asked him if he
would write a short piece which he could give Sullivan for
setting. Gilbert had recently been disappointed in a deal
with Carl Rosa—Sullivan's fellow-student at Leipzig. He
had dramatised a story which he had published in the paper
Fun, and Rosa had agreed to set the work himself and "star"
his wife, Madame Paripa Rosa, in the principal part. But

Death intervened, Madame Paripa Rosa passed away suddenly, and the postman dumped the returned libretto through Gilbert's letter-box.

But for this episode D'Oyly Carte's scheme of the partnership might never have matured. Gilbert was busy with other work; one or two failures had caused him to labour feverishly at new libretti. Carte's suggestion brought to mind the manuscript which had been offered to Carl Rosa, and Gilbert sent it to the Royalty. A few days later, he went down to Sullivan's flat with the manuscript in his pocket and read it to him. Even then he appeared to be dissatisfied with the work, which was called *Trial By Jury* and was a satire on the Breach of Promise Court. Sullivan, however, was delighted with it and composed the cantata in two weeks.

D'Oyly Carte produced *Trial By Jury* at the Royalty on March 25th, 1875, with Nellie Bromley as the Plaintiff, and Frederic Sullivan as the Judge. The piece was put on after Offenbach's *La Perichole*, in which Fred Sullivan also appeared. From the first night there was no question about the success of the piece. It drew all London, for it possessed a freshness and cleverness absent from current comedy. There was a brilliance and verve in the music which *La Perichole* lacked. Crowds thronged the theatre; even standing room was exhausted at every performance, and the piece ran triumphantly for more than a year. Meanwhile, *La Perichole* waned in favour and was withdrawn, and in its place *La Fille de Madame Angot* ran in double harness with *Trial By Jury*. More money passed into the Royalty Theatre during the first twelve months of the partnership D'Oyly Carte had created than its till had known for years.

Sims Reeves, who was then singing in Sullivan's serious works, saw that his friend was turning towards light opera, and, when *Trial By Jury* was an assured success, he sent Sullivan one of his characteristic letters:

"MY DEAR ARTHUR,—

"I shall look forward with the greatest interest for a large Comic Opera. I trust Rosa will give you the opportunity of giving to the world something to astonish the natives, and make the teeth of the furreneers[1] gnash, and tear their beards. Go on and win, old fellow. . . .

"Yours ever,

"IL VECCHIO TENORE ROBUSTO SENZA IL TREMOLO."

But Carl Rosa was not to have the opportunity, for both Gilbert and Sullivan had decided to settle down—as far as their collaboration was concerned—with D'Oyly Carte, and Rosa never ceased to bemoan the opportunity he had missed.

Neither of them, however, showed any haste with regard to the preparation of a successor to *Trial By Jury*. In the summer, Sullivan went off to Italy with Sir Coutts and Lady Lindsay, and left London's theatre crowds to swelter at the doors of the Royalty. For some weeks he lazed at Cadenabbia on Lake Como.

"The air is so soft and beautiful," he wrote to his mother. "We are very thinly clad, too, with things we bought in Paris, suits of batiste, very light and cool. This morning Lindsay and I got up and bathed in the lake at six o'clock. Then we returned to bed for two or three hours and dozed. Breakfast at 9.30. Our rooms are *en suite* overlooking the Lake, with a wide stone covered-in balcony which makes a beautiful room where we sit and take our meals. It is all very beautiful and sweetly lazy."

The mood of idleness passed. With sudden resolve he packed his trunks and returned by Geneva and Paris to London. He worked hard at some new songs, and produced five in as many weeks. Two of them, *Let Me Dream Again* and *Thou'rt Passing Hence*, reached a sale of thousands of copies in a few months. Years afterwards a legend passed through the drawing-rooms that *Thou'rt Passing Hence* was composed on the death of his brother, but Frederic Sullivan lived some time yet to sing that song.

The passion for work, the restlessness which would not be stilled save by work, sent him all over the country conducting concerts. He wrote to his mother from Glasgow:

"Here is my engagement list for this week. Monday, Rehearsal. Tuesday, rehearsal and concert, Glasgow.

[1] Offenbach.

77

Wednesday, rehearsal and concert, Greenock. Thursday, rehearsal and concert, Perth (start at 9 in the morning and sleep there). Friday, rehearsal and concert, Dundee (and sleep there). Saturday, return to Glasgow. Rehearsal at 2, concert at 7.

"That's pretty well, with travelling. I am dead tired to-day. Next week I shall be knocked up, I fear.

"There's a wretched creature on the floor above me who plays the piano a little. He, or she, has been playing *my* hymn tunes all this afternoon. I hope they don't do it out of compliment to me, for they put their own harmony which, to say the least of it, isn't as good as mine."

For some time efforts had been made to associate Sullivan with a national training school of music, but his ardour for composing and for concerts claimed all the energies he possessed, and he persistently refused. "There are so many things I want to do for music," he wrote, "if God will give me two days for every one in which to do them."

But his friend the Duke of Edinburgh, who loved music better than his royal state, urged Sullivan to submit. He did more, he brought the Prince of Wales into the argument. The three of them met in a room. For a long time the conversation lay a long way from music. The Prince of Wales and Sullivan entered into an animated discussion. The Duke stood aside, saying little. Then, seizing an opportunity, he brought the Prince and Sullivan round to business, and in a few moments he had attained his object. Sullivan became Principal of the National Training School of Music, and out of it emerged, in the fullness of time, the Royal College of Music.

No one appreciated Continental music and musicians more than Sullivan, but he stubbornly refused to engage a foreign performer if one of British birth and training could be found to fill the post. In spite of his cosmopolitan temperament he adhered to this creed, often against the advice of those associated with him. "I am not going to give English concerts performed by foreigners," he wrote. But the means of training being distinctly limited in the seventies, his ambition was not always easy to achieve. Occasionally he had to call in the aid of foreigners. When he meditated going to the Continent in order to find an oboeist, the novelist Anthony Trollope wrote to him:

"MY DEAR SULLIVAN,—

...c you going to Paris? So report has it in that Capital. If you do, will you make yourself acquainted with an American lady, one Miss Dalany. She writes to me begging that I will introduce you to her. She sings really well—*very well* indeed; she is not beautiful, but is very clever and agreeable. Do call on her like a good fellow.

"Yours always,

"ANTHONY TROLLOPE."

Though the letter led to an engagement, Sullivan was not so fortunate with his oboe player.

"I am in despair about an oboe player," he wrote. "This new military law (compulsory service) [1] plays the deuce with all engagements. I had a letter from Dubois saying he didn't think the Zoo [2] will do very well. No more do I."

The shortage of British musicians, which was hindering Sullivan at every turn, convinced him of the urgency of national training in music of all forms. He applied himself assiduously to the task of finding and training new talent. He spent days at the task, and sat up half the night composing so that his work should not fall in arrear. Young musicians, who usually possessed more ambition than talent, besieged him at his house till the ring of his door-bell was a sound of dread.

He had now become the most forceful figure in English music, not only in London, but throughout the country. He would leave his composing, go to the north to conduct a concert, then hurry to the station to catch the train back even before the audience had filed out of the hall. The strain, and the demands of his body for rest—demands that were flung aside—militated against his health. Since 1872

[1] Conscription had been introduced into France after the Franco-German War.

[2] The *Zoo* was a trifle composed by Sullivan in 1875 and performed at the St. James's. It was never printed, and much of the music was used up again by the composer in his later Savoy operas.

he had suffered from stone in the kidney which afflicted him at intervals with bouts of relentless agony. In the train, even when conducting his concerts, the enemy would wake and assail him, but his work never faltered. "I did not hear the applause, I did not see the audience," he wrote after a performance, the latter half of which had been conducted during an attack, "for the tears were rushing out of my eyes in agony."

In April, 1876, his work received official acknowledgment. He received a letter from Professor George Macfarren:

"MY DEAR SULLIVAN,—

"It is the pleasantest privilege of the office I hold at Cambridge that I have to tell you the Council of the University yesterday agreed to sanction a grace offering you the honorary degree of Doctor in Music. You will please regard this as a testimony to your earnest work in Art, and I trust as an assurance that your highest productions are appreciated."

Three months later—in June—Sullivan went to Cambridge to receive his degree. His joy was unbounded. The honour of this recognition of his serious music made a deep impression upon a sensitive soul.

"The deed is done, and I am Mus. Doc.," he wrote to his mother after the ceremony. "Now I am dressed in a black silk gown (evening dress) and a trencher hat, and am going to dine in the hall at my own College (Trinity), and then to an evening party at the Master's, Dr. Thornton. God bless you.

"Yours Affectly.,
"A. S., Mus. Doc."

The tide of success had lifted him high; now it appeared to race and bear him with it. The clamour for his work increased. His concerts were more crowded than before. The winter of 1876–7 found him going ceaselessly from place to place with greater enthusiasm than ever, travelling in unheated, comfortless trains, snowed up in the Highlands, driving in wretched horse-cabs through weather that forced the cold into his bones, yet his blood was aflame with the desires of his music. The more he urged his body against fatigue, the greater the response in melody his brain appeared to yield.

The year 1877, which was to be one of the most remarkable in his life, drew on. Hardly had the laughter and music of the New Year's party he had attended in the North of England passed, than tragedy stalked into the year which appeared to be so laden with promise. Frederic Sullivan was taken ill towards the middle of January and the brother rushed to the bedside. He did not believe that Frederic could pass out at thirty-nine; his vitality had never seemed to wane. Even when bad health hurt him cruelly, when bad luck knocked loudest at the door, Frederic had always laughed. It was Frederic who found the jest in life, Frederic who followed the younger brother in his travels with the jovial jibes in every letter which nothing could subdue. When Arthur was at the Chapel Royal, at Leipzig, and back in London, it was Frederic who kept that wonderful spirit and ecstasy burning, who adorned his letters with sketches of Arthur marching into Paris, monocle, side-whiskers and all, and Arthur marching out, Arthur conducting imaginary concerts, Arthur in every conceivable position of ridicule— letters conceived and illustrated in a splendid spirit of fraternity rare even in brotherhood.

Fortune had never been kind to Frederic Sullivan. He had many talents and worked ceaselessly, but without great reward to himself, for the Fates were shy. For many years he was employed in an architect's office. On one occasion his firm competed for the erection of the present Treasury offices, and Sullivan drew the plans. When they were finished he went home and slept for twenty-four hours. The plans which Sullivan had made were adjudged the best, and £1,000 was given for them. But the contract to build was withheld from the firm with which Sullivan was engaged because it had not sufficient money to carry out the work. The blow almost broke Sullivan's heart.

He had a great sense of humour, and when he suddenly appeared in *Trial By Jury*, London realized that a new comedian of talent had, as it were, come up in a night. From

81

a wage of £250 a year he sprang to £500, and almoſt believed himself to be a rich man. Gilbert was so enchanted with Frederic Sullivan's performance in the piece that he wrote the principal part in his next play with Arthur Sullivan— *The Sorcerer*—especially for him, but Frederic Sullivan was dead before his brother had composed a note of the music.

He was ſtrangely like his father. The happy-go-lucky nature, which had no reproach againſt the unkindliness of Fate, was the counterpart of Thomas Sullivan's. They lived together for so many years, these two, that the younger man possibly acquired the philosophy and temperament of the elder. Night by night they would go down to the kitchen and sit for hours smoking because Mrs. Sullivan could not endure the smell of tobacco. In these hours they looked at Life through the same eyes, and became unconsciously akin in all their thoughts.

Frederic married early in life and quickly surrounded himself with a young family. He had a passion for his children. In some families the father is merely the parent; in others he is the friend who can in some myſterious fashion slip his years, and make his children believe that he is only their age. Frederic Sullivan had that gift. He had a habit of giving each of his children a penny to spend, and returning the penny spent to the child that had made the beſt bargain.

All through those days and nights of mid-January Arthur Sullivan waited beside the bed of his brother. Death with its fateful wings appeared to lurk in the hot shadows of the room.

· So closely had their lives been knitted that the ſtill figure in the bed seemed as a part of himself that lay in jeopardy. Presently, in one of the lone hours of waiting, he recalled some verses which had attraΔed him a few years before when they had appeared in *Household Words*. His brother appeared to have drifted into slumber. Arthur Sullivan drew together some odd sheets of paper and sketched out the complete setting from the firſt bar to the laſt of *The Loſt Chord*. He drafted it from beginning to end while he sat beside the bed of the brother who was so soon to pass.

It was his laſt composition for many months. When, on

The Partnership Begins

January 18th, Frederic Sullivan died, his brother ceased to compose.

Just as his *In Memoriam* had been his tribute to the memory of his father in 1866, so was *The Lost Chord* his tribute to his brother in 1877. When it was published a few months later the song swept through England as an inspiration. At first the mother of the dead authoress of the words—Adelaide Procter—objected to its original title, and so it was changed to *The Lost Chord*. The inevitable penalty of popularity followed—it was parodied, to Sullivan's disgust, by Edward Solomon.[1] *The Lost Chord* eclipsed in a few months in its sales all the songs of England for over forty years.

Mrs. Ronalds, one of the sweetest singers in Society and Sullivan's life-long friend, sang it at the musical gatherings at her house on Sundays. Her Sunday *Salons* at 7, Cadogan Place were a feature of London's life. All musicians appeared there, all lovers of music in the highest walks of life were her guests. She did for music what Cardinal Ottoboni achieved at Rome in the days of Handel. She gathered about her the most brilliant musical circle of London.

Mrs. Ronalds was the greatest influence in Sullivan's life. She had amazing personality and also a fine understanding of music. By birth she was American—a member of an old Boston family named Carter—and she married Pierre Ronalds in 1859. But it was not a happy marriage, and they came to Europe only to separate. Pierre Ronalds returned to America, and his wife went to Algiers.

Ultimately she became associated with the Empress Eugenie's circle at the Tuileries, where her wonderful voice and rare beauty attracted the attention of two capitals. With the fall of the Empress she migrated to London, and was immediately accepted as one of the most talented women in Society. She was, indeed, among the few untitled people who had the privilege of calling informally at any time upon the Prince and Princess of Wales.

The influence of Mrs. Ronalds upon Arthur Sullivan has

[1] When the parody appeared, Sullivan wrote to Solomon: "I wrote *The Lost Chord* in sorrow at my brother Fred's death, don't burlesque it."—S. Adair Fitzgerald: "Story of the Savoy Opera."

often been discussed and usually misunderstood. She was at all times his mentor, and he consulted her in most things, almost in everything. When abroad he wrote to her daily, and, if no letter or telegram was forthcoming, his day was spoiled. It was a friendship the fidelity of which lasted till death, and, during its many years, was never broken for a single hour. After the death of his mother the friendship became even closer, its influence more deeply felt.

It was the Prince of Wales who remarked that he would travel the length of his future kingdom to hear Mrs. Ronalds sing *The Lost Chord*. In later years the first phonograph record ever played in England was that of Mrs. Ronalds singing this song, and it was performed in Sullivan's drawing-room. All musical society was there to hear the new invention—actors, musicians, singers, Clara Butt and all that uprising school of young singers that seemed to encircle her. When the instrument scratched its indecorous way into the first notes of *The Lost Chord*, and the voice of the singer rang through the room, clear, resonant, nearly a hundred people stared at each other in blank amazement. They might have been early Britons stained with woad, and somebody, some magician, had by a freak dropped down among them the first motor-car. No one spoke. The song—yes, it was clearly Mrs. Ronalds singing, and yet she stood there smiling at them.

The song finished on the grand "Amen." A man went up to her and said: "God gave somebody a brain to invent this instrument so that we should never forget your singing. But it was quite unnecessary."

A pretty compliment, but the speaker lacked vision. A new epoch in musical recording, a new addition to music had begun, and had begun with *The Lost Chord*.

Sullivan gave one of his manuscript copies of *The Lost Chord*—those scribbled notes that had come from the depth of his suffering—to Mrs. Ronalds. It was a fitting tribute to her, who, for more than twenty years, was the most cherished singer of his song. When, in the fullness of time, she followed him to the grave, the manuscript was, by her instructions, buried with her.

The Partnership Begins

But should it be otherwise? She sang the song to his liking as no one else ever sang it, and of all those who rendered it during the many years when it was the most widely sung melody of the world, put into it the sorrow he knew when he composed it. He openly said that she alone brought tears to his eyes with his own notes. It belonged to her. And, by all the rights of understanding of one artist for another, it was hers.

*   *   *   *   *

For weeks after his brother's death Arthur Sullivan did nothing. The burden of grief bore upon him so heavily that the effort to work and the inspiration to compose appeared to have left him. Then, in the late Spring, he began his music of *The Sorcerer*. At first the work was unequal; it came from him only with difficulty, and much of it he destroyed or recast. The fires were slow to rise.

In March he received a letter from Lewis Carroll, the author of "Alice In Wonderland," asking him if he would be prepared to set some words to music, to which Sullivan replied that, with the commitments before him, and knowing nothing of the work Carroll had in mind, he thought the chances of a collaboration were obscure. Carroll then wrote to him as follows:

"Christ Church, Oxford,
"*March* 24*th*, 1877.

'Dear Sir,—

"I thank you for your letter. I thought it needless to trouble you with any particulars till I knew if my proposal were at all possible. And now, though your answer gives little or no ground for hope, I think I may as well, before giving up all hope, tell you what it is I want, as perhaps it might change your view of my question.

"I am the writer of a little book for children, 'Alice's Adventures in Wonderland,' which has proved so unexpectedly popular that the idea of dramatizing it has been several times started. If that is ever done, I shall want it done in the best possible way, sparing no expense—and *one* feature I should want would be good music. So I thought (knowing your

85

charming compositions) it would be well to get 2 or 3 of the
songs in it set by you—to be kept for the occasion (if that
should arrive) of its being dramatized. If that idea were
finally abandoned, we might then arrange for publishing them
with music.

"In haſte,

"Faithfully yours,

"C. L. Dodgson.

('Lewis Carroll')."

Sullivan's reply was not encouraging; he ſtated that the
ſum he would require to compose the songs would be considered absurdly extravagant. But Lewis Carroll was not
deterred. He wrote again.

"Guildford.

"*March* 31*st*, 1877.

"My dear Sir,—

"I have again to thank you for a letter which like the laſt,
is nearly final, but juſt leaves the gates of Hope ajar. Excuse
my troubling you with more queſtions, but I should much
like to know what the sum is which you say would be thought
'absurdly extravagant' for the copyright of the musical setting
of a song, and also what the terms would be supposing you
had a 'royalty' for every time it was sung in public. For my
own part, I think the 'royalty' syſtem the beſt of the two
usually, but the other has the advantage of finality.

"You speak of your readiness to enter on the matter if ever
I should carry out the idea of dramatizing 'Alice'—but that is
juſt what I don't want to wait for. We might wait an
indefinite time, and then, when the thing was settled, have to
get our music prepared in a hurry—and, worse ſtill, *you*
might not then be able or willing to get something ready
beforehand; and what I know of your music is so delicious
(they tell me I have not a musical ear—so my criticism is
valueless, I fear) that I should like to secure something from
you while there is leisure time to do it in.

"Believe me,

"Very truly yours,

"C. L. Dodgson."

The Partnership Begins

It was certainly not the fault of Lewis Carroll that the collaboration—and it might have been a great collaboration—failed to mature.

Meanwhile, D'Oyly Carte had not been idle. Situated as he was at the Royalty, he saw that his dream to exploit Gilbert and Sullivan as collaborators was restricted by his own lack of independence. Therefore, at the end of 1876, he decided to go into management on his own account. He prepared a wonderful prospectus which was to be sent out to procure capital. Ultimately he formed a company which he called The Comedy Opera Company, to take over the Opera Comique Theatre in Wych Street, Strand. But his appeal to the collaborators to provide him with a piece was not immediately fulfilled. Gilbert for some time was uncertain as to a suitable theme, but at length he decided to dramatize a story he had contributed to the Christmas number of the *Graphic* called *The Elixir of Love*.

Thus did *The Sorcerer* come into being. Sullivan received the libretto a few days after he had definitely refused Lewis Carroll's request to set "Alice." It was Carte's intention to produce *The Sorcerer* during the first week of September, but he experienced considerable difficulty in getting suitable singers. Sullivan nevertheless worked hard to get the music finished and on August 18th he wrote:

"Alfred Cellier has just been here offering to help me, but I can get along now pretty well. Don't expect me to-morrow as I must have a quiet day's work. I shall then be able to get it finished by Tuesday or Wednesday. It comes out *Monday week*."

The delay in engaging the artists made him put the work aside for a while, and he did not actually finish it until the beginning of November. On the first of that month he wrote:

"I am just putting the last few bars to my opera, and to-morrow begin the scoring. I have been slaving at this work, and I hope it will be a success. Everything at present promises very well. The book is brilliant, and the music I think very pretty and good. All the company are good and like it very much."

Sir Arthur Sullivan

One of the most interesting engagements made for *The Sorcerer* was that of George Grossmith, and it was Sullivan who brought him into the company. Grossmith's own story of the engagement—an engagement which was to contribute enormously to the success of the Gilbert and Sullivan operas —is as follows:

"In the latter part of 1875 I was taking the part of a juror in *Trial By Jury* at the Haymarket for a benefit; and the late Arthur Cecil introduced me to Sullivan. Afterwards I met him in Society, and on one occasion went round to his rooms after a dinner party. The following year I received a note from him asking, 'Are you inclined to go on the stage for a time? There is a part in the new piece I am doing with Gilbert which I think you could play admirably. I can't find a good man for it.' "

So Grossmith received his first engagement with D'Oyly Carte, and when *The Sorcerer* was put on in November, he appeared as John Wellington Wells. Although his inclusion in the company had been opposed by all the directors except D'Oyly Carte and, of course, Gilbert and Sullivan, the first night of the piece decided them all that he must remain a permanent member of the company. As the Gilbert and Sullivan partnership grew up so did Grossmith grow up with it.

Immediately *The Sorcerer* had been launched, Sullivan left London for Paris. The object of the journey was to see the President of the Exhibition Commission, but he also wanted to rest. He decided to remain in the Capital till after Christmas. No word had come from Gilbert concerning a successor to *The Sorcerer*, for the Opera Comique was crowded at each performance. Meanwhile letters arrived from Carte telling of the success of the piece, and direful news of the trouble he was having with his co-directors at the theatre. *The Sorcerer* ran till May, 1878, 175 performances in all, but Carte was harassed continuously throughout the run by directors who in the afternoon wanted to close the piece down, and by the next morning wished to keep it going.

On Christmas Day Sullivan wrote from Paris to his mother in London:

The Partnership Begins

"It is very wet and miserable-looking outside, but my fire and *café-au-lait* tend to give an artificial cheerfulness to my rooms. The Dramatic profession of London has mustered in great force for Christmas. I meet someone I know at every turning. Of course they all go back for their Boxing Day performances, and a nice crossing they will have, if it is anything like the one I had. I had a cabin and lay down, so kept my balance all the way. Silva [his valet] looked green and yellow when we arrived at Boulogne. '*Ah, Monsieur, quelle traversée épouvantable!*' said he. I swaggered and said I had not noticed it—but I was deuced uncomfortable all the way.

"I have gone out of mourning for to-day, and shall put it on again to-morrow till the end of the year. But I don't see why I should wear black on dear old Fred's birthday. So I brighten up and shall drink a glass of wine to his memory, bless him, just as I should to his health if he were alive. He would have done the same for me I know. It is of no use grieving and repining. Those who are left have cares and responsibilities, and must brace themselves up and face them courageously. I hope I shall come back strong and well, for I have much to do this forthcoming year. Now good-bye, and God bless you.

"Yrs. affect.

"A."

Four days later Gilbert's outline for the new piece reached him in Paris. It was *H.M.S. Pinafore*. The possibilities of the play made a magic appeal to Sullivan. The Gilbertian wit of *The Sorcerer* had lost much of its force upon a public which as yet did not understand him—indeed one critic termed him a poseur of indifferent merit!

Sullivan started for home. On New Year's Day the tidal train bore him back to London. Back to work.

CHAPTER IX

"H.M.S. Pinafore"

H.*M.S. PINAFORE* was the first of the great Gilbert and Sullivan successes, and never did a play come so near to being a dismal failure. It was produced immediately *The Sorcerer* was withdrawn in May, 1878, and, within the first two months of its life, orders to close it down were given and countermanded by the directors no fewer than six times. D'Oyly Carte was in despair, not because *Pinafore* might be an ill-starred adventure, but because his constant upheavals with the directors made the battle for the life of the piece a difficult one. Yet in the darkest days, when it seemed as if the opera would have to be withdrawn, he never lost his faith in *Pinafore*. That he ultimately made a lot of money out of it was a deserved reward for his fidelity.

When on Saturday, May 25th, *H.M.S. Pinafore* or *The Lass That Loved a Sailor* put out to sea—metaphorically speaking—at the Opera Comique, the town declared that the part of Sir Joseph Porter, First Lord of the Admiralty —so brilliantly played throughout the run of the piece by George Grossmith—was a caricature of Mr. W. H. Smith, who had risen from a newsboy to be head of the Admiralty. *Pinafore* set the political dovecotes fluttering. Indeed, that Gilbert did caricature W. H. Smith in Sir Joseph Porter is a common legend to this day. But the letter which he sent to Sullivan in Paris with the plot of the opera is sufficient evidence that, instead of caricaturing a politician of whom he openly expressed his dislike, he did his utmost to prevent this intention being attributed to him. He wrote:

"H.M.S. Pinafore"

"24, BOLTONS,
"27th Dec. '77.

"DEAR SULLIVAN,—

"I send you herewith a sketch plot of the proposed Opera. I hope and think you will like it. I called on you two days ago (not knowing that you had gone abroad) to consult you about it before drawing it up in full. I have very little doubt whatever but that you will be pleased with it. I should have liked to have talked it over with you, as there is a good deal of fun in it which I haven't set down on paper. Among other things a song (kind of 'judge's song') for the First Lord— tracing his career as office-boy in cotton-broker's office, clerk, traveller, junior partner and First Lord of Britain's Navy.

"I think a splendid song can be made of this. Of course there will be no *personality* in this—the fact that the First Lord in the Opera is a *Radical* of the most pronounced type will do away with any suspicion that W. H. Smith is intended. . . . Barrington will be a capital captain, and Grossmith a first-rate First Lord. The uniforms of the officers and crew will be effective—the chorus will look like sailors, and we will ask to have their uniforms *made for them* at Portsmouth.

"I shall be anxious to know what you think of the plot. It seems to me that there is plenty of story in it (*The Sorcerer* rather lacks story) with good musical situations.

"Yours,
"W. S. GILBERT."

This enthusiasm was shared by Sullivan, but *Pinafore* went down in the composer's memory as the most trying work he ever achieved. Throughout almost the whole of the time he was composing, he was in the grip of terrible pain from his internal trouble. In later years he said: "It is, perhaps, rather a strange fact that the music to *Pinafore*, which was thought to be so merry and spontaneous, was written while I was suffering agonies from a cruel illness. I would compose a few bars, and then be almost insensible from pain. When the paroxysm was passed, I would write a little more, until the pain overwhelmed me again. Never was music written under such distressing conditions."

Sir Arthur Sullivan

A great house gathered for the first night. All seats were sold out days beforehand, and a crowd—far greater than the unreserved seats could accommodate—was turned away. The play went merrily through its first performance; the clever dialogue, the music sparkling in new turns of melody, the joyousness, the atmosphere, made one of the greatest *premières* of the partnership. But no one knew that the man who had provoked this atmosphere of sheer delight by the gaiety of his music had created that music out of agony. None of those who went out into the hot May night imagined Arthur Sullivan—who now, every one admitted, alone could do these things—crawling from his desk to a sofa twisted with pain, and, after an hour of suffering, dragging himself back to his desk again to laugh in his music, and to make the world laugh, while the devil's pincers tore at his body. Others had known the same road of torment. Mozart, Schubert, Handel— they gave, as Sullivan gave, beauty to the world from the hideous hours.

Oddly enough, *H.M.S. Pinafore* did not become an immediate success. The enthusiasm of that first night fell away; the unstinted praise of the critics was forgotten. A tropical summer broke over London. The streets became a purgatory; the stifling theatres as waiting-places on the fringe of hell. The receipts of the Opera Comique fell in June to £100 a night. The directors became alarmed; they gave a fortnight's notice to close the play down. But, suddenly, the receipts bounced up again, even while the heat from days of brazen skies clung with foreboding and menace about the theatre. Both Gilbert and Sullivan watched the play of the barometer, and the unaccountable barometical variations of the directors. Sullivan had always found that his work was judged on its merits. It drew or it failed. But the indecisions of these directors were beyond his power of judgment. The notices were withdrawn. The next week—the first in July—the receipts fell in one night to under £40. The notices were put out again.

The company performing *Pinafore* was kept in a state of continual nerves. In vain did D'Oyly Carte argue at the Board table that the play would make money if they would leave it alone to fight the heat. If his extraordinary personality had not swayed the other directors when they quivered like reeds in the wind, *Pinafore* would have been a record of disaster.

Then an accident happened. Sullivan, who was conductor of the Promenade Concerts started by the Gatti Brothers at Covent Garden, conducted an arrangement of the *Pinafore* music which had been prepared by Hamilton Clarke to whom he had given a commission for the work. He put it in his programme. He may have done so out of curiosity in order to discover its effect on the public; he always admitted that he did so with uncertainty. But the music was liked. Having heard it, people went down to the Opera Comique to see the play. By the end of August *Pinafore* was one of the best successes London had known for years. It was proof of the old adage that the best art to be successful needs advertisement, and by utilizing this method Sullivan advertised with success the merits of his work.

The Opera Comique now became crowded every night. Months passed, and *Pinafore* rolled merrily on to packed houses. America—with which country no adequate copyright law existed—pirated *Pinafore*. Eight theatres in New York were playing it at the same time, and filling their houses every night.

The *Pinafore* music then became rapidly known in every corner of England and America. The London publishers of the music—Metzler—issued edition after edition. In New York, one publisher after another sold out varying editions of the score of the songs. One man in particular in New York, who had been a copyist in a music publisher's office, bought a press, purloined *Pinafore*, sold it in cartloads, paid off all his establishment expenses, and retired a rich man, having built up from this escapade—this dishonest adventure—a business that achieved much in furthering the issue of other music.

But, meanwhile, New York had played havoc with *Pinafore*. The theatrical managers introduced into the play endless diversions of their own. There was a song inserted about a new design in trousers—a design which was swaying the sartorial opinions of New York at the moment. There was a song that had been inspired by a new supper dish which neither Gilbert nor Sullivan nor the British public had ever heard of. Some thousands of barrel organs churned out Gilbert and Sullivan all over New York—including the song about the trousers—and New York felt sure that Gilbert and Sullivan were good! The eight theatres that were playing *Pinafore* were all situated within a quarter of a mile of Fifth Avenue, and each version carried at least one song of which the words and often the music were unknown to the parents of *Pinafore*. And there was no law to end the scandal.

At the end of July, 1879, the situation in London became grave. The lease of the Opera Comique to the Comedy Opera Company ran out. D'Oyly Carte was in America, and he had left in his place at the theatre Michael Gunn, a young man of decided business acumen, to keep the Carte flag flying. Gunn decided to continue *Pinafore* without a querulous board of directors.

Meanwhile, Gilbert and Sullivan had discussed the advisability of going to America to circumvent, if they could, the piracy of their work, which was pouring fortunes into the coffers of eight theatres. In vain Sullivan protested in the Press about the ways of the American pirates. The law, or rather the lack of it, continued, so did *Pinafore* in New York. To his friend, C. K. Remington of Buffalo, Sullivan wrote:

"DEAR MR. REMINGTON,—

"It is very good indeed of you to send me so many interesting scraps about the *Pinafore* in America. I am gratified beyond measure at its success there, but there is one matter of great regret to me. Not the money question, although I don't pretend for an instant that I should not prefer to be paid for my work. No, my regret is that my music is not performed as I wrote it.

"Orchestral colouring plays so great a part in my work that to deprive them of this is to take away from the attraction. ... For a very small sum a manager might have had a copy of my score, and my work would have been given to the American public as I wrote it, instead of in a garbled form.

"H.M.S. Pinafore"

"An American lady once said to me, 'No, I don't think I will dine with you because I shall meet none but my own countrymen; you've a mania for Americans.' Well, I'm glad to say that, in spite of the success of *Pinafore*, this mania continues.

"ARTHUR SULLIVAN."

Sullivan's health was suffering, and, in consequence, his departure for America was delayed for some time. The trouble that produced *Pinafore* from a welter of pain had been gaining ground. In order to prepare himself for the journey he had submitted to an operation.

On August 1st, 1879, the Duke of Edinburgh wrote to him:

"MY DEAR SULLIVAN,—

"I cannot tell you how glad I was to read in your letter that you were relieved from your sufferings by a successful operation. The Prince of Wales has asked me to join his congratulations to mine. I hope you will now take great care of yourself, and pick up plenty of strength for your journey to America. . . .

"ALFRED."

The board of directors of the Comedy Opera Company was still in a state of turmoil. These directors saw—or thought they saw in the absence of D'Oyly Carte in America—an opportunity to "jump the claim." On the night of July 31st, 1879, a raid was made on the Opera Comique by the hirelings of these directors, and an attempt was made to seize the scenery during the evening performance. A letter from Gilbert to Sullivan, dated August 6th, described the events.

"By the way, on Friday night they broke into the theatre with a mob of 50 roughs, during the performance, and tried to carry off the properties. Barker resisted their approach, and was knocked downstairs and seriously hurt. There was an alarm among the audience who raised a cry of 'Fire'— appeased, however, by Grossmith who made them a speech from the stage. Barker has applied for summonses and the case comes on next Monday. . . . I hear the performance at the Aquarium was wretched, and that very few audience were present. J. G. Taylor plays Sir Joseph as a low comedy

95

D*

part, and the soprano is a contralto so has to take her high notes an octave lower. That's all the news.

"W. S. GILBERT."

The attack on the Opera Comique failed, and in the litigation that ensued the Master of the Rolls wrung the withers of the directors by declaring that the case was an audacious attempt to rob Gilbert and Sullivan of their property. The disgruntled directors then decided on a new attack. They opened with *Pinafore* at the Imperial Theatre, Westminster. It is to this opening that Gilbert referred in his letter. They scratched a company together. Then they grew bolder, they moved it to the Olympic Theatre in Wych Street, Strand, which rubbed shoulders with the Opera Comique.

Gilbert and Sullivan then issued their manifesto in which they made it clear that the company playing at the Opera Comique alone performed their authorized version, and that the players were those they had selected.

London enjoyed the quarrel, and *Pinafore* drew from it a great advertisement. Moreover, London discovered through the Press that this, the most English of plays, was a triumph in New York. Crowds packed the Olympic; greater crowds thronged the Opera Comique, and the confusion caused chatter in the drawing-rooms. The battle for the scenery, a gang of hectoring raiders trying to strip the theatre during the performance, was a ten days' sensation. It acclaimed the value of Gilbert and Sullivan opera when mobs of people fought over the rights. To the playgoing public *Pinafore* became more and more an opera to be seen.

Meanwhile, Gilbert had made considerable headway with the successor to *Pinafore*, although as yet there was no reason to suppose that it would be required for a considerable period. Early in August he wrote to Sullivan about the libretto of *The Pirates of Penzance*:

"I've broken the neck of Act II, and see my way clearly to the end. I think it comes out very well.

"By the way, I've made great use of the 'Tarantara' business in Act II. The police always say 'Tarantara' when they desire to work their courage up to the sticking point. They are

96

naturally timid, but, through the agency of this talisman, they
are enabled to acquit themselves well. When concealed in
Act II, and the robbers approach, their courage begins to fail
them, but a recourse to Tarantara (pianissimo) has the desired
effect. . . .

"W. S. Gilbert."

As soon as Sullivan received the libretto from Gilbert he
began the composition, not in Act I, but in the middle of
Act II. He would have completed the composition of the
Pirates whilst *Pinafore* was still drawing full houses, had not
another project intervened. In D'Oyly Carte's office one
morning Gilbert and Sullivan resolved to go to America
immediately, in order to make some attempt to share in the
profits which were pouring into the New York theatres by the
pirating of *Pinafore*. "I will not have another libretto of
mine produced if the Americans are going to steal it," Gilbert
declared in a fit of spleen. "It's not that I need the money
so much, but it upsets my digestion!"

Together with Alfred Cellier—the conductor of the Opera
Comique—and Blanche Rooseveld—a Covent Garden
soprano of great quality who was to play lead—they left
England in November. The night before sailing Sullivan
wrote to his mother:

"This is the *very last* sheet of notepaper in the house, and
the *very last* letter I write before I go away. I have had
an awful day, never alone, and never ceasing work, except
for dinner, from 9 this morning till 1 a.m. now. At least
30 people I have seen. I was writing and working all last
evening, and finished a song *Edward Gray*, which I have
promised for a Tennyson Collection."[1]

The voyage was trying in the extreme; even Gilbert re-

[1] In another letter to his mother at this time he said: "If you had come in
last night you would have found me in company with *Edward Gray*—a song
of Tennyson's I had to set before I went away." Surely there is no better
proof of the manner in which Sullivan was able to withdraw his thoughts from
all surrounding influences when composing. In spite of all the upheaval of
packing, the natural excitement of farewells on account of the coming journey
to America, he was able to sit down and employ the last hours before starting
in composing a song of such distinguished beauty and feeling as *Edward Gray*.

marked that the humours of life were confined to the country
he had left, and not to the seas it was supposed to rule.
Clay had preceded them to America, and was waiting to
meet them on the quay when the boat came in.

Their invasion of America was the talk of New York.
Everybody expected a splendid battle between the owners and
the pirates. There would be the devil to pay!

Both author and composer were fêted everywhere. "On
Saturday we dined at the Lotus Club," Sullivan wrote in his
first letter home. "It was a splendid reception, and although
both Gilbert and myself were very nervous, we spoke very well,
and, I am told, at once gained the goodwill and sympathy of
our hearers who comprised the most prominent men in New
York. The Judge of the Police Court in his speech said
that, to shew his hearty goodwill, and to mark his feeling of
gratitude for the many happy hours we had given him, he
hoped we might soon be brought before him as drunk and
disorderly, so that he might have the satisfaction of letting
us off!"

"We have engaged a first-rate chorus, and the Principals
are the best who have ever been got together for the immortal
Pinafore," he wrote a few days later. "We open on Monday
week (Dec. 1), and the rest depends upon the public. . . . I
must do the Americans the justice to say that they are most
wonderfully kind and hospitable. The moment a man sees
you, he wants to know what he can do for you, and means it
too. Of course it is an exciting state of existence—too
exciting for me. I live in a semi-public state all the time,
everything I do watched, every word I say noted and publicly
commented on, so that I get bewildered and dazed, and long
for a little rest and quietness, but I fear it is out of the question
here."

The confusion which American homage brought to him was
reflected in his next letter: "Americans for three hours this
afternoon. I've talked to more Americans half the night, and
I'm told that there are still more Americans whom I haven't
talked to coming to-morrow morning. What I want to know
is—where do all these Americans end!"

When they opened the Fifth Avenue Theatre the opera

created a sensation, insomuch as the various versions with unlicensed American additions had left people wondering what *Pinafore* really was. Eloquent testimony of this was the criticism of a journal which said: "We've seen it as a comedy, we've seen it as a tragedy, but the play these Englishmen have brought over is quite a new play to us, and very good it is."

It was soon obvious that with eight theatres playing *Pinafore*, all the barrel-organs of the city grinding out its music—music which, in printed form, was in every music-shop—the financial fruits had been taken by the pirates. There was nothing left but for Sullivan to complete his music to *The Pirates of Penzance*, and produce the opera in New York before it fell into the hands of those managers who would purloin and play it free of royalty. With the exception of the portion of Act II which Sullivan had written before leaving England, he composed the whole of *The Pirates of Penzance* at his hotel in New York. He worked at the music ceaselessly.

"I told you about our magnificent first night of the 'Pinafore' here," he wrote to his mother. "We have been going fairly well since then, but the houses are not good enough to pay us, and so we are hard at work rehearsing the new piece, as that, we hope, will bring great houses. I am writing night and day at the last Act—the second is done and in rehearsal. I cannot really enjoy myself until it is produced, as I cannot go anywhere or do anything. I fear I left all my sketches of the last Act at home, as I have searched everywhere for them. I would have telegraphed for them, but they could not have arrived in time. It is a great nuisance as I have to re-write it all now, and can't recollect every number I did. We hope to get it out in a fortnight from next Saturday—27th. I think it will be a great success, for it is exquisitely funny, and the music is strikingly tuneful and catching."

Then two days later:

"Our houses at the *Pinafore* have fallen off very much this week. All the theatres are doing badly, and we shall have no profits until the new piece comes out—so Gilbert and I are reducing our expenditure. We shall begin by not paying the postage of our letters home! We hope to have the new Opera out on the 27*th* or 29*th*. It is called *The Pirates of*

Penzance, or Love and Duty.[1]   I can't help feeling sanguine of success although we ought never to be sanguine."

A few days before Christmas he wrote again:

"It is 4 a.m. and I tear myself away from my scoring to get this off by the steamer 'City of Boston' which leaves at 11 a.m. We are tremendously hard at work, rehearsing all day, writing all night. I have finished the Opera of course, and am now scoring for dear life. It comes out on Tuesday the 30th. If it isn't a success it won't be our fault, for everyone thinks it lovely—those who have heard it at rehearsals. If it is a success, of course it will pay us very well . . . on the 8th of January I go to Baltimore to 'A Grand Concert of Welcome' given in my honour. All my own works which I conduct."

Soon after he landed in America Sullivan began to keep a diary, and he kept these diaries carefully until his death. They cover a period of twenty-one years, and reveal, as no other record can reveal, his method of working. He put all his thoughts into these diaries, his impressions of things as they happened, his impressions of people, of plays, the story of how he composed his operas, and the records of the first nights of their production.

The first entries in the diary, made while he was working on *The Pirates of Penzance* in New York are of interest.

"10th December.—Writing all day. Gilbert, Cellier, Cecil Clay called. Cellier stayed and finished 2nd Act. I wrote till 4.30.

"13th December—Conducted matinée at theatre (Pinafore). Came home and wrote. Had no dinner.

"14th December.—Wrote all day. Went to the Grants afterwards. Came home and wrote.

"15th December.—Rehearsal of music of 1st Act at the theatre. Wrote afterwards. Dined at the Manhattan Club with Gilbert. Went round to theatre. Then home to work.

"16th December.—Wrote in the morning. Interrupted

---

[1] When *The Pirates of Penzance* was afterwards produced in London, the alternative title was *The Slave of Duty*. In Gilbert's original manuscript of the libretto used by Sullivan for setting it is given as *A Sense of Duty*.

by constant callers. No dinner. Went to concert of the Mendelssohn Glee Club; heard 'The Long Day Closes.' Admirably sung and encored.

"17th December.—Began scoring of Opera. Went to rehearsal 11—4. Came home tired. Couldn't work. Dined at Bett's. Then home. Wrote Trio (2nd Act) and Ruth's Song (1st Act) and went to bed at 5 (a.m.)

"18th December.—Rehearsal at my own rooms of Principals, 11.30 till 3.30. Very tired. Went to bed at 5.30 till 7. Then up, had a walk, dined with Gilbert. Came home; scored 2 numbers of 1st Act. Went to bed at 4.

"19th December.—At work all day, scoring. Went to 'Pinafore' afterwards. I conducted. Came home with Cellier; stopped at Dorlon's to have a chop; saw Sothern there. Wrote till 6 a.m.

"20th December.—Conducted at matinée. Came home at 9.30 and wrote till 4 a.m. The roysterers (Gilbert and Clay) came in of course about 1.

"21st Sunday.—Came home and worked till 5.30 (a.m.)

"25th. Christmas Day.—Worked all day. Dined at Grant's. Came home and worked till 5.30 (a.m.)

"26th December.—Writing. First Act rehearsed with Band only.

"27th December.—Finished full score at 7 a.m. on morning of 28th, Sunday.

"29th December.—Full band rehearsal 10.30, 2nd Act. First Act, full dress. Rehearsal at night again, 8 o'clock, of 2nd Act. Full dress. In despair because it went so badly. Finished at 1.

"30th December.—Full Band rehearsal of 2nd Act at 10.30. Went much better—lasted till 1.30 only. Full dress rehearsal at 8. Press and some friends there. Excellent rehearsal; everyone enthusiastic. Over at 1. Came home with Cellier, Clay and Gilbert; all set to work at the Overture. Gilbert and Clay knocked off at 3 a.m. Cellier and I wrote till 5 and finished it.

"31st December.—(First Night of 'The Pirates of Penzance.') No rehearsal, except Band at 11 for Overture. Home at 1.45 to breakfast. Too ill to eat. Went to bed to try and get sleep, but could not. Stayed in bed till 5.30. Gilbert came. Got up feeling miserably ill. Head on fire. Dressed slowly and got to New York club at 7.30. Had 12 oysters and a glass of champagne. Went to Theatre. House crammed with the élite of New York. Went into the orchestra, more dead than alive, but got better when I took the stick in my hand—fine reception. Grand success. Then home—could not sleep, so did not go to bed till 3.30. Felt utterly worn out."

It was on the last night of 1879 as the diary records, that Gilbert and Sullivan sprang a surprise on New York with the production of *The Pirates of Penzance* at the Fifth Avenue Theatre, and within twenty-four hours a copyright performance was given at Paignton in South Devon, England, thereby protecting the English copyright.

The reception of *The Pirates of Penzance*, from the moment the curtain went up, was amazing. Sanguine Sullivan may have been, but he could not have foreseen this headlong rush to success. New York playgoers declared that there had been no such *première* within their memory. Journalists sat outside his rooms for interviews; theatrical managers from all the principal cities of the States telegraphed offers for the opera to be produced at their theatres. Whatever America had stolen, America was now ready to repay. The telegrams piled up; the journalists became more insistent than ever. Sullivan did nothing except to write one letter to his mother.

"45 East 20th St., N.Y.
"2nd January, 1880.

"Dearest Mum,—

"At last I am out of my penal servitude and find a little breathing time to look around me, and write home. Since I last wrote to you I have had the usual tremendous strain upon me before producing a new work, only more so. For I found that all my sketches for the 1st Act which I had made before leaving home had been left behind in England.

"The 2nd Act I brought with me complete, so they set to work rehearsing that while I wrote the 1st Act. Then I had the whole opera to score, of course—so that the last three weeks have been imprisonment with hard labour, never going to bed before 5.30 in the morning, sometimes later. However it was finished at last, even the Overture, and brought out the night before last with a success unparalleled in New York as our telegram will have told you.

"We had long and wearisome rehearsals, but fortunately our Company and all the Chorus are charming people and devoted to us, and spared themselves no pains or trouble to do their work thoroughly well. All except the Tenor who is an idiot—vain and empty-headed. He very nearly upset the piece on the first night as he didn't know his words, and forgot his music. We shall, I think, have to get rid of him.

"On Tuesday night there was a full dress rehearsal to which most of the Press and a few personal friends were invited. To my surprise it all went very smoothly indeed, and those who were there were wildly enthusiastic. It was over at *one*, and then I came home and, assisted by Clay and Gilbert as copyists, Cellier and I finished the Overture. I got to bed at 5, and was up again at 9 for a Band rehearsal.

"I was dreadfully ill all day. I could hardly hold up my head—it ached and burnt like iron. I could eat nothing, and when I went into the Orchestra at 8 I felt more dead than alive, and I looked so, everybody told me.

"When the curtain went up after the Overture, I began to pull myself together and thought only of the piece. There was no doubt about its success, we took *nine* encores, and might have had more if I liked.

"The laughter and applause continued through the whole piece until the very end, and then there were thunder calls for Gilbert and myself after every Act. Its success was undoubted and instantaneous, and the next day (yesterday) both performances (being New Year's Day there was a *matinée* as well) were crowded. We anticipate immense business for the next few weeks.

"What do I think of the piece myself? The *libretto* is ingenious, clever, wonderfully funny in parts, and sometimes brilliant in dialogue—beautifully written for music, as is all Gilbert does, and all the action and business perfect. The music is infinitely superior in every way to the *Pinafore*—

'tunier' and more developed, of a higher class altogether. I think that in time it will be more popular. Then the *mise-en-scène* and the dresses are something to be dreamed about. I never saw such a beautiful combination of colour and form on any stage. All the girls dressed in the old-fashioned English style, every dress designed separately by Faustin, and some of the girls look as if they had stepped out of a Gainsborough picture. The New York ladies are raving about them. The 'Policemen's Chorus' is an enormous hit and they are cheered tremendously when they march on with their Bulls-Eyes all alight, and are always encored. I am sanguine of its success in London, for there are the local allusions etc. which will have twice the force they have here. . . .

"So the New Year opens auspiciously for me."

The American laws at that period offered no security whatever to the author and composer. Sullivan had to keep the music in manuscript form because the American law decreed that, directly it appeared in print, it became the property of anyone. After each performance at the Fifth Avenue the music had to be carefully collected and locked in a safe till the following evening. Attempts to obtain the music by nefarious means were carried on ceaselessly, even to the extent of placing expert musicians in the audience to take down the themes as they were played, in the hope of ultimately piecing the entire music of the Opera together.

But the defence was stronger than the attack. The Fifth Avenue Theatre was packed nightly, and the theatrical pirates were foiled, at least for the time being.

One evening Gilbert and Sullivan stood together on the steps of the theatre talking business. A man passed who, recognizing the pair as Englishmen, apparently resented their presence. He spat on Gilbert's boot. Gilbert ceased to talk. He looked down at his boot; he looked at the disappearing back of the aggressor. Then, turning again to Sullivan, he said, imitating the American drawl: "Waal, I guess I like the manners of the feller. They are so fresh!"

On January 8th, after a concert given at Baltimore in his honour, Sullivan wrote to his mother:·

"H.M.S. Pinafore"

"Mount Vernon Hotel, Baltimore.

"Here I am; the Concert is over, and I have to be up at six to-morrow morning to go off by the 7.10 train. So before going to bed I write a line for Saturday's steamer to tell you that all has gone well, and that I am delighted with the Baltimoreites. . . . *The Pirates of Penzance* is still doing enormous business every night and likely to last, so that at last I really think I shall get a little money out of America. I ought to, for they have made a good deal out of me. We are going to send out two Companies, one for New England, and another to the South—Washington, Baltimore, etc. Strike whilst the iron is hot."

The interest in the *Pirates* soon convinced the partners that extra companies could be sent out, and before a fortnight had elapsed some changes were made in the plans. Much of the labour of organization and rehearsal fell upon Sullivan, and in writing home towards the end of January he said:

"Although our work is nominally over, and we ought to be resting, yet the very success of the piece keeps us hard at work, for, in order to strike whilst the iron is hot, and get all the profit we can while everyone is talking about it, we are sending out three companies to other towns in America, and these have to be selected, organized and rehearsed. . . . All this involves a lot of work and constant anxiety. But we don't mind it; we all work like slaves, D'Oyly, Cellier, Gilbert and myself. Cellier is at Philadelphia this week rehearsing the chorus over there, and I am doing the rehearsals here. The houses here have been excellent, and I believe will keep up through Lent. You have probably received our telegrams about the receipts and profits. Of course we can't expect them to go on at this rate, but we shall reap a good harvest all the same, I hope and believe. In the meantime the excitement is kept alive by articles and correspondence in the newspapers about conspiracies to pirate the opera."

As the weeks passed the work rapidly increased; the clamour for the *Pirates* came from every town in the States. Had Sullivan been wise he would have abandoned—in view of the attacks of bad health to which he was so completely a victim—all social and public functions, for the strain was becoming greater upon him than he could bear. He was found one day lying in his room almost unconscious with agony; that same evening he spoke at a public dinner given in his honour. He would rehearse all day, attend a Society dinner in the evening, then return to the theatre and carry on rehearsals late into the night.

In his speeches he spoke with a fearlessness of expression which might have made enemies for him but for the good temper behind his words. He attacked the American law which permitted the wholesale piracy to which he had been subjected; he even went so far as to reprove the American women in English Society.

"The many charming American women who visit England," he said, "have no cause to complain of the welcome they receive in English Society. Their nationality is a passport that opens all doors to them. As this is the case, and no pleasant attractive American can ever complain of being left out (if only fairly accredited) why are they so ill-natured about each other? The moment they get settled in English Society, their chief object seems to be to keep the newcomer out, and if possible oust those who are already admitted.

"The other day a friend of mine was in a house where some Americans were congregated. It was touching to see their affection towards each other. They 'dear-ed' and 'darling'd' and 'Hattie-d' and 'Sadie-d' in a manner that very much moved my friend who is a man of simple, affectionate nature. But one of them left the room for a short time, and the interval was too precious to be wasted.

"Down came woman's wrath and just anger against the offending creature who by her natural charm, great kindness and patience under trying domestic circumstances had made and kept many good friends—patience under slander arising from jealousy. . . . No, dear charming ladies, you will not acquire a greater social importance yourselves by trying to depreciate others. Don't let me have to speak again, I pray you!"

Sullivan's five months in America were now drawing to a

close. He had decided to go to the Western States and Cuba with Gilbert, but it was necessary that they should return for the Spring production of *The Pirates of Penzance* in London —a production which could not be deferred longer without missing the season. They changed their plans. With Gilbert and D'Oyly Carte he went to Buffalo to launch a new company and then to Niagara, after which he left his two friends who were returning to New York, and proceeded alone to Ottawa.

"Here I am, seated at my window watching the great Niagara dashing and foaming within fifty yards of me," he wrote on February 23rd. "This is my first day of rest for a very long time. Up till Friday last, the day we started, we worked night and day like niggers. . . . It isn't only the rehearsals that take up time, it is the whole of the details which are so worrying—band parts, conductors' parts to get ready. However, we got all in order and finished our last (dress) rehearsal at 4 last Friday. Then came a hurry and scurry to get off by the 6 train—people, dresses, music, baggage. . . . The Company consisted of about 60 all together, with Gilbert, Carte and myself. We arrived at Buffalo at 8 on Saturday morning in a violent snowstorm. Of course our first thought was 'Bad house this morning.' We played at 2, and it wasn't a very good house, nor was it a good performance—everyone was nervous and made mistakes. But at night the house was crowded, and it went very well. Gilbert and I got a good reception, and everyone seemed pleased. We said 'Good-bye' to our company in the morning, as they were going on to Cincinnati to play this week, and we three 'bosses' took train to Niagara."

At Ottawa a sleigh met him at the station and took him to Government House to stay with Princess Louise and the Marquess of Lorne. Then after a few days' tobogganing —"I wasn't sure whether I had got my body on or left it behind," he wrote—he hurried back to New York, and with Gilbert and Carte embarked on the *Gallia* for England on March 3rd.

The *Pirates* was produced at the Opera Comique on April 8th with George Grossmith in the part of the Major-

General. The success of the American production was
repeated.   After a first night, boisterous with enthusiasm, the
play settled down into an unbroken run of over four hundred
performances.

CHAPTER X

A Baltic Journey and " Patience "

ALTHOUGH for some time the success which had followed his light opera music had created an irresistible attraction to this form of composition, Sullivan had no intention of neglecting more serious work. He was not unjustly conscious of the fact that he had become a pivot of English music in all its forms. In 1878, for instance, he had been chosen as the Royal Commissioner for Music at the Paris Exhibition. The French adopted many of Sullivan's suggestions and made him an officer of the Legion of Honour. Finally, they gave a concert in Paris at which only his music and that of other English composers was played.

The Prince of Wales had watched Sullivan's work at the Conference, and was not in ignorance of his influence on the music of the Exhibition. A few months later he sent Sullivan a signed photograph with this autographed letter:

"As the labours of the Royal Commission for the Paris Universal Exhibition of 1878 have now come to a close, I desire to acknowledge the valuable services you rendered as a member of the Staff of this Commission, and, while expressing my personal obligations for the zeal and efficiency with which you have performed the important work assigned to you, I have much pleasure in presenting to you the accompanying portrait as a memento of our connection with the work of the Paris Exhibition which has been attended with such satisfactory results.

"ALBERT EDWARD. P.
"*President of the Royal Commission for the
Paris Universal Exhibition of 1878.*"

But apart from his *Henry VIII* music for Calvert which was produced in Manchester in 1878, Sullivan composed no serious work again until 1880. Whilst in America he had received from the Council of the Leeds Festival an invitation to compose a full-length work for the Festival in the autumn, and, since the success of *The Pirates of Penzance* left him free from opera, he accepted it. Nevertheless he found difficulty in the choice of a subject. He studied the Scriptures only to decide that the Bible had been so freely used for oratorios that he must look elsewhere.

Eventually he decided on *The Martyr of Antioch*, the religious drama by the late Dean Milman of St. Paul's. The *Martyr*, as the Dean, true poet as he was, had written it, was quite unsuitable for composition, so, with the consent of the Dean's sons, Sullivan made selections from the work and persuaded Gilbert to put them into verse.

It was a curious commission for a writer of "Bab Ballads" and light libretti, but so attuned had the minds of the partners now become, that Gilbert knew exactly what Sullivan required, and he gave it to him very quickly. When the *Martyr of Antioch* was produced at Leeds it was acclaimed a triumph. The beauty of such numbers as "Come, Margarita, Come," of the Funeral Anthem, "Brother, Thou Hast Gone Before Us," gave the certain assurance that, in spite of his divergence into light opera, Sullivan as a composer of religious work was greater than ever. Again did the highbrow critics hurl taunts at Sullivan from their armchairs, reproving him in the fashion of their colossal wisdom with throwing away his talents on "theatrical frivolities" when he could produce majestic music. Sullivan merely smiled; had not Gilbert already intrigued him with a scheme for a work called *Patience*, and convinced him that here was another great success waiting for them to take?

Gilbert was proud of his association with *The Martyr of Antioch*, although he never collaborated with Sullivan in work of this kind again. Shortly after this festival he wrote a gracious letter to Sullivan:

A Baltic Journey and "Patience"

"24, THE BOLTONS, SOUTH KENSINGTON.

3rd Dec., 1880.

"DEAR SULLIVAN,—

"It always seemed to me that my particularly humble services in connection with the Leeds Festival had received far more than their meed of acknowledgement in your preamble to the *libretti*—and it most certainly never occurred to me to look for any other reward than the honour of being associated, however remotely and unworthily, in a success which, I suppose, will endure until music itself shall die. Pray believe that of the many substantial advantages that have resulted to me from our association, this last is, and always will be, the most highly prized.

"Very truly yours,

"W. S. GILBERT."

Probably not the least valued of the congratulations which poured in upon Sullivan after the production of the *Martyr* was a letter from Joseph Barnby. What memories it must have recalled of the battle in the final stage of the Mendelssohn Scholarship against his friend, who now, as he, was one of the most admired musicians of England! Barnby wrote:

"Sincere and hearty congratulations on the achievement of a great work. No matter what the public may say of it, you have created a work which is an honour to England."

Meanwhile, Gilbert was working away at the libretto of *Patience*, but toward the end of the year he decided to alter it. "I don't feel happy about it," he wrote to Sullivan. "I mistrust the clerical element. I feel hampered by the restrictions which the nature of the subject places upon my freedom of action, and I want to revert to my old idea of rivalry between two æsthetic fanatics."

He met Sullivan and promptly changed his plot. He worked at *Patience* anew, treating the piece from a different angle. Sullivan went down to Nice to spend Christmas, and took a portion of the newly-constructed *Patience* in his bag. The entry in his diary at the beginning of 1881 is the best evidence that *Patience* was not destined to be completed in haste, as was the case with so many of the operas that came from the partnership. In more than one way the piece was well-named.

Sullivan wrote thus in his diary:

"The year 1881 opens when I am still at Nice. Having brought with me some numbers of the new opera G. and I intend doing (*Patience*) I occasionally try to find a few ideas; amongst others I sketch Bunthorne's song 'A Good Young Man,' but the sunshine and my natural indolence prevent my doing any really serious work. I enjoy myself doing nothing, with many visits to Monte Carlo."

Sullivan left Nice for Italy on January 11th, together with a friend who had a scheme concerning local and suburban tramways at Turin. They discovered the City official whose word on trains in Turin was law. He insisted on going with them to obscure and distant villages in order that they should see the roads through which the trams must pass, and interview the "Syndic." " 'The Syndic,' " Sullivan writes in his diary, "and the 'Ex-Syndic' are both hearty jolly farmers. They can't speak anything but Italian, so *I* am interpreter (save the mark!)"

The business eventually came to nothing, and Sullivan returned to Paris towards the end of January. He was still in holiday mood, and the *Patience* libretto in his bag claimed his attention in vain. He dined at Bignon's on the Avenue de l'Opéra, went to see *Divorçons*, then the rage of Paris, and which he thought "deliciously funny." The musical circle finding him in its midst swept him into a round of gaiety, but by the middle of February he was back in London.

Three things occupied him on his return. He was busy in the daytime with the rehearsals of *The Martyr of Antioch* at the School of Music. He spent hours in solicitors' offices going into details of the lawsuit which D'Oyly Carte, Gilbert and himself were bringing against the Comedy Opera Company.

He did not attack *Patience* with the old diligence. He would compose a few numbers, then leave them. He was at this time undoubtedly interested to a greater extent in his serious music. It is probably true that he rejoiced more over the great success of *The Martyr of Antioch* than over the far greater financial success of *Patience*. That wonderful storehouse of melody for light opera, which was his, had been, as yet, but lightly drawn upon. The themes that responded to his every mood, the joyousness of life, the serious and the tender moments which life gives in turn, brought from him music of differing expression, and beautiful in its manifold phases. It is also true that Gilbert was giving him wonderful pegs on which to hang his notes.

The case against the Comedy Opera Company began on March 10th. Henry Irving, Palgrave Simpson—all the stars of the theatrical firmament were there. Charles Russell[1] fought the case for D'Oyly Carte and the collaborators, and he won it, without a single witness for the plaintiffs being called. From that moment the Comedy Opera Company had no right to perform the work of Gilbert and Sullivan. It went into liquidation, and the verdict gave Gilbert, Sullivan and Carte freedom. This cemented the great trilogy which was to provide London for fifteen years with the best light opera in all the varying history of its theatre.

With the lawsuit out of the way, Sullivan settled down to work. He gave *The Martyr of Antioch* at the Albert Hall early in April, the Prince of Wales being present. "The chorus surprised me," he wrote after weeks of rehearsal. "It was truly magnificent." Then he turned again to *Patience*. Parts of the opera were actually in rehearsal before he had begun to think about the rest of the work. He worked night after night till 5 in the morning. The opera was to be produced on April 23rd; on the 13th he began the scoring. Ten days in which to score an opera that was going to run for a year and a half! They laughed at him, and told him sagely that the curtain could never go up on the 23rd.

He was rehearsing one part of the opera at the same time as he was scoring the rest of it. Here is his diary entry for April 20th:

"Rehearsal at 12, then home to write Tenor song, afterwards cut out. Duke of Edinburgh called to see me, stayed while I wrote and dined. Went to the theatre at 7.30 to dress rehearsal. Came home late. Scored Tenor song and

---

[1] Afterwards Lord Russell of Killowen.

sketched out Overture. To bed 5.30 a.m. Finished all scoring of the Opera."

And only three days to the production! His doctor hectored and bullied. But no warnings assuaged his ardours.

On the 21st—two days before the production—Sullivan sketched out the Overture. He finished it the next morning in time to have the parts copied and rehearsed at night. On Saturday, April 23rd, the play was produced at the Opera Comique. A few lines in the diary relate what happened:

"Crammed house at Opera Comique. Enthusiastic reception on entering the orchestra. New piece ('Patience') performed for first time. Went splendidly. Eight encores. Seemed a great success. Called at the Fielding [1] for a lemon and soda. Talked a little to Randegger, John Hare, Aide, etc."

Walter Browne, who played the part of Colonel Calverley in the production of *Patience*, was selected by D'Oyly Carte for the part, but he did not know Sullivan, and was a little uncertain as to what the composer would think of his voice. He was told to go to Carte's office in Beaufort Buildings where Sullivan would arrive in due course and test his singing. Browne obeyed instructions, but Carte was not there. Instead, Browne found a man in Carte's office strumming on the piano.

"I have come to sing to Mr. Sullivan," he said.

The other looked up, but went on playing.

"Well, I hope for your sake you're in good voice," he said. "Best thing you can do is to try your songs over with me before he comes in."

Browne did so. He sang them through. Then D'Oyly Carte entered.

"Hullo, Sullivan," he said to the man at the piano.

Patience proved altogether too great a draw for the Opera Comique; hundreds of people were turned away regularly every night. It was obvious already that no further light opera would be required from Sullivan for some time to come. There was no immediate urge to work. Music, "that most brutal of all mistresses" as he had once termed it, was now

[1] A small club in Covent Garden.

returning him rich recompense for his years of slavery. No longer was there any need of economy, and yet he practised it and broke into violent fits of generosity towards others at the same time. The strict economical discipline of the Leipzig years was not to be forgotten as one might some uncomfortable chapter of one's youth. Royalties were now coming in from many sources. The year previous he had made little short of ten thousand pounds—half of which he had received from *The Pirates of Penzance*—and, as the months passed, this figure was quickly exceeded.

In June, 1881, the Duke of Edinburgh invited Sullivan and Fred Clay to go as his guests to St. Petersburg, travelling on *H.M.S. Hercules* to the Baltic. He had no important work in hand, and he had also no desire to work. He said frankly that he was going to compose nothing further until Gilbert came along with a new libretto, or a Festival Committee became so insistent in its demand for a fresh work that he must yield in order to be rid of the nuisance. This, however, was only a brief phase. He had not been at sea two days before he was organizing concerts on board, and actually singing songs himself out of *Pinafore* to a nautical audience. He did not realize—probably he did not fully realize at any time—that music was the one thing in life he could never do without, since it was so much a natural part of himself. To slip this other self for a while, to rush off to the Riviera, or some haunt where his work was forgotten, never yielded him any lasting satisfaction. Before long he came back to his music.

The *Hercules* put in at Copenhagen. The King of Denmark had long been an admirer of Sullivan's music, and the Court orchestra possessed almost every page of music Sullivan had ever written, with standing orders that Sullivan was to figure in the programme at dinner at least once a week. A kingly welcome awaited the Duke and Sullivan when they reached the capital. A banquet, to which more than a hundred people sat down, was given at the royal hunting-box situated about an hour and a half's journey away from the city. It was a banquet worthy of a royal court. The food and wines were without compare, the music Sullivan's, and the speeches full

of international cordiality, heightened by the ties of blood
between the two royal houses of England and Denmark.
Sullivan wrote in his diary: "The King proposed Queen
Victoria's health and the Duke of Edinburgh's in English.
The Duke responded. The band played 'God Save the
Queen,' repeating each part which caused some uncertainty
about our sitting down."

They left Copenhagen and passed on to Cronstadt. The
presence of a group of British ships of war in a Russian harbour
stirred the Russian people. There was an orgy of salute-
firing, flag-dropping, and all the circumstance of royal occasion.
Russian officers, diplomats, uniformed and be-medalled,
crowded on board and were plied with champagne. The
Czar's private yacht was waiting to bear the Duke and his
guests to Peterhof. "Here," says Sullivan, "carriages met
us at the pier to drive us to the house prepared for us, one
of the Imperial villas kept expressly for the reception of
Royal guests and relations. Everything very comfortable,
though plain, but no baths!"

The sanitary arrangements at the Palace were primitive
in the extreme. At the foot of each bed was a concealed
lavatory of which Sullivan was unaware. Starting to go in
search of a lavatory during the night, he was turned back
by a Cossack who was sleeping on his doormat, and the soldier
entered his bedroom to show him the contrivance.

Another round of State banquets and more playing of the
Sullivan music, but it is doubtful if he derived as much pleasure
from these compliments as he did from hearing the Czar's
choir which he described in a letter home.

"This morning we started again at 9 and went to the Winter
Palace to hear the famous Imperial Chapel Choir who were
all in full dress—red and gold—waiting for us. The Duke
said to me: 'Doesn't it remind you of when you were in the
Chapel Royal?' and it did. There were about 80, and *blasé*
as I am with music, I confess to a new sensation at hearing
them. It's like nothing else. They have basses with the
most wonderful voices going down to the *low A*, and the
effect of their singing was thrilling. Sometimes it was
exactly like an organ only more beautiful. They sang for

an hour, and I could have heard them for a couple of hours more."

The impression he received from the singing of the Russian choir coloured his composing at a later stage. Many of the unaccompanied quartets, etc., in his Savoy operas are the outcome of that impression. Some of the numbers in these operas which the public admires are directly due to the influence of Russia.

A great diversion greeted the departure of the British ships the next day.

"The Emperor and Empress came on board, and, oh! my stars! wasn't it splendid to see the yards all manned and the guns all firing Royal Salutes! Then we weighed anchor and here we are in a thick fog—all the signals going like Blackwater fair, guns, steam whistles and bell-buoys. If we don't all run each other down we shall arrive at Kiel on Thursday."

When they reached Kiel they were entertained by Prince William (afterwards Kaiser William II) and Prince Henry of Prussia, both of them musical enthusiasts who were familiar with Sullivan's work.

"When I got into the carriage," Sullivan relates in his diary, "Prince William bowed to me and sang 'He polished up the handle of the big front door.' I burst out laughing and so did everyone. It was too funny."

For some time D'Oyly Carte had been engaged in building a new theatre in London—a theatre where he could do justice to Gilbert and Sullivan and other light operas. The Savoy was ready at the beginning of October, and *Patience* was switched over from the Opera Comique to the Savoy in eight hours, so that there should be no break whatever in the run of the piece. D'Oyly Carte was unquestionably the most far-seeing theatrical manager of his time, and there were no luxuries in theatre construction and comfort of the early eighties which were not to be found at the Savoy. It was the first theatre in London to be lighted with electric light, an experiment which Carte deemed to be a little uncertain, for he had arranged an alternative means of illumination in case the electric light should prove unsatisfactory. There were no fees of any kind. The decorations were tasteful in the extreme. When on the night of October 10th, the curtain went up on *Patience* the Savoy was filled with a Society audience that had scrambled for seats. Sullivan conducted the performance himself, and when the curtain fell he took the Prince of Wales behind the scenes and presented every member of the company to him. On leaving the theatre Sullivan went to the station and caught the night train to Norwich, where he conducted a performance of *The Martyr of Antioch* at the Festival at 10 o'clock the next morning.

Nine days after the opening of the Savoy, Gilbert called upon Sullivan to discuss the successor to *Patience*.[1] The Diary reads:

"19th October, Wednesday.—Gilbert came and sketched out an idea of a new piece [*Iolanthe*]. Lord Chancellor, Commander-in-Chief, Peers, Fairies, etc. Funny, but at present vague."

More than a year was to pass before the piece Gilbert had in hand was required, for *Patience* had an unbroken run of 408 nights. Moreover, Sullivan had no desire to work, and he was engaged in moving into Queen's Mansions, Victoria Street, which was to be his final home. At the end of the year he went off to Egypt, and arrived at Port Said on December 31st. Throughout the night he tossed in bed unable to sleep. The Casino next door had an orchestra of German girls who played with such vigour all through the night that sleep was effectually driven away from him. He went on to Cairo.

"How I do wish letter-writing was made a crime punishable by death, and telegrams reduced to five words a penny," he wrote. "How much happier we should all be. This is the most enervating place in the world I think—if you once begin to be lazy you can never stop, but are carried on with a mad impetus until from sheer exhaustion you write a letter or read one.

"I can't do any proper work here, but it doesn't matter. On Friday I went to see the Howling Dervishes, and a pretty

---

[1] *Iolanthe.*

sight they were! I drove to a small mosque in the midst
of a lot of ruined and half-completed structures in old Cairo.
We were shown into the mosque by an attendant, sat down
on chairs and looked at our friends the Dervishes. It was
not a pleasant sight, or one calculated to make one say proudly,
'I, too, am a man like these,' but it was interesting. They
stood in a circle, one boss Dervish in the middle, a sort of
conductor whose motions they followed, and at one side were
one or two gifted vocalists who sang real Arab music accompanied by tom-toms. This collection of human beings then
howled and gasped (breathing 'Al-lah') and swayed their
bodies backwards and forwards and sideways, their long hair
waving in the air, giving them a wild and mad appearance.
They went on for twenty minutes without stopping, then a
minute or two quiet while a verse of the Koran was read,
then off they went again."

Egypt so impressed him that he had ideas of writing an
Egyptian symphony, indeed a statement that he was doing so
appeared in a musical paper in London which provoked him
to comment: "Tell my dear old friend (the Editor) that I am
not writing an Egyptian Symphony at present, but as soon as
I can get an orchestra in London of 'Kanouns,' 'Neis,' 'Uts,'
etc. with really good players I will see about it."

The Arab music interested him; he attempted to catch the
notes and transfer them to his diary, no doubt with the
possible Egyptian Symphony in mind. But he found the
task almost impossible; the music was so much part of the
Eastern atmosphere that it was hopeless to attempt to transfer
it successfully. A note in his diary (January 14th, 1882)
describes his impressions:

"After dinner went to Tigrane Bey's house (Nubar Pasha's)
with Osman Pasha to hear the Arab music. Six musicians
were in waiting for us, and Osman said they were the best
in Cairo, that there were none so good anywhere. Only one,
the chief singer, was in Arab dress. They all sat cross-legged
on a divan. Four played and two sang; occasionally they
all joined in the chorus. The instruments were the 'Out,' a
kind of large mandoline, six *bichord* strings tuned and played
with a quill. The 'Kanoun,' a kind of *trichord* zither, with a

scale of three octaves, quills on both hands, and the 'Ney' or 'Ni' a perpendicular flute from which I could not elicit one single sound. I cannot understand how it is blown, although I watched and tried frequently. There was also a tambourine which was only tapped very gently to help the rhythm. The music is impossible to describe, and impossible to note down. I came away dead beat, having listened with all my ears and all my intelligence."

For three months he remained in Egypt. He revelled in the colour; it stirred, he said, his bones of laziness so that he had no wish to return to his work. Edward Dicey was in Egypt then—a Commissioner on the Dual Control, and Dicey was one of Sullivan's oldest friends, and an executor of his will. "Every day I see something fresh," he wrote; "a mosque, an old house, or a bit of characteristic life, so that I never lose interest. I sigh for the good old days of the late Khedive Ismael, who spent money regally (and borrowed it freely, too!) ruined the country, but made the fortunes of his friends and favourites. If he were here I should get the appointment of Director of the Music, or Bandmaster General, and should be Sullivan Pasha with £5,000 a year and a large income from taking bribes as well!"

New friends he made in plenty. The cosmopolitan society of Cairo hailed him as a kindred spirit. Princes and Pashas, ambassadors, financiers and government ministers welcomed him to their tables. Of these occasions he made breezy notes in his diary, such as the following: "Dined at Blum Pasha's. Dinner of 14. Took in Miss G—— (plain and 40) to dinner. Saw the ugliest woman I ever set eyes on—a Miss O—— from Hamburg. Left early." Germans and Greeks, Russians and Italians mixed in a social fraternity, and they soon discovered that the composer of the music now so well known in all European capitals was the greatest cosmopolitan of them all.

In the middle of February he went to Alexandria to conduct a concert after one rehearsal. "The Chorus," he says in his diary, "consists of about 48 amateurs, principally English and was very fair, reflecting great credit on their conductor,

A Baltic Journey and "Patience"

Mr. Swallow, formerly in Hall's Band, now a successful rag and bone merchant of Alexandria. The orcheſtra consiſted of 3.2.1.1.1. ſtrings, 2 Flutes, 2 Horns, 2 Cornets, 2 Trombones (who had the Fagotti part, but I ſtopped that) and drums. We rehearsed Mozart's '12th Mass.' Fairly good. The principal Soprano, Signorina Foriani, excellent. 'The Messiah' (selection) was lamentable. Band and soloiſts all at sea. I was in despair. Worked 3½ hours and then went home to dinner."

His mother in England received from him endless pen-pictures of his life in Cairo—letters rich in description, and biting sometimes in sarcasm. "Yeſterday we drove out to Heliopolis," he wrote, "a place about an hour's drive on the edge of the desert, to see the Blunts [1] who are bitten by the Arab mania, and live in tents, ride on camels, dress like Arabs. There they were in tents pitched in the desert, juſt like two children playing at being Arabs."

In another letter he described the "Carpet" procession, the great celebration of bringing back the sacred Carpet from Mecca by the pilgrims.

"We drove to a ſtreet of the bazaars where Moses had hired a house for me, and from the windows we saw the 'Carpet' procession pass. Regiments of soldiers came firſt, cavalry and infantry, then two or three ſects with banners, and laſtly the camel with the carpet in a splendid palanquin of gold cloth. The Sheik of the Caravan, a fat old man, naked down to the waiſt, who was half drunk with 'Hashish,' seated on a camel directly behind, then several camels bearing Sheiks, drummers, etc.

"Leaving there at 10 we proceeded to the Citadels where the procession was to be received by the Khedive, who arrived in a salvo of guns. We ſtood in the open portico of the palace with him, and then the army marched paſt, followed by the procession as before. Thousands of people about on the houses, in the ſtreets, and open places, on the sides of the water, etc., glowing with picturesque colours in the brilliant sunshine. I jotted down some of the tunes."

At the beginning of March, the Duke of Clarence and

[1] Wilfrid Blunt.

121

Prince George (King George V) arrived in Cairo, and Sullivan's diary records his meeting with them.

"Dined at the hotel and went to Malet's [1] directly afterwards to meet the young Princes. We played riotous games and separated at midnight. The Princes enjoyed themselves very much, were in riotously high spirits, and knocked me about a good deal. I was in good spirits myself."

He returned to London in the middle of April, and settled into his new house in Queen's Mansions, 60 Victoria Street. Even then he did not willingly take up his work again. *Patience* was at the height of its appeal, Carte was in jubilation, and there appeared to be no hurry to arrange for a successor to the Opera.

With May, his fortieth birthday came and passed, and, close behind it, as yet unseen, was the grim figure of Tragedy. Only three days after this birthday his mother, whilst at her son's house, had complained of feeling ill. Since 1876 she had lived at Fulham with Frederic's widow. Now she had come to hear Courtice Pounds sing, and when the songs had been sung and the singer had gone, she went on to a luncheon with her son, only to leave before the meal was over and go home to bed. In two days her state was critical. Then she rallied—the doctor declared that all danger was over.

Throughout these days Sullivan lived in a frenzy of anxiety. He remained day by day in the Fulham house and slept—when he could sleep—on the drawing-room sofa. The third night he sat through the hours till dawn, unable to close his eyes. He was numb with fear. The announcement that all danger was past left him inert and stupefied, as a condemned man might be when the prison gates mysteriously open and set him free.

But the respite was of brief duration. On the following day Sullivan's servant, Louis, who had been sent to Fulham for the latest details, returned with the news that Mrs. Sullivan had become rapidly worse. She had been kept under morphia throughout the night. Arthur Sullivan hurried to the bedside, but even as he looked at her he knew she was sinking. She drifted from recognition of him into a comatose state,

[1] Sir Edward Malet.

then, as if some fierce spirit in her were battling against the journey it was so soon to take, she would rally sharply, receive a little nourishment from his hand, and slip under the influence of renewed lethargy into heavy sleep.

After this vigil Sullivan went back to Queen's Mansions from Fulham at four in the morning. At 8.15 his niece Amy roused him with an urgent summons to return at once, and his diary describes the end of that journey.

"I knew the worst was at hand, if not already over. I put on my clothes rapidly and was at Fulham before 9. The blinds were all down. I rushed upstairs and was alone in the room—alone that is, with dear Mother's lifeless body—her soul had gone to God."

The blow fell upon him with shattering force. Only now did he really discover how important was the part she had played in his whole existence. She had been a power behind him—a pivot around which his own life, as those of his brother Frederic and his father before him, had circled. No musician ever gave greater devotion to the woman who had borne him, unless a comparison can be found in the allegiance of Handel to the blind lady at Halle who hobbled round the room with a stick. On June 1st Mrs. Sullivan was buried in Brompton Cemetery, and Thomas Helmore—Sullivan's old master at the Chapel Royal—conducted the service.

Sullivan's diary bears this brief entry so poignant with grief: "Home, feeling dreadfully lonely."

He was in truth the loneliest soul in London that day, and his music could not help him.

CHAPTER XI

"Iolanthe" and "Princess Ida"

WITHIN three days of the burial of his mother, Sullivan began the music of *Iolanthe*. It was, he said, the only thing to do, otherwise, the sense of his loss would make a craven of him.

But the music progressed slowly. He would work half through the night, only to tear up what he had written when he came back to his manuscript on the following evening. He was also deeply absorbed in family affairs. His brother Frederic's widow and children were now absolutely on his hands—he was, if it may be so described, a father by proxy to the little family at Fulham, and, in addition to providing for them as he had done since Frederic's death, he decided to adopt his nephew Herbert Sullivan.

From this decision sprang a companionship which endured unbroken and unspoiled until death. The affection ripened with the years, until it reached that great accord which belongs to parentage and is returned by an only son. If the composer were out late at night, it was the nephew who would wait up for him till the familiar whistle sounded outside the window, and an equally familiar whistle answered it. If the nephew were late, it was Arthur Sullivan who sat up, busy scoring with a " J " pen, till he heard the familiar whistle outside the window and gave the reply.

The work of *Iolanthe* proceeded very slowly till August. Meanwhile, the houses for *Patience* remained crowded, and it seemed as if the play might even run through the winter. In America it was being played at a number of theatres, and the music was being sold by a score of publishers, for the American law had decided that to print and sell the piano-

score of a composer's opera was not to infringe his copyright!
Consequently *Patience* appeared throughout the States in all
forms of print, and the last man to receive any benefit from
it was Sullivan.

The American infringement was becoming such a serious
thing to grapple with that, towards the end of June, Sullivan
met Gilbert and Carte in private conclave, and it was decided
that they would rehearse the new opera secretly in London,
and send a company under D'Oyly Carte, fully rehearsed, to
New York to stage it simultaneously with the London production. At the same meeting it was agreed that Gilbert
and Sullivan should have £1,750 per annum each for the
Country and Colonial rights for five years.

Sullivan then left London for Cornwall to stay with Lady
Molesworth who had promised him all the seclusion he needed
in order that he might proceed with his composition. He
spent the first three days of his visit in his own room composing odd numbers. He would then appear at luncheon as
might some unexpected person secreted in the household,
after which he took his walk with the other guests and played
his hands at cards.

He composed the finale of *Iolanthe* in the first two days
of August, long before Gilbert had supplied him with the
completed libretto. The day following he began the " Invo-
cation " (No. 3) and finished it before lunch the following
morning. After breakfast on the next day he retired to his
room and began the " Peers' March." It was a day of heat
and sun, but all the lure that Nature could offer did not draw
Sullivan even to the garden. At dinner he appeared again,
went through the meal with his accustomed good humour
and then played poker, and drew a royal flush in Hearts!

They lost him again the morning following. The lively
spirit whose conversation kept the table quiet as they listened
had not been heard of. The servants did not know if he
had even breakfasted. But some one discovered him in the
garden during the afternoon watching the pigeons. He had
completed the "Peers' March." When asked where he had
been, he said he thought "it would be a good year for the
cider!" They could draw no more information from him.

It was his habit when composing to live almost entirely with his work, and those about him knew very little of what he was doing.

When he left Cornwall he paid a rapid visit to Germany to drink the waters at Bertrich, and on the night of his return sat with Gilbert till two in the morning piecing together Act II.

He was dissatisfied with the first Act of *Iolanthe*, and he wrote to Gilbert and told him so. A meeting was arranged at Exeter. They met in the coffee-room of the Half Moon Hotel, for Gilbert was yachting, and it was a convenient half-way house. They ate ham and eggs at one o'clock, and sat there all through the afternoon reconstructing the Act. The two heads drew closely together. They ordered dinner and seemed to become more absorbed in their conversation, whispering with that quietude which suggested that nothing short of high treason would be the outcome. They reconstructed Act I in the coffee-room, and Gilbert then handed over the manuscript of Act II and shared a cab to the station with his partner. That evening Sullivan supped at the Beefsteak Club, where no one was aware that the light opera which was to entrance London for the greater part of a year had been settled by the traveller.

Sullivan loved the Beefsteak Club; he usually supped there. A year previously, Prince Christian had proposed him for the Marlborough Club, and, with the Duke of Edinburgh as seconder, he was given membership. But the Garrick was his club-home. He would dine there, and go on to the Argos or the Portland for his hand at cards. Till the end of his days he clung to the Garrick, which held his friends, and the atmosphere of which was his own.

August in passing found him busy on *Iolanthe*, and he began his first rehearsals late in September. At the end of the month, although he was rehearsing Act II, he had really composed but a small portion of Act I.

He finished the first Act of *Iolanthe* at a quarter to five on October 3rd, and made some changes in the *Finale*. The next day he sketched out a portion of Act II which had been untouched, and composed after dinner that night *Fold Your*

Flapping Wings, Heigho, Love is a Thorn,[1] *He Loves,* and *When Britain Really Ruled,* in one night, and went to bed at five o'clock in the morning! Then he lazed for three days.

The brief interval of rest only brought in its wake a fierce burst of energy. He went to rehearsals at the Savoy of such work as he had composed, he sat up till five and six in the morning composing more work, and actually rehearsed it two days later. He told D'Oyly Carte to prepare his plans and decide the date of sailing for America. The music would be ready before the boat. It was the promise of a giant. D'Oyly Carte looked at him and said: "You really mean that you can do this?" "Yes," said Sullivan, "the music will be there."

During the next three nights he composed till four in the morning, then an attack of the old kidney trouble, brought about by the severe strain on his physical resources, sent him to bed. But on October 20th—eleven days after he had given his promise to Carte—he had completed Act II, and two days later he began the scoring. The complete disregard which he had for himself, even when an attack had warned him that the enemy waited at his elbow, is demonstrated by the entries in his diary:

"October 25th. Wednesday.—Dined at Marlborough Club. Home to work till 6 a.m.

"October 26th.—Wrote and finished score of 2nd Act (including new quartett) at 4.30. Only Finale (repetition of Trio No. 9) and Overture to do now.

"November 5. Sunday.—Tried to write new duet (No. 5) 1st Act, but failed. Walked out at 5. Began duet again at 1 a.m. Composed and scored it. Finished at 4.10 a.m.

"November 7. Brighton.—Conducted performance of *The Martyr* in the evening. Albani, Trebelli (who sang abominably), Lloyd, King and McGuckin. Very fair performance. Audience enthusiastic."

His time was now occupied in rehearsals. Only the Overture remained incomplete. It had dissatisfied him. He worked at it, tore it up, sat through many nights with it again.

---

[1] These two numbers were ultimately omitted.

E*

Sir Arthur Sullivan

He actually began to re-compose the Overture afresh on November 21st—just five days before the date billed for the first performance. A day later—November 22nd—he worked at the rehearsal of *Iolanthe* all day, was present at the last performance of *Patience* in the evening, then went back to Queen's Mansions and worked at the *Iolanthe* Overture from midnight till 7 a.m.

Iolanthe was complete, but his energies did not relax. He concentrated on the rehearsals. He went to the Band rehearsals the day following and did not leave the theatre until two in the morning. He rehearsed the full company for the last time on the evening following till 1.30 a.m., and then enjoyed a festive supper with Tom Chappell, his old friend and publisher, at Rule's in Maiden Lane.

It may have been the American piracy that inspired the precaution, but throughout the rehearsals of *Iolanthe* both Gilbert and Sullivan had taken extreme measures to prevent any part of the piece, even its title—from becoming known. The music was locked away in the Savoy safes after each rehearsal. But, in spite of the precautions, more information concerning *Iolanthe* leaked out before the appointed day than was the case with any other Savoy opera. One paper published some of the designs of the costumes, another entered into elaborate descriptions of the costumes and plot.

To defeat the inquisitive the play had been purposely incorrectly named. It was called *Periola* at all rehearsals until the day when it came into dress rehearsal for the last time. Then it was re-christened *Iolanthe*. The company was in confusion by the introduction of the new title. It meant the changing at the last moment of *Periola* for *Iolanthe* in the actual words which they had to speak. They protested to Sullivan ; mistakes would be made. It was obvious that no company could absorb a changed character without mistakes.

Sullivan went through the last rehearsal and ignored the protests. They might never have been uttered. They had gone in at one ear and out at the other. But when the rehearsal ended, and everybody was preparing to go home, he called the company together on the stage and he said this:

"Iolanthe" and "Princess Ida"

"Never mind, so long as you sing the music. Use any name that happens to come first to you. Nobody in the audience will be any the wiser, except Mr. Gilbert and he won't be there!" Nor was he.

It was just the manner of Arthur Sullivan. They cheered him off the stage. They cheered him at the stage-door when he went on to Tom Chappell's supper at Rule's. They cheered him when he arrived to conduct the first performance the following evening. But they did not know—no one knew —that when he stepped to the rostrum to conduct his first performance of *Iolanthe*, disaster had crept into his house through the post. Just as he was setting out for the theatre where he was to be acclaimed and encored, a letter was slipped into his hand informing him that the brokers who had the investment of his savings had gone bankrupt. All his savings amounting to over £7,000 had been lost.

Most men, in the circumstances, would have dismissed the cab and returned to the house. Sullivan tore up the letter and went to the theatre. How ironical the cheers that met him at the stage-door when his heart was lead! They welcomed him to a new success that was going to give him more money than he possessed already. Little players of junior parts saw in him the man—he might be rich—he ought to be rich—who had given them music that would keep them in employment for months on end.

He made his way through the crowd at the stage-door. He returned the smiles. The attendant's wife had been ill through childbirth; he inquired after her. He had never been sweeter in his understanding of the people who worked for him, the beloved figure of the Savoy. None knew that tragedy lay under his smiles.

Depressed, his mind very far away from the business of a first night, he went into the Orchestra. The entry in his diary was brief:

"November 25th. Saturday. — First performance of *Iolanthe* at the Savoy Theatre. House crammed. Awfully nervous; more so than usual on going into Orchestra. Tremendous reception. First Act went splendidly. The second dragged, and I was afraid it muſt be compressed. However it finished well, and Gilbert and myself were called and heartily cheered. Very low afterwards. Came home."

Five hours after the production of *Iolanthe* at the Savoy, the piece was produced in New York, and on both sides of the Atlantic it settled down to a long run. In two days all seats for the reſt of the year were booked at the Savoy. When eventually the music was published by Chappells it sold by the thousand copies every day, in spite of the faƈt that some of the critics had condemned the piece. Publication of the music was delayed so as to synchronize with America. So great, indeed, was the demand in London that before the play had been running a month, Tom Chappell called on Sullivan to say that 10,000 vocal and pianoforte scores had been sold from Bond Street on the previous day, the ſtaff remaining till midnight in order to complete the despatch of the copies ordered.

It was during the early performances of *Iolanthe* that an incident took place at the theatre which gave proof of Sullivan's good-nature. His fur-lined overcoat was missing from the green-room, and had obviously been ſtolen. In spite of the outcry, the coat was missing for a week. One of the "dressers" then called to see Sullivan, and told him that, his wife having recently given birth to her seventh child, he had ſtolen and pawned the coat for two pounds, in order to pay the doƈtor. The man ſtood there, a figure of woe, holding the pawn-ticket in his hand and expressing his contrition. He expeƈted a burſt of anger from Sullivan, but it did not come. Inſtead, Sullivan put his hand in his pocket and, producing a five-pound note, held it out.

"I'm sorry you're in trouble," he said to the "dresser." "But as it happens I am in need of that coat during the cold weather. Here's five pounds. Go and get the coat out of pawn, and keep the change to buy something for your wife and baby. And, for heaven's sake, don't say you're sorry again!"

Before *Iolanthe* had been running little more than a week, Mr. Gladſtone went to see it. The Gilbertian satire of political life, his gibes at the Court of Chancery, and the humours of George Grossmith's Lord Chancellor delighted him. Two days later he wrote to Sullivan:

"10, DOWNING STREET,
"*Dec.* 6, '82.

"MY DEAR SIR,—

"Though I am very sorry that your kind wish to bring me to the Savoy Theatre on Monday should have entailed on you so much trouble, I muſt thankfully acknowledge the great pleasure which the entertainment gave me.

"Nothing, I thought, could be happier than the manner in which the comic ſtrain of the piece was blended with its harmonies of sight and sound, so good in taſte and so admirable in execution from beginning to end.

"I remain, my dear sir,
"Faithfully yours,
"W. E. GLADSTONE."

On January 2nd, 1883, Sullivan left London for Paris. He found the French capital surging with the sensation of Gambetta's tragic death which had juſt occurred. The wildeſt ſtories were afloat. Suspicion and mud were heaped upon Mademoiselle Léonie who had been in the room with Gambetta when he was shot. But, as it chanced, Sullivan's housekeeper, Adèle, was married to Paul Violette, Gambetta's *valet-de-chambre*, and Violette had been present with the great Frenchman very shortly before the tragedy occurred. On the evening of the 8th, Violette himself came to see Sullivan and gave him details of the tragedy which Sullivan put down in his diary.

"Paul Violette (Adèle's husband, and *valet-de-chambre* to Gambetta) came to see me at ¼ to 8. He told me all the details of Gambetta's accident and death. Indignantly denied that Mad. Léonie had been in the slighteſt way concerned in the matter. She was in the room with G. when Paul went out. Paul had been handling the revolver and examining it with Gambetta; a few minutes after he left the room he heard a report and ran into the room. As he juſtly says, there was no time for G. and Léonie to have had a dispute between the time he left the room and the accident."

The affair became the scandal of Europe; every Parisian journal recapitulated it with a wealth of rumour, imagination and detail.

During 1883, Sullivan composed little until the latter part of the year. His actual output during the early months was an anthem *Who Is Like Unto Thee?* and the carol *Hark! What Mean?* He began and finished the former in four days in August, and within a week wrote the first music to *Princess Ida*. He completed two choruses and two songs—*I am a Maiden* and *The Ape and the Lady*—on the day he began to work.

Gilbert's libretto was a new version of Tennyson's poem, which the former had first put into dramatic form in 1870, to score only a moderate success with it. He now took out his old play and refurbished it, but even the second version was far behind the high standard he was accustomed to give his collaborator.

It was in February that Gilbert first showed the renovated Act I to Sullivan, for the diary recorded on February 8th:

"Went to Stanley's office to meet Carte and Gilbert and sign agreement for 5 years. Drove Gilbert to Savoy (had a slight breeze and explanation *en route*) and read 1st Act (or Prologue) of the 'Princess.'"

Ultimately Gilbert satisfied Sullivan with the libretto, for when he read the final version of the *Princess Ida* on July 31st, Sullivan wrote in his diary:

"Eastbury (Pinner) to stay with the Gilberts. Went through libretto of new piece (Princess) at night, made several alterations and modifications. 2nd Act in good order, only wants a song for the Princess. 3rd Act very nearly complete. Left 1st Act with him to make some alterations. Like the piece as now shaped out, very much."

At the end of April Sullivan attended a dinner given by Alfred Rothschild to the Prince of Wales. Florence St. John and Violet Cameron were singing. During the evening the Prince came up to Sullivan, shook hands and said: "I congratulate you on the great honour we have in store for you."

Sullivan believed he knew precisely what the Prince implied, for he wrote in his diary: "I suppose he meant he is going to place me on the Council of the R.C. of Music!"

He was wrong. Four days later he received the following letter from Mr. Gladstone:

"10, DOWNING STREET,
May 3, '83.

"DEAR MR. SULLIVAN,—

"I have the pleasure to inform you that I am permitted by Her Majesty to propose that you should receive the honour of Knighthood, in recognition of your distinguished talents as a composer, and of the services which you have rendered to the promotion of the Art of Music generally in this Country.

"I hope it may be agreeable to you to accept the proposal.

"I remain,
"Faithfully yours,
"W. E. GLADSTONE."

Sullivan's acceptance led the Prince of Wales to announce when he opened the Royal College on the following Monday that the Knighthood was to be conferred. After the function he approached Sullivan and urged him to persuade George Macfarren to accept a Knighthood at the same time. Macfarren at first was obdurate. His obstinacy continued for days; he prated that his Art was the only honour he desired. But eventually he yielded, and on May 22nd, the three who had done so much for English music—Sullivan, George Grove and Macfarren—went together to Windsor Castle to receive the honour from Queen Victoria.

It was at this period that Sullivan caused a private telephone to be fixed up between Queen's Mansions and the Savoy Theatre. To listen to a play by telephone was an experience as yet unknown. On his 41st birthday—May 13th—he gave a dinner party and sprang a surprise on his guests. The Prince of Wales was present, the Duke of Edinburgh, the Marquis of Hartington, the Earl of Kenmare, Ferdinand Rothschild, Millais the painter, Gilbert and Burnand.

Madame Albani and Tosti took part in the musical programme. Never, the Prince declared, as he presented him with an enamel match-box, had Sullivan given a more successful birthday dinner.

Without the knowledge of his guests Sullivan had secretly arranged for the entire Savoy company to go to the theatre— it was Whit-Sunday—in order to perform selections to which those who sat around his table could listen by wire. Very carefully he watched the clock. At 11.15 he rang up the Savoy. In a few moments more the Prince of Wales was seated in an armchair, his cigar dead and stale between his fingers as he listened for the first time in his life to a play being performed in another part of London.

With the exception of a few days spent in Leeds, rehearsing and conducting the Leeds Festival, Sullivan employed the whole of the Autumn of 1883 on the new opera *Princess Ida*. The Leeds Festival that year had been a great success, even Sullivan declared that he only heard "five trifling errors, three wrong notes by the Band, and two entries missed also by the Band, inaudible and unknown to anyone but myself. This is surely extraordinary in a week's performances."

And yet, to him, the rehearsals had been too short, too crowded, too hurried. He was always punctilious about rehearsals; he never left anything to the lucky chance of the first night of the actual concert. An imperfection, a flaw ever so trifling which none but the trained ear would observe, was, to him, as some loud clamorous discord. He probably brought more out of an orchestra or a choir than any man of his time, not by boisterous hectoring, but by his sheer placidity, his means of *leading*, not bullying. He rarely, if ever, lost his temper. Highly-strung as he unquestionably was— and how many men of genius are immune from the plague of nerves?—he was always the master of his emotions. If he felt temper, he did not display it; if he were ruffled, the even tone of his voice never varied. When humorous incidents occurred, as they frequently did, he was the first to observe them. He was sensitive to a degree in avoiding any upsetting publicly of the feelings of those who were performing his work. Sometimes he would privately rehearse a player at

Queen's Mansions, rather than hold him up to ridicule or compel constant repetition of a song before the assembled company on the stage.

During the rehearsals for this particular festival at Leeds, an amusing incident occurred. Mr. F. R. Spark, who was Secretary to the Leeds Festivals for many years, records it in his history of the Leeds Festivals of 1858–89. Sullivan had decided for the purpose of the work which was being rehearsed that the choir should be separated into two parts, one to express the anguish of lost souls, and the other the ecstasy of the saved. Sullivan said: "Ladies and gentlemen, I want the choir divided, and in order that this may be done, I want the 'wicked' to stand up, and the 'righteous' to keep their seats." A few of the "wicked" stood up and looked nervously about the tittering choir. Their ludicrous position, their loneliness as self-acclaimed sinners, changed the tittering to a roar of laughter. Then dropping his *bâton* Sullivan laughed longer than they.

Occasionally, only occasionally, rehearsal incidents were more serious. One occurred at the first rehearsal of *Princess Ida*. Gilbert read the piece to the Savoy Company at the beginning of December, and this was one of the very few "readings" of the Savoy operas from which Sullivan was absent. The play then went into active rehearsal. Before long an actor attempted to force his way against the composer's wishes in a certain song. Sullivan endured this for some time; he struggled with his displeasure until it got the mastery of him.

"Mr. ——," he said very calmly, laying down his *bâton* with that quiet smile of protest the company knew so well, "there is something very radically wrong with that song. Either you do not understand it, or I don't."

"I think *I* understand it," the singer replied.

"Perhaps you do," Sullivan retorted. "That's the worst of being a composer. One always begins at the wrong end of the stick. In future, I shall start at the other end. I'll get you to sing my songs first, then I'll compose them afterwards." The rebuke was followed by an awful silence, then the rehearsal went on.

The firſt performance of *Princess Ida* was fixed for the firſt week in January, 1884. Sullivan, however, was late with the music. His health was worrying him, and, juſt as portions of the play had been put in rehearsal, Frederic Clay had a paralytic ſtroke shortly after Chriſtmas, whilſt walking with George R. Sims in the Strand at midnight, after conducting the *première* of his own play *The Golden Ring*, at the newly opened Alhambra. A second ſtroke intervened on the day following. Clay, one of the moſt lovable men who had come into Sullivan's life, lay for many months speechless and in a ſtate of coma. Sullivan was so diſturbed by the tragedy that, in spite of the approach of the night of production, he was unable to work.

At Chriſtmas his sister-in-law married B. C. Hutchinson, and left England for California, leaving his nephew Herbert Sullivan, who lived with Arthur Sullivan from this date.

Rehearsals and the composition now became so concentrated that he scarcely slept. He rehearsed the piece with Gilbert late into the night, and then returned to Queen's Mansions to compose till daylight. The following day the same round began again. He was not conscious of the effect upon him which the ſtrain provoked. He had desultory attacks of pain. When he did reach his bed, sleep was often denied to him. This fanaticism for work, the squandering of all physical powers in order to carry out the dictates of a brain that was his maſter, was running up a bill which some day would claim its reckoning. Whilſt he was working at the laſt numbers of the *Princess* on December 31ſt midnight chimed, but he did not hear it. The New Year entered without his even raiſing his eyes from his work to greet it. But a quiet knock at the door and the sound of the door opening made him look up. Cluſtered on the threshold were the servants—they had come to wish him a Happy New Year!

On New Year's Day he completed the music which four days later was to be performed when the *Princess* was produced. He reheaſsed the Orcheſtra in the morning, put in many hours at a dress rehearsal afterwards, then trudged home through a snowſtorm—he was unable to get a cab—to compose the two songs, *I Built Upon a Rock* and *Nothing to Grumble At.*

But his health was breaking. Now that *Princess Ida* was finished, his tired brain and overdriven body collapsed. The day before the production he attended a full-dress rehearsal that lasted till 2.30 a.m. He went home and got into bed, but before daylight he was attacked by violent pain and a doctor was summoned. Morphia was injected. It might have been water, for it was of no avail.

Saturday dawned. That night the crowds would be hustling at the Savoy for admission to the first performance. He lay in bed, inert and helpless, seeing these things happening in some panorama that swept across his mind. Happening without him. The doctor departed knowing full well that his patient was too ill to get up, therefore his warnings against so doing were unnecessary. But towards the afternoon Sullivan crawled out of bed, dropped to the floor, then struggled to a chair. He had made up his mind.

His diary completes the story of that evening:

"Saturday, January 5th, 1884.—Resolved to conduct the first performance of the new Opera *Princess Ida* at night, but from the state I was in it seemed hopeless. At 7 p.m. had another strong hypodermic injection to ease the pain, and a strong cup of black coffee to keep me awake. Managed to get up and dress, and drove to the theatre more dead than alive—went into the Orchestra at 8.10. Tremendous house —usual reception. Very fine performance—not a hitch. Brilliant success. After the performance I turned very faint and could not stand."

He was brought home by Frank Cellier and his nephew, Herbert Sullivan, and put to bed in acute pain.

So was the first night of *Princess Ida*, like that of *Iolanthe*, a night of affliction for Sullivan. None of those who listened to the joyous music of the *Princess* that evening realized that its composer—who with such ease seemed to carry the performance in his hand—was at breaking point.

CHAPTER XII

" The Mikado "

THREE weeks after the production of *Princess Ida*, Sullivan wrote to D'Oyly Carte and said that he would compose no more pieces for the Savoy. He had, he said, tired of that form of composition. Though this communication must have come as a bombshell to Carte, he did not take it at first too seriously. With Miss Helen Lenoir, destined to be the second Mrs. D'Oyly Carte, he went to see Sullivan on the day he received the letter. They dined *à trois*. Relations were never more friendly. But Sullivan was adamant. D'Oyly Carte left the dinner-table believing at last that things were more serious than he thought, and Sullivan went off to Paris.

Towards the end of March *Princess Ida* showed signs of drooping. It was even then apparent that the play would never attain the success its predecessors had known. The words were as witty, the music as charming, but, for some reason unknown, the opera had not the same appeal to the public.

Meanwhile, D'Oyly Carte became anxious about the partnership. By his agreement, made a year before, he could compel Gilbert and Sullivan to produce a play at six months' notice. The future looked ominous. D'Oyly Carte had built the partnership; he resolved that it should not break down without a struggle. He entirely disregarded Sullivan's decision, and wrote to him in Brussels:

"Savoy Theatre,
March 22nd, 1884.

"Dear Sullivan,—
"The business here, as you will have observed, shows signs of dropping. It may of course pick up again after Lent,

but it may not, and in any case it seems probable that we shall want a new piece for the autumn.

"By our agreement I have to give you and Gilbert six months' notice in case of a new opera being required.

"Will you please accept this note as fulfilling the required formality.

"I am sending a duplicate of this note to Gilbert.

"Yours sincerely,
"R. D'OYLY CARTE."

The letter brought matters to a head. Had it never been sent, or had there been no agreement which gave Carte the right to send it, the greatest of all the Savoy operas might never have been written. The partnership would have drifted to an end.

In a few days Sullivan replied from the British Legation in Brussels:

"MY DEAR CARTE,—

"Your letter of the 22nd inst. has reached me, in which you give me formal notice that you may require a new opera in six months' time. I ought therefore to tell you at once that it is impossible for me to do another piece of the character of those already written by Gilbert and myself. The reason for this decision I can give you verbally when we meet. When I return to town, I must, of course, talk the matter over with Gilbert and hear what his views on the subject are."

Before two more days passed Gilbert wrote to Sullivan:

"MY DEAR SULLIVAN,—

"I learnt from Carte yesterday, to my unbounded surprise, that you do not intend to write any more operas of the class with which you and I have been so long identified. . . . You are of course aware that by our agreement entered into on the 8th February, 1883, and extending over five years, we are bound to supply Carte with a new opera on receiving from him six months' notice, and, if from any reason we fail to do so, we are liable with him for any losses that may result from our default.

"During your absence I have busied myself with constructing a *libretto*; I have even gone so far as to write some of the numbers and to sketch out portions of the dialogue. . . . In all the pieces we have written together I have invariably subordinated my views to your own, you have often expatiated to me, and to others, on the thorough good feeling with which we have worked together for so many years. Nothing, as far as I am aware, has occurred to induce you to change your views on this point, and I am, therefore, absolutely at a loss to account for the decision."

Sullivan's reply written from Paris on April 2nd was a frank explanation, and reveals exactly what was passing in his mind about his light music.

"I will be quite frank. With 'Princess Ida' I have come to the end of my tether—the end of my capability in that class of piece. My tunes are in danger of becoming mere repetitions of my former pieces, my concerted movements are getting to possess a strong family likeness.

"I have rung all the changes possible in the way of variety of rhythm. It has hitherto been word setting, I might almost say syllable setting, for I have looked upon the words as being of such importance that I have been continually keeping down the music in order that not one should be lost.

"And this my suppression is most difficult, most fatiguing, and I may say most disheartening, for the music is never allowed to arise and speak for itself. I want a chance for the music to act in its own proper sphere—to intensify the emotional element not only of the actual words but of the situation.

"I should like to set a story of human interest and probability, where the humorous words would come in a humorous (not serious) situation, and where, if the situation were a tender or dramatic one, the words would be of a similar character. There would then be a feeling of reality about it which would give a fresh interest in writing, and fresh vitality to our joint work. . . . I hope with all my heart that there may be no break in our chain of joint workmanship.

"Yours sincerely,
"ARTHUR SULLIVAN."

To this letter Gilbert replied two days later in terms of sharp reproach:

"Your reflections on the character of the *libretti* with which I have supplied you have caused me considerable pain. However, I cannot suppose that you have intended to gall and wound me, when you wrote as you did. I must assume that your letter was written hurriedly.

"When you tell me that your desire is that I shall write a libretto in which the humorous words will come in a humorous situation, and in which a tender or dramatic situation will be treated tenderly and dramatically, you teach me the ABC of my profession. It is inconceivable that any sane author should ever write otherwise than as you propose I should write in future."

Sullivan reached London on April 9th, and immediately telephoned to Gilbert and asked for a meeting. The following afternoon Gilbert arrived at Queen's Mansions, but the meeting led to no result. Never had the partnership been in greater jeopardy. At the end of the day Sullivan made the following entry in his diary:

"Thursday, April 10th.—Gilbert came at 2. Two hours' conversation. He proposed to me as subject of new piece, the same idea that I had already declined two years ago, based on the notion that by means of a charm (formerly a coin, now a lozenge) a person would really become the character he or she represented themselves to be. Thus a young woman playing an old woman's part would, by taking the lozenge, really become an old woman for the time, and so on. I was obliged to reject the subject, as it makes the whole piece unreal and artificial. Long argument on this part— no concession on either side—complete deadlock, though quite friendly throughout."

Gilbert then wrote and suggested that he should retire from collaborating with Sullivan in the next Savoy opera, hoping thereby to straighten out the *impasse*. He said:

"What do you say to this—provided that Carte consents. Write your opera to another man's *libretto*. I will willingly

retire for one turn, our agreement notwithstanding. It may
well be that you are cramped by setting so many *libretti* of
the same author, and that a new man with a new style will
start a new train of musical ideas. I suggest this because I
am absolutely at a loss to know what it is you want from me.
You will understand how faintly I grasp your meaning when
I tell you that your objections to my libretto really seem
arbitrary and capricious. That they are nothing of the kind
I am well persuaded—but, for all that, I can't fathom them.
"Yours truly,
"W. S. GILBERT."

It was a generous suggestion, but happily Sullivan refused
to accede to it. He declined to break with his friend, and,
apart from all question of sentiment, there was not another
collaborator who could adequately fill Gilbert's place. "I
yield to no one in admiration of your matchless skill and
genius," he wrote to Gilbert in reference to his works. He
was sincere in the belief that Gilbert was a master of his craft,
and they had shared too many triumphs together to permit
of the intrusion of another partner. Sullivan replied:
"Your letter of to-day has just come. Such a proposal as
you therein make I could not entertain for a moment. Nor
do I see why, because an idea which you propose to me fails
in my judgment to afford me sufficient musical suggestion,
we should necessarily come to a standstill. You must remember that you proposed the same idea to me before *Iolanthe*
was written, and that I then expressed the same views with
regard to it as I hold now."
On the same day as Sullivan dispatched this letter he wrote
in his diary:

"Saturday, April 12th, 1884.—Carte came, then Miss
Lenoir joined us, to discuss *modus vivendi* with reference to
deadlock with Gilbert.
"I wrote to Gilbert to mention an insuperable difficulty in
his proposed subject, also referred to his letter I had just
received; declined, of course, to accede to his proposal that
I should write the next 'Savoy' piece with another author.
I cannot understand the position he takes—viz.:—because

I do not like the subject he proposed, he is at a loss to
find another, and that my objections seem arbitrary and
capricious. The case stands thus:

"Gilbert gives me the outlines of a piece. I do not
like it.

"1st. Because it is going back to the elements of topsy-
turveydom and unreality which I had hoped we had now
done with, and about which I had written most earnestly in
my letter to him of the 2nd of April.

"2nd. It bears a strong resemblance to 'The Sorcerer,'
inasmuch as in both pieces by means of a charm, people all
fall in love with each other *à tort et à travers,* and if, as is possible, we revive 'The Sorcerer' after the new piece, people will
not fail to observe the resemblance.

"3rd. Any element of romance and tenderness which
Gilbert might introduce must, by its surroundings, be unreal
and artificial, and this reacts on me most disadvantageously.
I *cannot* do any more of that class of work.

"In answer to all this G. says that he cannot look for another
subject, as he fails to see what I want, that if this does not
suit me, it is impossible for him to find one that will. And
so there we are."

The following Tuesday Gilbert called on Sullivan. The
diary records what took place between them.

"Tuesday, April 15th, 1884.—Home to meet Gilbert.
Long talk. He sketched out the piece (in dispute) with
considerable modifications, proposing to give it a very serious
and tender interest in addition to its grotesque and humorous
elements, and to keep the two elements totally distinct. There
still remains the machinery of the 'charm' which is to me so
objectionable musically. It was arranged that he should send
me a sketch of 2nd Act, and that then, after giving it my most
earnest consideration, if I still found the subject uncongenial
to me, I should say so, and he would then look about for
another idea altogether."

For some days, no further movement was made on either
side, but on the 26th, according to the diary, Gilbert called
again.

"Gilbert brought me a sketch plot (written out) of new piece. He read it. There is much I like in it, but I don't like the lozenge and its consequences, and I stick to my objection—it takes away all the reality and interest. Besides, it has too strong a family likeness to 'The Sorcerer'—everyone must be struck with it, and will say (even more than they do now) that we are repeating ourselves. I told Gilbert to let me have it and study it carefully, and that I would let him know the result. I don't think I can ever get over my distaste for the charm."

After a few days Sullivan returned the plot and "wrote a long letter to Gilbert begging him to put aside the plot he proposes, and give me another. If I were to say 'very well, I accept it, just as it is,' I should go into it," he said of the plot he returned, "without that interest and enthusiasm which has hitherto characterized all my work with you, and should be doing both you and myself a great injustice. . . . After 20 years' hard work in my career, I am not going to depart from a privilege I have always acted upon, viz.: never to force myself to try and do that which I feel I cannot do well."

The finality of the letter brought an equally final reply from Gilbert:

"MY DEAR SULLIVAN,—

"Your letter has caused me the gravest disappointment. I explained my plot to you a week since, you distinctly expressed your satisfaction with it, and I have worked at it during the week in the absolute belief that all difficulties had been finally overcome. You now write to tell me that you wish me to construct a piece which shall not deal with the supernatural or improbable.

"Anxious as I am, and have always been, to give due weight to your suggestions, the time has arrived when I must state— and I do so with great reluctance—that I cannot consent to construct another plot for the next Opera.

"Yours truly,
"W. S. GILBERT."

The following day Sullivan wrote:

1885 31 Days   14 SATURDAY [73–292]   [14] March

BREAKSPEARS.
UXBRIDGE.

(*Left*) The entry in Sullivan's diary after the first night of "The Mikado."
(*Right*) Portion of a letter from Gilbert to Sullivan informing him of the title first chosen for the opera which was eventually called "The Yeomen of the Guard"

"The Mikado"

"MY DEAR GILBERT,—

"The tone of your letter convinces me that your decision is final, and therefore further discussion is useless. I regret it very much.

"Yours sincerely,
"ARTHUR SULLIVAN."

Carte was in despair. The partnership seemed to be smashed, and the two friends were separated by—a lozenge! He hurried from Sullivan to Gilbert, and from Gilbert to Sullivan, without avail. Their friendship remained unviolated, but as collaborators they had now become as distant as the Poles. Happily this severance was to endure only for five days, for on May 8th Sullivan wrote in his diary:

"Gilbert wrote to propose piece on lines I suggested. Wrote and accepted with greatest pleasure, and said, under the circumstances, I undertook to set it without further discussion."

Sullivan's letter ran as follows:

"8 May, 1884.

"MY DEAR GILBERT,—

"Your letter of to-day is an inexpressible relief to me, as it clearly shows me that you, equally with myself, are loth to discontinue the collaboration which has been such a pleasure and advantage to us.

"If I understand you to propose you will construct a plot without the supernatural and improbable elements, and on the lines which you describe, I gladly undertake to set it without further discussing the matter, or asking what the subject is to be.

"Yours sincerely,
"ARTHUR SULLIVAN."

A day later, Sullivan's diary reads:

"Letter from Gilbert. All unpleasantness at an end."

Out of this disturbance and turmoil came *The Mikado*.[1]

[1] Mr. Adair Fitzgerald in his book "The Story of the Savoy Opera" asserts that the idea for the *Mikado* came to Gilbert through a Japanese sword, which hung on the walls of his study, suddenly falling down. If this be so, then the incident must have taken place between May 3rd, when Gilbert refused to supply a new plot, and May 8th when by a sudden change of front he offered a new plot—that of the *Mikado*.

Possibly Time has proved that, in urging a departure from the plots they had used hitherto, Sullivan was right, for *The Mikado* broke fresh ground, and the partnership, that had seemed in such jeopardy, became stronger than ever.

Gilbert was engaged with the libretto throughout the autumn and winter, and, now that the skies of the future had cleared again, Sullivan resolved to wait until the work was handed over to him completed before taking up his pen to compose. In the spring his name had been mentioned as a conductor of the Birmingham Festival, indeed three conductors alone were left in the running after several Committee meetings—Sullivan, Randegger and Richter. Many of the Committee wanted a British rather than a foreign conductor, but, to the surprise of every one, the choice ultimately fell upon Richter. It was Joseph Bennett, the eminent musical critic of the *Daily Telegraph*, who apprised Sullivan of what had happened. The Birmingham Committee would not "play second fiddle" to Leeds, and, such was the antagonism between the two Festivals, that Sullivan was rejected on account of his close association with the Leeds Festivals. The affair drew from Sullivan the *bon mot*: "it was said Birmingham was a sort of boa constrictor of music—it devoured a mighty meal every three years, and then relapsed into a state of coma in order to digest it."

Sullivan spent the summer on a round of visits. He appeared at Ascot, at Newmarket. He was a favourite guest as a diner out. At a dinner-party given at the end of July, thirteen sat down to table, among whom were Mr. Gladstone, Sir William Harcourt, Sir Charles Dilke, Lord Leighton, and de Staäl, the Russian Ambassador. Considerable agitation prevailed when the number was discovered. A wave of superstition rose high. Who would dare ill-fortune by rising first? The Grand Old Man of Politics stared impassively across the table, but he made no sign to move. It was Sir William Harcourt who got up first—and outlived Mr. Gladstone by many years!

After the settlement with Gilbert in May, *Princess Ida* began to pick up again, and ran till October 8th. It had been decided that *The Sorcerer* and *Trial by Jury* should be revived to keep the theatre open until *The Mikado* was ready, which, since Sullivan had not yet begun the work of composition, could not take place before the spring of 1885. They served their purpose admirably, and were played to crowded houses all the winter. Moreover, *The Sorcerer* was simultaneously revived in New York and became an immediate success, whereas when it was first produced there in 1877 it had been a dismal failure. Such are the changes of fortune when subsequent success advertises the qualities of that which has been previously despised!

In the middle of August Sullivan went down to Stagenhoe in Hertfordshire for ten weeks, and began composing some new numbers for *The Sorcerer* revival. He wrote a new introduction to the 2nd Act with choruses, etc., in one night (September 11th). Two days later he broke away from the Opera and wrote a new version of the song *A Shadow* for Madame Patey. This also was completed in one night. Cellier visited him to go over *The Sorcerer* music, and a fortnight before the revival was due Sullivan returned to London and plunged into the work of rehearsal.

Once *The Sorcerer* had been started off again, Sullivan did nothing. He still waited for Gilbert. He went to Zurich, taking his nephew to enter him at the Polytechnic. November came, and with it an event of considerable musical significance, the first performance of *Parsifal* at the Albert Hall. Wagner had completed the work two years previously, and it was now to be performed for the first time in London by the complete company from Bayreuth, Joseph Barnby conducting. Sullivan wrote his opinion of *Parsifal* in his diary that night:

"Saturday, November 15th, 1884.—Went to hear *Parsifal* at the Albert Hall. Finale to 1st Act impressive and noble. 'Flower' scene graceful and scored with delicate charm—other little bits here and there of great beauty and originality. But the whole is heavy, gloomy, dull and ugly—very undramatic, as, except by means of the worn out 'leitmotiven' trick, there is nothing characteristic in the music sung by each individual. The music of one individual would do just as well for any other."

Five days later Gilbert and Sullivan came together again in collaboration. The meeting took place at Gilbert's house, and Sullivan made a brief note in his diary:

"Thursday, November 20th, 1884.—Dined with Gilbert and his wife. Went through 1st Act of new piece. Made several important suggestions with which Gilbert agreed. Act still in an incomplete and somewhat crude condition, but will shape out well. Left at 2 a.m. Some words for music ready."

At first the music came very slowly and at intervals. Not that his music failed him—it never actually failed him—but there were occasions when he took a little time to settle down to his subject and get its atmosphere. The first number of *The Mikado* he composed was *Three Little Maids from School* which, with a Quintett, he wrote complete in one day (December 21st). Then in January his work on the Opera was disturbed by the death of his sister-in-law (Frederic's wife) at Los Angeles. "Those poor children," he wrote in his diary. Now with tragedy at their door he made up his mind quickly. As soon as *The Mikado* was finished and produced, he would go to America to look into their affairs.

He concentrated on his work with fresh impulse, and with the coming of February became almost a hermit. By February 18th, when Gilbert read the play to the Company at the Savoy, Sullivan had completed most of the music for Act I. He attended the reading, then hurried back to Queen's Mansions to compose the next numbers that would be required, working, as was his custom, each night until daylight appeared round the curtains of his sitting-room.

Between February 21st and March 1st, he did not emerge from his room except to attend the Savoy rehearsals, save that on February 26th he conducted for the first time a Philharmonic Concert. His diary records the measure of his concentration:

"March 2nd.—All these days since February 21st writing and rehearsing (Mikado). No drives, parties, or recreations of any kind."

"The Mikado"

And again on March 3rd:

"Worked all night at Finale 1st Act. Finished at 5 a.m. 63 pages of score at one sitting!"

Three days later he finished scoring Act II at 5.45 in the morning. He composed the song *Flowers That Bloom in the Spring* one evening between tea and dinner.

The completed music of *The Mikado* was in the hands of D'Oyly Carte just a week before the date fixed for the first night. One may suppose that there was no need for this rush, that the first night might have been postponed. But Sullivan always worked best in light opera when the calendar stared him in the face. His temperament, unlike the usual temperament of genius, was willing to yield to discipline when discipline was required. Because he loved his music he was always as happy under the discipline that brought production as in those days when he was a free agent to enjoy himself in leisure. Never in the whole of his life—even when racked with spasmodic attacks of pain—did the business of his composing ever prove irksome. When he was ill, the suffering of the mind was greater than that of the body because his work had been stopped.

On Saturday, March 14th, 1885, the opera was produced, and Sullivan's diary is the best testimony of what occurred.

"New Opera, 'The Mikado' or 'The Town of Titipu' produced at the Savoy Theatre with every sign of real success. A most brilliant house. Tremendous reception. All went very well except Grossmith, whose nervousness nearly upset the piece. A *treble* encore for 'Three Little Maids' and for 'The Flowers That Bloom in the Spring.' Seven encores taken—might have taken twelve."

The friendship was complete; the partnership was never stronger. It had produced a play that was destined to run over 600 nights.

CHAPTER XIII

More Adventures in America and "The Golden Legend"

ON June 20th, 1885, Sullivan sailed for New York, and D'Oyly Carte followed by the next steamer. Already news had reached the Savoy that a piratical theatrical manager named Duff intended to produce the *Mikado* on Broadway, and was even prepared to fight a lawsuit to prove that, the law being what it was, he had the right to pirate the work. Now it was said that Sullivan was coming to New York to produce *The Mikado* himself. But Duff was not to be hurried or driven from his purpose. He had not yet begun to rehearse *The Mikado*, which he proposed to produce in September, whether Sullivan was present in the States or not.

Sullivan, however, had no intention of staying in New York, or, if he had, the interviewers who overflowed into his hotel apartments quickly made him change his mind. In vain had he taken refuge in a private room at the Custom House, leaving a New York friend to get his luggage through the Customs. The interviewers tracked him to his hotel. Only for a few days did he tarry. The thermometer was climbing and hung languorously near 100° in the shade. He met his old New York friends, saw a few plays, supped at Delmonico's, then went off to the West almost before New York was aware of his coming.

When he reached Chicago the reporter nuisance began again. The first pair interviewed him when he reached his bedroom and had just begun to take his clothes off. He proceeded to Denver; from thence to Salt Lake City. At Grand Junction *en route* he was detained for a day without

food owing to an engine smashing down a bridge. At Salt
Lake City a friend took charge of him.

"We drove about the town for a long time," he wrote,
"saw all the Brigham Young family, houses, cemetery, etc.,
bought Mormon books, a little desk etc. at the Zion Co-
Operative Stores, went to the great Tabernacle and played
for an hour on the great organ, a really good instrument
(3 manuals, etc.) made by a local Mormon, a Swede. The
next day (Sunday) I went to the Tabernacle to service. The
hymn-tune was my arrangement of St. Ann's tune! . . . I
arrived at San Francisco Monday morning. I saw all I
could, and should have enjoyed my stay there very much but
for the ceaseless and persistent manner in which I was interviewed, called upon, followed and written to. . . . Went
through Chinatown with a detective, Devitt, a great character, saw the theatre, and went into the vilest dens. Got home
at 1.30."

At Los Angeles he found his brother's children healthy
and comparatively happy, in spite of the tragedy of the mother's
death which had so recently thrown the family into mourning.
Welcome indeed was the uncle, who, travel-stained, walked
into the little home on that August morning. He picked
up the family *en bloc* and took it for a wonderful tour through
the Yosemite Valley. If he had cares he forgot them in the
splendour of the scenery, the isolation and freedom.

Whilst making the journey Sullivan learned that Carte's
case against the plagiarists of *The Mikado* had been heard in
New York and failed. "All that one can do," he wrote, "is
to try and prevent a man doing an injustice after he had done
it! So *The Mikado* is open to everyone—free to be played
by every miserable penniless scoundrel in the States!"

In one respect at least, Carte had stolen a march on his
enemies. The day he lost the case, he produced *The Mikado*
to a crowded house at the Fifth Avenue Theatre, and Duff,
with his preparations less advanced, had to postpone staging the
stolen piece till the following week. The Press was unanimous
in favour of Carte's production, and the stolen version appeared
unheralded, and had, in consequence, hard work to pay
expenses.

Sir Arthur Sullivan

When Sullivan left Los Angeles at the end of August he made his way slowly back to New York. *The Mikado* was now doing big business at the Fifth Avenue, and Carte was in his element. Sullivan took the train from town to town, heard local music, played on endless organs, was fêted in some towns where he was recognized, and passed like an inquisitive tourist through others that knew him not. One amusing incident occurred at a small mining town, and thus he relates the story.[1]

"For the purpose of this story we will call it 'Cut-throat Euchre Gulch.' On arriving the driver said to me, 'You are expected here, Mr. Sullivan,' and sure enough there was a small knot of prominent citizens gathered at the store where we stopped.

"They looked hard at us——went up to a tall man and said: 'Are you Mr. Sullivan?'

" 'No,' he said.

" 'Then which one is?'

" 'That'——pointing to me.

" 'How much do you weigh?' a man asked me.

" '162 pounds,' I replied, astonished at the question.

" 'Hell!' the man exclaimed. 'Then how did you come to give hell to John H. Shehan?'

" 'I didn't,' I said. 'I didn't give hell to John H. Shehan.'

" 'What, not down at Pittsburg?'

" 'No.'

" 'Aren't you John L. Sullivan, the Slogger?'

" 'No.'

" 'Who are you, anyway?'

" 'I am *Arthur* Sullivan.'

" 'Arthur Sullivan ? Oh, you're the man as put *Pinafore* together?'

" 'Yes, I am.'

" 'Well, we're just as glad to see you as the Slogger anyway. Let's have a drink.'

" So," said Sullivan, "we parted with many assurances of mutual regard, and a hearty invitation on their part to spend as much of my time as I could at 'Cut-throat Euchre Gulch!' "

[1] Sullivan's autograph notes.

More Adventures in America

At another small town recognition brought Sullivan an invitation to a ball. It was a dreary affair—bad music—a stolid company that lacked the first knowledge of dancing. Bored to death, he stole away to a quiet corner, and a kindred soul—a man—came up and offered him a cigar. Sullivan took it gratefully.

"Can I smoke in here?" he inquired cautiously.

"Oh, yes, everyone smokes here," replied the other. "It isn't very lively, is it?"

"No," Sullivan agreed. Here was a companion in adversity; he hazarded a suggestion. "Let's 'jump'?" he said.

"Well, I can't," the other replied. "I'm giving the ball!"[1]

Down in one of the small towns near the Mexican border he found a judge—an Englishman—who ruled the place with the despotism of an uncrowned monarch. The power of this man amazed him. He had an assistant—an Indian. The judge was a sort of "Pooh-Bah" who filled any post there was to be filled, including those of Sheriff, Coroner and all the rest. Wherever there was any power to be wielded he was the figure in the limelight. Sullivan very soon struck up a friendship with him.

One day, when in the act of talking to Sullivan, the judge broke off to give an order to his assistant, and said: "Go and tell Don Juan Baptista I want to try him for that murder case."

The assistant went away. Presently he returned and said with great humility:

"J. B. is engaged with a hand of cards and a drink. He says he'll be up in half an hour."

The judge was an Englishman and a sportsman. He waited the half-hour.[2]

When Sullivan reached New York towards the end of September, Carte was playing to better houses than ever, and making money fast. The pirated version of the opera, on the other hand, was about to be withdrawn; for weeks it had been run at a loss. New York had begun to admire Gilbert, Sullivan, and D'Oyly Carte for the spirited manner in which they had come across the Atlantic to produce their opera in

[1] Sullivan's Diary.   [2] Sullivan's Diary.

153

their own way, although the law gave the opera to the fellow who lurked round the corner, and who could play it without paying a cent to anyone. Nor did New York hide its pleasure at the fact that these people from London were being recompensed for their enterprise.

Directly Sullivan returned to New York he arranged with D'Oyly Carte to give a Gala performance which he would personally conduct. Bouquets were to be given to every lady in the audience. Illuminated programmes—a flower-laden theatre—none of those accessories that would make towards a great night were forgotten. It was intended to be the final blow to the pirate.

The performance took place on September 24th. "House crammed with a fashionable audience," Sullivan wrote in his diary. "Bouquets given to all the ladies. Very bright and spirited performance. Great enthusiasm. And I had to make a speech."

If there were a few javelins thrown at the enemy in Sullivan's speech, they were certainly not without justification. It was this speech, reported throughout the American Press, which ultimately brought into being an examination and revision of the copyright laws—laws which have, by their adjustment, led to the affording of proper protection to any man who puts up a play in America which America wants to see. Sullivan made his speech from a box, and he said:

"Although I have made it a rule through my life never to address the public when I appear before them in an artistic capacity, I am impelled to break through my rule to-night by the kind reception you have given to my friend Mr. Gilbert's and my work. As I am speaking for Mr. Gilbert as well as myself, I can only regret that he is not here to share with me your congratulations, and to thank you in words far more eloquent than I can hope to use.

"We owe it to the extraordinary energy of our good friend and colleague, Mr. D'Oyly Carte, that our opera has been put before the American public in a manner sanctioned and approved by us—produced in fact under our personal supervision, and in a style which thoroughly and accurately represents that which we wish to represent.

More Adventures in America

"We should have been grieved indeed if you received the first impressions of our work from a spurious imitation—an imitation in which the author's intentions are ignored for the very good reason that the performers don't know what our intentions are, and in which the music, through having been patched up from a pianoforte arrangement, must necessarily be mutilated, and a misrepresentation of the meaning of the composer. . . . To-night you see our work exactly as we intended it should be performed.

"It may be that some day the Legislation of this magnificent country may see fit to afford the same protection to a man who employs his brains in Literature and Art as they do to one who invents a new beer-tap, or who accidentally gives an extra turn to a screw, doing away with the necessity of boring a hole first. On that day, those unfortunate managers and publishers, who, having no brains of their own, are content to live by annexing the brain properties of others, will be in an embarrassing and piteous condition. Like Hamlet, their occupation will be gone, and I, for one, will give them my warmest sympathy and condolence.

"But, even when that day comes, we, the authors and creators, shall still trust mainly (as we do now) to the unerring instinct of the great public for what is good, right and honest, and we shall still be grateful for your quick sympathy, your cordial appreciation, and your generous recognition of our efforts to interest and entertain you."

Having said which, Sullivan, Carte and the entire company departed for supper at Delmonico's.

Less than a fortnight later *The Mikado* was produced at McCaull's Opera House, Philadelphia, under the direction of Sullivan and Carte. The former made a brief criticism of the performance in his diary:

"Monday, October 5th, 1885.—Attended first performance of *Mikado* at McCaull's Opera House. Very fair. Digby Bell (Koko) bad and exaggerated. Miss Ricci (Yum Yum) plain, but fairly good. Miss Prince (Pitti) nice and taking. Mr. Donough (Nanky) very good, also Katisha (Laura Joyce). Tremendous house, piece enormously successful. I was called for after 1st Act and bowed continually from my box, then had to make a speech. Great enthusiasm. Entertained afterwards at supper by McCaull at the Bellevue. Ex-Gov. Curtin, Hoyte, Gov. Bunn, Gen. McCarty (Fenian) and several others to meet me."

At the end of October Sullivan was back in London, only to find that as far as light opera was concerned, there was nothing for him to do. *The Mikado* was playing to capacity every night at the Savoy; three companies were touring it in the provinces. The music was everywhere. It was being sung in Mayfair drawing-rooms and village halls; military bands were playing it; organs at street corners drew warmer patronage than ever for their music. Then the Japanese authorities made vain overtures to have the play stopped on the ground that it poked fun at the Emperor of Japan.

The Mikado, some said, would run for years. It did. It ran for almost two years at the Savoy, and, long after the curtain had dropped upon it there, the touring companies played it continuously year after year. Every corner of the States was toured by *The Mikado*. Alfred Cellier went out to Australia and launched the piece there, and it spread like a flame. It was produced in Berlin in English, and the audience was almost riotous in its enthusiasm. Holland, staid, unemotional, found a piece called *Het Mikado* filling its theatres when all the attractions of a dull season had failed. *The Mikado* almost became a theatrical epidemic.

The production of the Opera in Berlin caused Sullivan to write to Prince William of Prussia (later Kaiser Wilhelm II) and invite his opinion of it. The Prince had considerable knowledge of music, and had already published musical conceptions of his own. The future Kaiser wrote to him, in English, as follows:

"POTSDAM.

"DEAR SIR,—

"Many thanks for your kind letter which I have just received, and for the interesting news it contains.

"For the moment I am unhappily unable to fulfil your wish because I am just recovering from a very serious and rather dangerous attack of ear-ache, which compels me to stay at home and be quiet. But as soon as I shall be able to stir to go to Reichenhall, I shall visit *The Mikado*. To-day the first performance will be viewed by my parents and all my sisters, whom I envy immensely their good fortune to see this charming piece of which I have heard and read so much in the English Press.

"I hope that for the arrival of the Crown Prince they will have 'polished up the handle of the big front door,' for he might have been a Roosian, etc., but he is a Proossian!

"I often think of our nice evenings at Kiel, and the charming musik on the yacht, which gave me the lucky opportunity of making your acquaintance.

"Yours truly,
"WILLIAM PRINCE OF PRUSSIA."

Obviously there was no need to consider the question of a successor to *The Mikado* for some time to come. Gilbert, however, was not content to wait till a letter from Carte announced the fact that the Savoy bookings were running down. He was elated—particularly elated over the success of *The Mikado*. He wanted to press on with a new libretto, and wrote to Sullivan directly the latter reached London:

"I don't like to ask you to reconsider the (as it seems to me) admirable plot I proposed to you last year. I content myself with assuring you that I see my way, right through it, to as complete a success as we ever achieved."

The letter disturbed Sullivan. The friendship with Gilbert had been so warmly rekindled, and the success of *The Mikado* had fanned it to a gentle and genial flame. To find this plot, which turned on the episode of the lozenge, cumbering his imagination again, agitated him for some days. Like most musicians, when he felt adverse to a theme, music failed to supply the deficiency. He firmly believed that failure lay in this plot which, like King Charles's head, was so constantly recurring.

At the end of a week he wrote to Gilbert. There was, he said, no end to the resources of this word-magician. But he begged him to put the "lozenge plot" in a pigeon-hole and forget about it for ever. The letter was so gracefully couched that Gilbert put the plot as gracefully away. But only for a time.

The January of 1886 came in—a January of snow. One morning, in the midst of a blizzard, a snow-covered figure battled his way against the driving sleet up to the steps of Sullivan's house. It was Gilbert, who brought with him the outline of an entirely new plot. So pleased was he with the theme, that he had hurried off to Sullivan before he had begun to work his story out. It was Sullivan who let him in, who tried to brush a mountain of snow from his overcoat. Gilbert appeared as a veritable visitor from the North Pole. They went in to their chairs and the fire. . . . Gilbert had brought the idea for *Ruddigore*.

They sat there, these two, the windows banking up with snow, scheming out the story. Lunch time came, was announced, and passed. Who wanted lunch? The twain were absorbed by the theme. An hour later the manservant announced lunch again. They went on talking; they talked as they ate, and *Ruddigore* was a practical entity by the time they had finished the meal.

There was no immediate need for *Ruddigore*; they both admitted it. *The Mikado* was never stronger. The official Japanese "breeze" about the dignity of the Emperor of Japan had come and gone. The conquest of Europe was complete. Queen Victoria wrote for the music. Henry Irving declared it to be the greatest triumph of light opera—British or foreign—in his memory. Massenet wrote and congratulated "a master."

Had Sullivan, in this hour of exaltation, committed his genius for all time to light opera, he would have found in the success of *The Mikado* every excuse for so doing. Well aware that the piece had many months yet to run, he then turned away from that form of music which had made his name acclaimed in every European country. He had committed himself to compose a new work for the Leeds Festival in October, and he told Gilbert frankly that he would write that piece before he set out upon the heavy labour of composing *Ruddigore*.

When February arrived, he had not decided upon a

subject for his Leeds Festival work until Joseph Bennett
called upon him and put forward a libretto of his own based
on Longfellow's *Golden Legend*. The idea appealed to
Sullivan at once, and he gave Bennett the sum of three
hundred pounds for the libretto. Even when the words
were in his hands he did not begin the work of composition
immediately. He attended a few race meetings; he went
about London with Liszt. He took the ageing Abbé to a
smoking concert of the Royal Amateur Orchestral Society,
of which the Duke of Edinburgh usually led the first violins,
and the *doyen* was enchanted. With Sullivan, incentive to
work appeared to be elusive.

Gilbert very soon became impatient with Sullivan's progress
on the music of *Ruddigore*, for the diary reads on April 3rd:

"Gilbert and Carte at 3. Gilbert attacked me about delay
in new piece—gave it to him back—finally arranged to defer
production of new opera till September or October."

It almost seemed as if he were obsessed by the burden of
work which hung over him—so obsessed that he could scarcely
bring himself to make a beginning. Only two days before
Gilbert reproved him for his lack of progress, Sir Philip Owen
had called upon him from the Prince of Wales, bringing with
him the manuscript of an Ode which Tennyson had specially
written for the forthcoming Colonial and Indian Exhibition.
The Prince wished Sullivan to set the Ode as a hymn.

"After much hesitation I consented to do it," Sullivan wrote
in his diary. " How am I to get through this year's work?"
A light opera, an oratorio, a hymn and the year already
warming towards summer. "Do they think me a barrel-
organ?" he wrote; "they turn a handle and I disgorge music
of any mood to order!"

He went to Yorktown in the spring and took a cottage
there. It chanced to be next door to that in which he had
lived two years of his youth during the period his father was
engaged at Kneller Hall. Here, on April 24th, he began the
work of composing *The Golden Legend*, and his diary reads:

"Saturday, April 1886. Yorktown.—Began composition
of 'Golden Legend'; got on very well for 1st day."

Throughout May he composed but little. "Work began to move again ('Sea Scene,')" he wrote on June 5. The day following he began framing what he had composed, and the next morning finished the frame of the Prologue (except the "Noĉte Surgentu"). Then for five days he idled, at the end of which he brought himself back to the task: "Began *scoring* Prologue—awful work."

"June 12.—At work again. Scoring. Awfully tedious and slow work."

He concentrated spasmodically on *The Golden Legend* till July, but, with the coming of that month, he continued his task all day, and usually half the night. The sheets of manuscript began to pile up. In vain did the London Season ſtrive to lure him. He became almoſt a recluse. Mr. Spark arrived from Leeds to see him about the Feſtival arrangements, found him scoring, and, when his visitor had departed, Sullivan continued scoring till 11 at night "with cold beef between." The diary bears teſtimony to the progress of the scoring:

"Auguſt 10.—Finished 3rd scene.
"Auguſt 11.—Began 4th scene (composition).
"Auguſt 13.—Gave Baird [1] scores of Prologue and 1, 2 and 3 scenes to get on with.
"Auguſt 14.—Finished frame of 4th scene.
"Auguſt 15.—Framed choral and Epilogue.
"Auguſt 16.—Scoring Epilogue.
"Auguſt 17.—Finished scoring Epilogue.
"Auguſt 18.—Composed 5th and 6th scenes.
"Auguſt 19.—Framing hard. Finished composition of 6th scene. Recomposed and scored 5th scene. Worked ten hours.
"Auguſt 20th.—Began scoring of 4th scene.
"Auguſt 21ſt.—Finished score of 4th scene (re-written).
"Auguſt 22.—Began scoring 6th scene.
"Auguſt 23.—At work scoring 6th scene.
"Auguſt 24.—Finished score of 6th scene. Only short solo in second scene (Ursula) to do now.

---

[1] George Baird and his son were his copyiſts all his life.

More Adventures in America

"August 25th.—Last day of work! At it all day for the introduction and solo in 2nd scene. Got it at 5 p.m. Scored it and finished at 7.45! Thank God."

Out of this strain, this overwhelming burden put upon a body and brain that continually rebelled, came a work of superlative beauty, *The Golden Legend*. It had been achieved —as Sullivan had so often achieved before—by sheer conquest of the mental over the physical. "Most people suffer and get well again. I suffer and don't," he wrote to Alexander Mackenzie.

That jewel in *The Golden Legend*, "O Pure in Heart," came into the work entirely by accident. Joseph Bennett explained it at a later date.

"Whilst the work was in progress we were necessarily in close association," he wrote. "No man could have been less sparing of pains than he, or more anxious to do his best at whatever cost. Lest this should not suffice, I will place in evidence some extracts from his letters. I had indicated a chorus on the lines beginning 'It is the Sea!' and the composer actually completed it. But he informed me soon after: 'I had to re-write "It is the Sea!" because I found that the chorus entirely robbed the next movement of its effect. The chorus I had written was, I really think, a fine piece of descriptive music, but it had to be sacrificed as the following number is what I rely on to bring about a broad and impressive effect. So I cut out the chorus, and gave it as a sort of melancholy reverie to Prince Henry.'

"This change, beyond question a wise one, brought about further good, for, as some choral relief was wanted a little later, the exquisite 'O Pure in Heart' took a place in the scheme of the work." Yet another chorus was sacrificed by the careless composer. As to this, Sullivan remarked: "wrote a chorus 'Let Him Live to Corrupt His Race,' but found it so unsatisfactory that I cut it out after it had gone to the printer. I could not get rid of the effect of the spirits in a pantomime. All the rest is as we left it at our last pow-wow. Shall we call it *The Golden Legend*? I suppose there is no better title. It has the merit of being known."

Sir Arthur Sullivan

In the first days of October Sullivan rehearsed the work at Leeds. Dvorak rehearsed his *Ludmila* there at the same time. When eventually *The Golden Legend* was produced on October 15th a scene of extraordinary enthusiasm took place. The audience stood up and waved programmes and hats; climbed on the chairs and shouted in a wild and incoherent babel. They pelted him with flowers. When he turned to bow his thanks to the choir for the splendid rendering of his work, he found himself under another cascade of bouquets. The choir had formed its own opinion of the work at rehearsal, and had accumulated bouquets under the chairs to hurl at the composer after the performance.

The newspapers reflected the enthusiasm of that day. *The Golden Legend*, they said, was the finest work of a serious nature produced in England for half a century, and in the opinion of one critic, Sullivan's reception was the grandest ever accorded to a composer at the Leeds Festival. It was a triumph not only for Sullivan, but for Madame Albani, Madame Patey, and Mr. Edward Lloyd who had sung the solos.

During the summer—an unusually hot one—the attraction of *The Mikado* seemed to flag. Gilbert and Sullivan saw no prospect of having a new piece ready to produce in the autumn, as had been planned originally. A discussion arose as to the revival of one of the earlier operas. But in September the Savoy began to fill rapidly again, and it was decided that *The Mikado* should fill the bill until the end of the year.

A few days after the performance of *The Golden Legend* Gilbert wrote to Sullivan from Uxbridge:

"I congratulate you heartily on the success of the Cantata which appears from all accounts to be the biggest thing you've done.

"I have just finished the libretto (subject to any alterations you may suggest) and I shall be in town for good. I don't expect you will want to turn to our work at once without any immediate rest, but, if you do, I can come up any day and go through the MS. with you."

Gilbert delivered the libretto of *Ruddigore* or *The Witch's Curse* complete on November 5th. It was then decided to produce the piece at the end of January, 1887, if Sullivan could compose the music in time. By the end of November he had finished all the choruses in Act I and they were at once put into rehearsal. The finale to Act I had also been sent to the printers. The whole of the first Act, excepting two songs for Grossmith, was completed by the middle of December, and when Christmas arrived the principals were rehearsing portions of Act II.

In addition to the heavy work of rehearsing and composing, Sullivan was engaged in rehearsing and conducting performances of *The Golden Legend* at the Albert Hall, Queen's Hall, St. James's Hall and Crystal Palace. He would go from a rehearsal of *Ruddigore* to a rehearsal of the *Legend*, then home to compose more of the opera during the night. All forms of his art were being exercised at the same time, and he could time his moods to the style of music he was rehearsing. From the superb numbers of the *Legend* he could return, completely attuned, to compose the lightest of music in *Ruddigore*. He always considered that this Opera contained some of the best of his light opera composition.

With the coming of January he scored the Opera at a feverish pace, evidence of which is found in the following diary notes:

"January 3rd.—Scoring. Ghost scene. 2nd Act.

"January 4th.—Scoring. Finished Ghost scene. Scored No. 1. Composed No. 7. (1st Act) and 7, 2nd Act (Grossmith's songs) and Finale 2nd Act.

"January 5th.—Scored Nos. 2 and 3.

"January 6th.—Scoring 5 and 6 (and hornpipe).

"January 7th.—Scored Grossmith's first song (No. 7).

"January 8th.—Began score of Finale 1st Act. Dined at 10.45; back again to write till 5 a.m.

"January 9th.—Scoring at Finale 1st Act. Finished it at 5.10 a.m. (Monday)!

"January 10th.—Wrote and scored Finale 2nd Act; ditto introduction and No. 1. 2nd Act.

"January 11th.—Gilbert called in afternoon to suggest new No. 6 in 2nd Act. Brought me new words at 9.30.

Finished No. 9 at 1 a.m. then wrote and scored new No. 6. 2nd Act.   Bed 6.10 a.m.

"January 12th.—Scoring 10, 11, 12, 1st Act.   Bed 7 a.m.

"January 13th.—Writing all day.   Scored Nos. 13 (1st Act) and 2, 3, 4, 8, 9, 10, 2nd Act.   Finished whole score at 4 a.m.

From that day until the production of the Opera on the 22nd, Sullivan attended rehearsals daily, and at night was occupied in making such alterations in the music as he deemed necessary.   Three days before the Opera was produced, the *Mikado* was played for the last time.   The curtain fell to shouts of enthusiasm which Sullivan did not hear, for he was conducting *The Golden Legend* at the Albert Hall that evening to an audience of 10,000 people.

Ruddigore was not to have the unqualified success on the night of production that had characterized its predecessors. Early in the performance two of the large pictures on the stage fell with a loud crash.   Sullivan's diary records his own impressions of the performance.

"January 22nd.—Production of *Ruddigore* at Savoy.   Very enthusiastic up to the last 20 minutes, then the audience showed dissatisfaction.   Revivification of ghosts, etc., very weak.   Enthusiastic reception."

Both the author and producer of *Ruddigore* were convinced that some radical changes must be made at once if the play was to be successful.   An emergency meeting of the three was held in Sullivan's house the next morning, when considerable changes and cuts were decided upon.   They sat through the day in solemn conclave right up to the hour when the evening performance was timed to begin.   The day following, the Finale was altered so that the ghosts were not brought back to life, and within twenty-four hours Sullivan had scored an entirely new Finale, and had put it in rehearsal. In some respects the feat was unique, for he virtually worked for thirty-six hours at a stretch with only brief interludes for meals.

Even with the alterations, *Ruddigore* made no great bid for popularity.   The title was against it.   A week after it had been staged Gilbert announced that he wished to change the name to "Kensington Gore," but Sullivan and Carte persuaded him that the play must now stand or fall on its merits, and that the change of title would have little effect upon its destiny. The Opera actually did run through to the autumn, and paid all those connected with it, but it was only a comparative success at that time. It ran 288 nights, which was considerably longer than *Princess Ida*.

At the end of February Sullivan left London for Monte Carlo in search of the sun, but met only leaden skies and days of driving rain. Outdoor exercise which he loved was denied him by the weather, so he began to work again. He spent a night working at his song *Ever*, which he completed at a quarter to two in the morning and went to bed. That night —February 22nd—was to be one of adventure. He tells the story in his diary:

"Not been very long asleep when at 6.6 a.m. was awakened by a tremendous shaking of the house, increasing in intensity —realized at once it was an *earthquake*. Ten minutes afterwards, another shock—short. Everyone terror-stricken, women rushing about and into the open-air in their nightdresses. At 8.30 another short shock. The first was the worst—it made me feel quite sick. The earthquake extended from Leghorn to Paris. The damage done to Mentone is considerable. Drove out there in the afternoon with Julius. At night there was a regular panic as another earthquake was expected. No one would sleep indoors. The place was alive with people all night—English Church crammed with people sleeping—all carriages hired also to sleep in. About 2 a.m. (24th) a slight shock occurred. I went downstairs, but soon returned to my sitting-room to sleep on the sofa, having given up my bedroom to Marthe. A few vibrations only during the night."

But the earthquake, startling in its suddenness and effect, produced a humorous incident which Sullivan always narrated with great enjoyment. After the first shock had passed, he put on his dressing-gown and hurried downstairs to the portico of the hotel. There happened to be staying in the hotel at the time a certain grand lady of considerable proportions, who wore a blonde wig. As Sullivan waited, the lady, running in panic downstairs, scurried past him. Gone the blonde wig. Gone all dignity. Gone the wonderful Parisian dress in which she had appeared that evening. All the raiment she wore was a red flannel petticoat and chemise, and Sullivan watched her rush madly to a "monkey-puzzle" tree, and, in her panic, try to climb it!

CHAPTER XIV

"The Yeomen of the Guard" and "Macbeth"

SULLIVAN remained at Monte Carlo until the beginning of March, then he left for Naples. No sooner did he arrive in the Italian City than he was attacked by his old malady. He took to his bed where he lay through the hours sleepless with agony. A doctor watched him night and day. Packets of correspondence came from England; the replies were sent by telegram. He had no strength to write letters, save only to his secretary, Smythe, in London.

The doctor told him at last that he could get up, but he must not travel. He got up, and promptly travelled back to Monte Carlo. But only for five days. Instead of dying on the train, as the Italian doctor had forecast—if the patient were so unwise as to experiment with trains in his condition —he set out for Paris, *en route* for Berlin.

For some time it had been suggested that Sullivan should go to Berlin to conduct *The Golden Legend*. The occasion was approaching. On the 22nd of March the Emperor William I, would attain his 90th birthday. *The Golden Legend*, so the Emperor was told, was one of the greatest works of Musical Art composed during his reign, and he must hear it. It was by an Englishman, but it did not matter. The Emperor weighed down with his war medals and memories of bygone campaigns from the War of Liberation down to the Franco-German War, nodded his head in agreement. The old monarch was like a corpse that had been fitted somehow with a resplendent uniform. He was very deaf, but he grunted or nodded his head to those who, ageing as he, had been his mentors through the years.

He subsisted on some form of diabetic bread. Important documents were read to him every morning to which he agreed with the same grunts and nods, the same blinking of the lifeless eyes set in a pallid face and buried almost under the Bismarckian eyebrows. He would sit during the reading—his white skeleton hands on the table, listening—or trying to listen—dreaming, probably of days long before Bismarck and Moltke had begun to read documents to him in the same fashion, whilst he sat, his hand upon the table in exactly the same pose.

Sullivan arrived in Berlin in a driving snow-storm, and spent the Emperor's birthday trying to reach the singer Pattini who was to play the part of "Elsie" in *The Golden Legend*. But the crowd in the streets was so great that he gave up the task, jostled his way back to the Hotel, and sat at his window watching the torchlight procession.

Much depended upon Pattini, and he did not know her. It was essential that there should be no hitch in a command performance at the Court of a nation which drew much of the sustenance of its genius from music. He may have had some misgivings about Pattini when he met her, "a little pretty soubrette; bright little voice, but does not give me the notion of singing 'Elsie,'" he had written. But he did not anticipate what was to follow. The social round interested him and quickly dispelled his worries. The Prince of Wales was there. Sullivan supped with Herbert Bismarck; he played the piano at a waxwork show organized by the Berlin aristocracy, where Princess Victoria posed as "Yum-Yum" in *The Mikado*.

Some foreboding of disaster came to him on March 25th, when he held a full-dress rehearsal of *The Golden Legend* at the Opera House. His diary notes:

"Crown Princess, Prince William and Princess Victoria there. Pattini sang, *à demie voix* in tune, but very uncertain as to time and phrasing. Went pretty well; but I felt that the whole thing was a very third-class sort of performance. Called on the P. of Wales in the afternoon to bid him good-bye.

Talked about Godolphin House, Newmarket. He would be pleased if I would take it."

The following night disaster descended, and his diary is the best means of expressing what he felt:

"March 26, Saturday.—Went to Opera House to look after arrangements and rehearsed for two hours with Pattini, who was very uncertain in her entries, and very shaky in her time. Called at Friedebergs and ordered some jewellery for the principal artists. Dined quietly at home. Went at 7 to the Opera; at ¼ past was ready—Pattini wasn't. She kept me ten minutes, then appeared without her gloves. I went on, and was cordially (not the English warmth) received by a crowded and brilliant audience. All the Royalties there. The performance itself is now a matter of history, alas! Everyone worked well and everyone sympathized with me —it was the most agonizing evening I have ever spent. The audience was very patient, and very kind to me. The last chorus created a great effect, and I was recalled enthusiastically three times."

The soloists had failed utterly. Pattini in particular. Sullivan knew early in the evening that the stars in their courses were set against him. To depart from Berlin like this, the merit of his work smothered under by the incompetence of his singers, was a hurt he was not prepared to endure willingly. As it chanced, Madame Albani was in Antwerp, and he sent her a frantic telegram appealing for help. She replied that she could not come till the following Saturday.

But she would come; that was enough. Sullivan immediately saw Count Hochberg and the high dignitaries of the Court who agreed to a second performance of *The Golden Legend*. Albani, hurrying from Antwerp, arrived on Saturday in time to sing without any rehearsal. The Opera House was crowded again. The fact that the piece was to be repeated after what had been quietly discussed as a fiasco, made it clear that a repetition of unhappy events would not recur. The diary records:

"April 2nd, Saturday.—Music with Princess[1] in the

[1] Princess Victoria.

afternoon. 7.30. 2nd performance of 'Golden Legend' in the Opera House. Full house. Royal family all there. Very good performance. Albani superb. Duet encored. Great enthusiasm and ovation at the end. Supped with Gye and Albani afterwards. Gave her a bracelet."

He amplified the last sentence in his diary the following day:

"I gave her a kiss and a diamond bracelet."

She had saved his reputation at the Court, and to the end of his days he gave her unstintingly of his gratitude.

"Went to the Kronp. Pal., accompanied the Crown Princess in a number of songs," the diary runs a day later, "stayed till 6. She is very sweet and gentle. Both she and Princess Vict. have most charming natures."

His last day in Berlin arrived. If any disappointment at the *débâcle* of the first performance remained in his mind, it was assuaged when, on Easter Tuesday, he was able to make this note in his diary:

"April 12, Tuesday.—Saw Prince and Princess Christian off at 7.45 a.m. Being Princess Victoria's birthday, I took her a basket of roses at 10. Met all the Royal Family standing on landing listening to the 'Kaiser Frantz' regimental band playing *Mikado* in the courtyard. Prince of Saxe-Meinigen sent for the bandmaster (Otto Jahn) and introduced him to me. After them came the band of the 'Cuirassiers' and also played *Mikado*, same selection! The Crown Prince chaffed me. Stayed till 12 looking at the flowers, etc., in Princess Yum-Yum's room."

When Sullivan returned to England he found that *Ruddigore* would soon be in need of a successor; indeed it was then doubtful if the opera would survive the summer. At the beginning of May Gilbert and Carte came to his house to discuss the situation. He wrote in his diary:

"May 9th, Monday.—Gilbert and Carte came. Former again urged his old plot to be considered, the one we almost split upon before. He read it to us and proposed various modifications of an important character. A sort of pro-

visional compromise was arrived at, that if, after he had
written part of it, it did not turn out in a manner that appealed
to me, or that it was not satisfactory for musical requirements,
no more should be said about it.   Revivals recommended for a
year or so before a new piece."

Gilbert returned to Uxbridge and concentrated himself
upon what Sullivan always called the "lozenge plot."   He
wrote to his collaborator in the middle of June, saying that
he had reconstructed it in a manner which would now meet
all his objections, and he was prepared to make even further
modifications if such were required.

Sullivan, however, was busy with the setting of an Ode,
written by Tennyson, which the Prince of Wales had asked
him to compose for the ceremony of laying the foundation
stone of the Imperial Institute—a ceremony which was to be
part of Queen Victoria's Jubilee celebrations at the end of
June.   In ordinary circumstances the setting of an Ode was
little more than a night's work to Sullivan.   To discover the
melody and sketch it was, at the pace his brain worked,
less than a full task between sunset and to-morrow's dawn.
But this particular setting tried him.

After his first night's work at the Ode he tore the setting
up at daybreak.   He abandoned the task for two days.   He
rehearsed at the Philharmonic, dined out, played cards at the
Portland Club, endeavoured by all means in his power to
forget the Ode and the occasion for it, so that his mind could
approach it *de novo*.   A few evenings later he returned to the
work again.   All through the day prior to starting afresh he
saw no one, and forbade the servants to admit a visitor.
He strove to get the "atmosphere" of the Ode deeply impressed on his mind.   At last he composed it in four hours!

The Jubilee with its bonfires, its myriad rockets, its portraits
of a Queen in fire blazing in the public parks, came and passed.
The Queen went to lay the foundation stone of an Institution
which was to be a permanent memorial of her Jubilee, and
the Ode was played while thousands stood bareheaded.   Into
the setting of the Ode Sullivan had woven the spirit of majesty
and greatness of an Empire.   Just as the mighty Handel

before him had composed special music for coronations, for royal weddings, for peace celebrations, so did Sullivan carry anew his mantle, and reflect in his notes the dignity of a Queen.

The following day the Prince of Wales wrote to him:

"MARLBOROUGH HOUSE,
"*July 5th*, 1887.

"MY DEAR SULLIVAN,—

"I must write you a few lines to thank you most sincerely for all the trouble you took in composing the music for the Ode yesterday.

"It met with universal approbation, and the Queen was specially delighted with it. All the musical arrangements, thanks to you, were admirable, and I thought the whole ceremony went off admirably.

"I am,
"Yours very sincerely,
"ALBERT EDWARD."

It was not until September that Gilbert again raised the question of the new Savoy piece. On a Sunday of rain Sullivan went down to Uxbridge. Gilbert was giving a small house-party. Luke Fildes, the artist, was present, Mr. and Mrs. Beerbohm Tree, and a number of others. After dinner Gilbert took Sullivan into his study to discuss theatrical matters, and left the others to their cards. Sullivan wrote:

"September 4th, Sunday.—At night Gilbert read me a scenario for proposed new piece. Clear, but I think very weak dramatically; there seems no 'go' in it. The 1st Act promises to lead to something, but that something doesn't appear in the 2nd Act which is the old story over again of whimsical fancies, and subtle argument, but it is a 'puppet-show,' and not human. It is impossible to feel any sympathy with a single person. I don't see my way to setting it in its present form."

All progress in the collaboration then came to a standstill. There was such division in the camp that the trio resolved to revive *Pinafore* when *Ruddigore* disappeared from the Savoy stage. For weeks Sullivan was confined to his bedroom with illness. When he was able to go out he conducted *The Golden Legend* at the Norwich Festival in mid-October—his first public appearance for many months. The situation was as acute, and apparently as lacking in any prospect of solution, as it had been before *The Mikado* was conceived.

On the last day of October Sullivan began to rehearse *Pinafore* at the Savoy, prior to a revival. The sands of *Ruddigore* were running low; the house was thinning every night. He was unaware of any intention on the part of Gilbert to attend this rehearsal, but as he walked on to the stage from one side, Gilbert—who had arrived late—emerged from the other. They met and exchanged greetings and the rehearsal proceeded. After it was over they had a long argument about the new piece.

"Gilbert told me," wrote Sullivan, "that he had *given up* the subject over which there had been so much difficulty and dispute (charm and clockwork) and had found another about the Tower of London, an entirely new departure. Much relieved."

Gilbert called his new libretto, *The Tower of London*. For months it went under that name, even after Sullivan had begun to set it. Then he changed it to *The Tower Warden*. A little later, on the advice of John Hare, the actor, he changed it again to *The Beefeater*.[1] It remained *The Beefeater* until a few weeks before it was produced, and then someone persuaded Gilbert that very few people were familiar with the fact that the janitors of the Tower of London were colloquially called "beefeaters." Gilbert therefore changed the title finally to *The Yeomen of the Guard*.

On the morning of Christmas Day Gilbert, accompanied by D'Oyly Carte, called on Sullivan, and the former read the

---

[1] Gilbert did not arrive at this decision until nine months after he had read the libretto to Sullivan. He wrote to his collaborator (September 16th, 1888): "The more I think of it, the more convinced I am that *The Beefeater* is the name for the new piece. It is a good, sturdy, solid name, conjuring up picturesque associations, and clearly telling its own tale, at once. The Tower Warden is nothing; no one knows, but the few, that Beefeaters are called Tower Wardens. I put the two names before Hare, without comment, and asked him which he preferred. He said: '"The Beefeaters," by all means.'"

completed libretto aloud. The plot appealed strongly to Sullivan. The story was packed with romance, and he had ever clamoured for romance. He was, at this stage, even more sanguine about the piece than the man who had designed it. The two minds were now closely attuned again.

"Gilbert read plot of new piece (Tower of London); immensely pleased with it," wrote Sullivan. "Pretty story, no topsy-turveydom, very human and funny also."

To Gilbert, his work on this libretto seemed an unending delight. He spent more time over it, gave it more thought and serious effort, than with any work he ever offered Sullivan. His interest in it was such that he was loath to let it go. It was, he afterwards declared, the best of all the operas he ever wrote for the Savoy. His questing after romance, his visits to the Tower of London—where he poked about among the centuries, and selected just those memories that had the richness of romance—were a continual pleasure to him. In January, 1888, he gave Sullivan seven numbers to set, including a part for Grossmith—"Jack Point" which he created specially. But the complete libretto did not reach Sullivan until June 8th, and then it was in a very rough state.

At the beginning of the year Sullivan decided to abandon comedy and confine himself to serious work entirely. He went to Monte Carlo and Algiers to consider the matter. It meant burning his boats at the Savoy for ever—a big resolve to take. It involved, too, breaking a collaboration with Gilbert which, if it had had its rough passages, was nevertheless built on a great friendship. Cellier's comedy-opera *Dorothy* had run at another theatre five hundred nights, and Sullivan felt that writing these light opera successes was an art which others—as *Dorothy* had proved—could share, if with lesser merit. With his serious music he would stand alone.

He wrote to Gilbert from Monte Carlo, and, with the frankness which one gives to a companion in Art, told him what was passing in his mind.

The letter filled Gilbert with quick alarm. He was absorbed with the libretto he was writing. It was his new offspring; and his best. His enthusiasm had reached the point of fever. But his partner had dropped a bolt from the blue and threatened to break up the Savoy partnership.

All through their association Gilbert had never really distinguished the two distinct forms of musical genius in Sullivan—the genius for the music of the operas, and the genius for the more serious thought of such works as *The Martyr of Antioch* and *The Golden Legend*. Gilbert appreciated the other side of Sullivan's genius, but believed that it was his light music that would place his collaborator with the immortals.

Sullivan's decision drew from Gilbert a long letter begging him to cast these dreams of serious music aside. He wrote to Monte Carlo:

"I can't, for the life of me, understand the reasons that urge you to abandon a theatre and a company that have worked so well for us, and for whom we have worked so well. . . . Why in the world are we to throw up the sponge and begin all over again because *Dorothy* has run 500 nights, beats my comprehension. The piece that we are engaged upon has been constructed by me with direct reference to the Savoy Company. Every member of it has been fitted to the ground, and now that the piece is half finished you propose to scatter the Company, abandon the theatre, and start anew with a new company in (I suppose) a new theatre. . . .

"We have the best theatre, the best company, the best composer, and (though I say it) the best librettist in England working together—we are world-known, and as much an institution as Westminster Abbey—and to scatter this splendid organization because *Dorothy* has run 500 nights, is, to my way of thinking, to give up a gold mine. What is *Dorothy's* success to us? It is not even the same class of piece as ours. Is no piece but ours to run 500 or 600 nights? Did other companies dissolve because *Mikado* ran 650 nights?"

It is characteristic of the friendship between these two that at the end of a letter—which was at the same time a reproach and a plea—Gilbert added a tip for the Monte Carlo tables.

"I hope you've been lucky at the tables," he wrote. "Try my system; it's very simple. Back red until it turns up twice in succession, then back black till it turns up twice—

then back red and so on. I tried it a dozen different times, with Napoleons, and always won."

Pending the completion of the new piece, Carte kept the Savoy Theatre open with revivals. *The Pirates of Penzance* was put on in March. On June 8th—the very day that Gilbert sent Sullivan *The Yeomen of the Guard* libretto complete—*The Mikado* displaced the *Pirates*. The public now associated the Savoy entirely with Gilbert and Sullivan, and, when a piece by Alfred Cellier, called *Mrs. Jarramie's Genie*, was staged before the revival of the *Pirates*, it proved a dismal failure, and was rapidly withdrawn.

When Gilbert wrote "we are world-known," he was merely recording an obvious fact. Plays of cleverness, plays brilliantly acted arose in London, had brief runs and disappeared. But neither slack seasons, nor the apathy which the public has for revivals, could thin the houses at the Savoy. Only one musical play—*Dorothy*—held up its head in rivalry against the drawing-power of the Savoy opera. Gilbert and Sullivan, aided by Carte's method of production, had built in these operas a national institution. Gilbert said that they were as much an institution as Westminster Abbey. In those days it may have seemed a flight of fancy. We who can judge these operas from the perspective of nearly forty years after, know that what he said in 1888 was true.

Sullivan returned to England and waited for the libretto. Gilbert's letter, so strong in argument, had convinced him that their future still lay along the same path. Social affairs engaged him, and he gave many sittings to Millais for his portrait.[1] Meanwhile he composed nothing, but conducted his concerts. On May 8th, he conducted a command performance of *The Golden Legend* at the Albert Hall.

A remark which Queen Victoria made to him at that performance germinated in his mind, and was the source of his later grand opera, *Ivanhoe*. In his diary he gives a brief note of the incident, quite unaware of its importance, of its bearing upon his work.

"May 8, 1888.—Grand performance of the 'Golden

[1] *Vide* frontispiece.

"The Yeomen of the Guard"

Legend' at the Albert Hall by command of the Queen, who was present. Very good performance. Afterwards the Queen sent for me and expressed her pleasure at having heard the work. Her first words were 'At last I have heard the "Golden Legend" Sir Arthur!' Later she said: 'You ought to write a grand opera, you would do it so well!' Her Majesty was very gracious and kind."

Sullivan began composing *The Yeomen of the Guard* in July, at Fleet in Hampshire, and by the middle of August part of Act 1 went into rehearsal at the Savoy. Then once again dissension was to break into the partnership. Sullivan found that a portion of Act 2 was musically ineffective, and promptly asked Gilbert to reconstruct the Act. Gilbert protested that it was rather late in the day to begin to make changes, but that he would do what he could.

"The reason I did not tell you of my requirements six months ago," wrote Sullivan, "is that I never saw a word of the 2nd Act until two months ago (June 8th). You brought me on that day the whole opera complete, 'in the rough' as you yourself said. The lyrics of the 1st Act I had had in my possession months before, but not a line of the second Act. I have devoted the last three weeks to the 2nd Act, and in the constant study and work have found (and not before) those points where the musical requirements had not been fully met. I delayed referring to you as long as possible (as I always do) thinking I could get over the difficulty, but finding I could do nothing without some modifications, I wrote to you."

The changes were rapidly made, indeed a portion of the second Act was in rehearsal before Gilbert had written the dialogue or Sullivan had composed a note of music for the rest of it.

It was not until the final stages of composition were reached in September that Sullivan resumed his habit of working all through the night on this piece. During the summer the progress of the opera did not interfere with his social round. He was still at Fleet. He went to race-meetings, and it was at Ascot that he heard on the course of the death of the

Emperor Frederick of Germany who had passed away at 11.15 that morning. He went to stay with the Empress Eugenie at Farnborough. He journeyed to Belfast, conducted some concerts and hurried back again. All the while, *The Yeomen of the Guard* was being carefully built up.

There was no system in his method of work, for the inspiration seemed to wait, as it sometimes waits for genius, in readiness for its call. Sullivan only had one "fad" when composing, and that was his "J" pens. He wrote all his music with "J" pens. And he would write continually to Gillott, the makers of these pens, and suggest that if a piece were put on to the point of the pen here, or a piece taken off there, it would be even a greater pen than it was, and the manufacturers always wrote delightful replies and sent super "J" pens.

The intrusion of people into his room, the breaking off of work in order to discuss some domestic concern, worried him not at all. It did not spoil the sequence of his thoughts, nor destroy his mood. He would lift himself out of his mood when the intruder entered, and as carefully replace himself in it when the door closed and he was alone again. He would talk to his nephew, when he happened to be sitting in his room, and compose even as he talked. All the while he smoked cigarettes from a long amber holder. He seemed to have a dual mentality—the one conscious of the world, the other absorbed in his music.

He invariably carried in his pocket a small writing wallet, such as one used for tearing off slips. In a crowded drawing-room he would laugh and joke with the rest, then, unobserved, draw apart, and, producing the note-book, jot down a few bars of a melody that had stolen in vagrant fashion across his mind during the conversation. From these pencilled notes were built up some of the most beautiful numbers in his operas. In his own room he would first draft out a sketch of the theme. He then added the vocal parts, and usually did not complete the orchestral parts till the players were actually rehearsing the vocal parts to which, as yet, there was no accompaniment.

Only once in the whole course of their long partnership did Gilbert suggest the air of one of the songs. This was Jack

Point's song: *I have a Song to Sing O* in *The Yeomen of the Guard*. The metre of the song had worried Sullivan for some time; he would compose a setting, then, in a fit of displeasure, tear it up. He told Gilbert eventually that the song was a nuisance, and he did not know what he was going to do with it. Gilbert was a great yachting man, and he made his crew sing all the chanties, he himself joining in. He happened to remember the time of an old chanty which had been running in his head, and which had given him the lilt for the words when he wrote them. He told his partner about this ancient and recurring theme. Sullivan asked him to hum the tune, and out of it he composed one of the most famous songs in the opera. "It was the only time in your life," he afterwards told Gilbert, "when you were responsible for the music as well as the words. I wish you would make a habit of doing half the music as well!"

The opera was down for production on October 3rd, but Sullivan had still much to do, and his diary reveals how he concentrated on his task in the early days of September.

"September 5.—Began scoring opera. Nos. 1 and 3.

"September 7.—Long music rehearsal at theatre. Rehearsed No. 1 and Finale Act 2.

"September 8.—Scoring No. 4 (Tower Legend).

"September 10.—Long rehearsal 1st Act at Savoy. Scored at night.

"September 11.—Left Paddington 12, arrived Hereford 5.31. Eight o'clock conducted performance of 'Golden Legend' in Shire Hall—crammed house. Very good performance, only band *rough*, a lot of fossils amongst them.

"September 12.—Scored Nos. 8 and 9 (1st Act). (Chorus and 'I have a song.')

"September 13.—Scored Trio (10) and Song (11) 1st Act.

"September 12.—Worked at cuts and changes in 2nd Act; also finished vocal score ditto.

"September 15.—Worked till 4. Wrote Recit., and scored that and Song (No. 11).

"September 16.—Scored 2, 5, (1st Act) 1 (2nd Act).

"September 17.—Scored No. 6 (patter) 2nd Act.

"September 18.—At home all day. Began scoring 2nd Act, finished at 5 a.m.

"September 19.—Scored 2, 3, 4, & 7 (2nd Act).

"September 20.—Went to rehearsal 1.30 (1st Act). Settled to cut No. 2. Tried new bell—all right. Home at 5. Scored No. 8 (Quartett 2nd Act). Went to theatre; rehearsed. Home to score; finished No. 9 and consequently all the opera at 5 a.m.!

"September 23.—Began sketching Overture.

"September 24.—Began scoring Overture.

"September 25.—First band rehearsal of new opera. 11.30 St. Andrew's Hall. Very heavy work—could not get through it all. *All* scored and copied except Overture. Went on with score of Overture—finished it at 3.30 a.m.

"September 29.—Wrote new song 'Is Life a Boon?' [1] Scored it, and took it to the theatre. Last night of the 'Mikado.' Great excitement, and tremendous enthusiasm for Barrington. Speeches before and behind the curtain."

Gilbert, even up till the last rehearsal, was uneasy about the opening of the opera. The comic element, he considered, was too long in making its appearance, and on the morning of the day fixed for the first performance he sent a letter to Sullivan by a messenger.

"39, HARRINGTON GARDENS, SOUTH KENSINGTON.
"*3rd October*, 1888.

"DEAR SULLIVAN,—

"I desire before the production of our piece to place upon record the conviction that I have so frequently expressed to you in the course of rehearsal, that unless Meryll's introduced and wholly irrelevant song is withdrawn, the success of the first act will be most seriously imperilled.

"Let me recapitulate:

"The Act commences with Phœbe's song—*tearful in character*. This is followed by entrance of wardens—*serious and martial in character*. This is followed by Dame Carruther's 'Tower' song—*grim in character*. This is followed by Meryll's song—*sentimental in character*. This is followed

[1] See page 266.

"The Yeomen of the Guard"

by trio for Meryll, Phœbe and Leonard—*sentimental in character*.

"Thus it is that a professedly Comic Opera commences.

"I wish moreover to accentuate the hint I gave you on Friday that the Wardens' couplets in the finale are too long, and should be reduced by one half. This, you will observe is not 'cutting out your music,' but cutting out a *repeat* of your music. And I may remind you that I am proposing to cut, not only your music, but my words."

It was not until a few minutes before the curtain went up on *The Yeomen of the Guard* or *The Merryman and His Maid* that author and composer met in the theatre to discuss the alteration suggested in this letter.

Sullivan thus describes his impressions:

"October 3.—Tired and nervous. Drove to the theatre at 8 to meet Gilbert and settle one or two points—arr. to cut down 2nd verse of couplet in Finale; to leave in Temple's song for the first night. Crammed house—usual enthusiastic reception. I was awfully nervous and continued so until the duet 'Heighday' which settled the fate of the Opera. Its success was tremendous; 3 times *encored*! After that everything went on wheels, and I think its success is even greater than the 'Mikado.' 9 encores."

Miss Geraldine Ulmar, whom Sullivan had first met in New York, played "Elsie Maynard," and in "Jack Point" George Grossmith found the greatest part of his life—a part which always remained his favourite. The newspapers were undivided in their praise, for the partnership had broken new ground. "There is no limit," said one critic, "to what these cunning fellows can do."

The morning after the production Sullivan received the following letter from the Duke of Edinburgh:

"H.M.S. 'Alexandra,'
"Nanplin,
"28th September, 1888.

"My dear Sullivan,—

"I have never had sign of life from you since I left England, but no doubt you have been so busy that you have forgotten

me altogether. You will remember two years ago my asking
you to send me some music for the Sultan's band, notably
amongst it selections from your Operettas. H.I.M. is so
pleased with the music that he questioned me much when I
was at Constantinople the other day as to the composer, and
requested me to forward to you the enclosed decoration as a
mark of his appreciation. . . .

"I think that about the favourite piece in the *repertoire*
of our band on board here is your music to 'Henry the VIIIth.'
I like it better every time I hear it.

"Yours very truly,
"ALFRED."

The year was drawing to a close, and Sullivan was about
to go abroad for rest when Henry Irving asked him to write
the incidental music for his forthcoming production of
Macbeth. He consented and began the music in November.

Irving's outline of what he wanted was brief, it was more
than a little vague. He wrote:

"MY DEAR SULLIVAN,—

"Trumpets and drums are the things *behind scenes*.

"Entrance of *Macbeth, only drum.*

"Distant march would be good for Macbeth's exit in 3rd
scene—or drum and trumpets as you suggest.

"In the last act there will be several flourishes of trumpets.

"Make all our trumpets speak," etc.

"Roll of drum sometimes.

"Really anything you can give of a stirring sort can be
easily brought in.

"As you say, you can dot these down at rehearsals—but
one player would be good to tootle, tootle, so that we could get
the exact tune.

"I'm at the present moment with the 'blood-boltered
Banquo' who's really making a most unreal shadow of himself.

"Ever yours,
"H. IRVING."

Early in December Sullivan went to the Lyceum with the
completed music, and began to rehearse with the orchestra.
Until then Irving knew nothing of what he had written.

Macbeth was to be produced on the 29th, and it was not until the night of Boxing Day that Sullivan finished the scoring after eleven hours' work. There could be no more than two full rehearsals, but such was Sullivan's grip on the orchestra that, at the second rehearsal, the performance was perfect. It might have been in rehearsal for a month. Irving was enchanted.

After the fall of the curtain, on the first night Sullivan wrote in his diary:

"December 29th, 1888.—Left at 7.15 for
"The *Production* of *Macbeth* at the *Lyceum Theatre*
            "Words by Shakespeare.
            "Music by Sullivan.
            "Produced by Irving.
                        "Great Success!
"Author, Composer and Stage-manager called enthusiastically.
"Only the two latter responded!"

CHAPTER XV

Storm—and "The Gondoliers"

WITH the coming of 1889 a definite change manifested itself in Sullivan's outlook. He wished to abandon light opera. It now gave him a sense of restraint. He had achieved, he felt, all that might be achieved in light opera, and within him an ambition, definite and demanding, clamoured for opportunity. He was really tired of doing what he could do so well. That he created a style of music without compare, possibly never occurred to him. If it had, it could not have cooled his desire for more serious things. He had wished to break free many times, but the *Mikado* and its success had bound him with fresh links to what he termed "this slavery." Queen Victoria's remark about his power to write grand opera had not been forgotten.

The same mood, more violent in its insistence, took control of him in January, 1889, as is evident from a note in his diary:

"January 9th, 1889.—Called, Carte, then Gilbert. Explained to latter my views as to the future, viz. that I wanted to do some dramatic work on a larger musical scale, and that of course I should like to do it with him if he would, but that the music must occupy a more important position than in our other pieces—that I wished to get rid of the *strongly marked rhythm*, and *rhymed* couplets, and have words that would give a chance of developing *musical effects*. Also that I wanted a voice in the *Musical constructions* of the libretto. He seemed quite to assent to all this."

These views came as no surprise to Gilbert. He had foreseen them. Gilbert gave himself to the wit of light opera and was a master of his craft. But he knew that in the still

184

hours some mischievous Puck was whispering stories of the magical Kingdom of Grand Opera in the ears of his partner. Sullivan's imagination in music had few limits, and of this Gilbert was aware.

Sullivan followed up his talk with Gilbert with a note some weeks later in which he said he had decided to compose a large work of dramatic and serious purpose before he contemplated anything else, and he hoped Gilbert would collaborate with him. To this Gilbert sent a sound and reasoned reply:

"39, HARRINGTON GARDENS, SOUTH KENSINGTON,
"20 *Feb.* '89.

"DEAR S.,—

"I have thought carefully over your letter, and while I quite understand and sympathize with your desire to write what, for want of a better term, I suppose we must call 'Grand Opera,' I cannot believe that it would succeed either at the Savoy or at Carte's new theatre [1] unless a much more powerful singing and acting company were got together than the Company we now control. Moreover, to speak from my own selfish point of view, such an opera would afford me no chance of doing what I best do—the librettist of a grand opera is always swamped in the composer. Anybody—Hersee, Farnie, Reece—can write a good libretto for such a purpose; personally I should be lost in it. Again, the success of the 'Yeomen'—which is a step in the direction of serious opera—has not been so convincing as to warrant us in assuming that the public want something more earnest still. There is no doubt about it, the more reckless and irresponsible the libretto has been, the better the piece has succeeded—the pieces that have succeeded the least have been those in which a consistent story has been more or less consistently followed out. Personally, I prefer a consistent subject—such a subject as the 'Yeomen' is far more congenial to my taste than the

---

[1] D'Oyly Carte was then engaged in building the Royal English Opera House (now the Palace Theatre) which he intended should be a house for serious opera to be kept open all the year round, except for a brief interval in the summer. He had told Sullivan that if he would write a grand opera it should be the first work produced there.

burlesque of 'Iolanthe' or the 'Mikado'—but I think we should be risking everything in writing more seriously still. We have a name, jointly, for humorous work, tempered with occasional glimpses of earnest drama. I think we should do unwisely if we left, altogether, the path which we have trodden together so long and so successfully. I can quite understand your desire to write a big work. Well, why not write one? But why abandon the Savoy business? Cannot the two things be done concurrently? If you can write an oratorio like the 'Martyr of Antioch' while you are occupied with pieces like 'Patience' and 'Iolanthe,' can't you write a grand opera without giving up pieces like 'The Yeomen of the Guard?' Are the two things irreconcilable?

"As to leaving the Savoy. I can only say that I should do so with the profoundest reluctance and regret . . . and I feel convinced that it would be madness to sever the connections with that theatre.

"If you don't care to write any more pieces of the 'Yeomen' order, well and good. But before launching a grand opera remember how difficult we have found it to get effective singers and actors for the pieces we have already done. Where, in God's name, is your Grand opera soprano (who can act) to be found?

"From me the Press and the Public will take nothing but what is, in essence, humorous. The best serious librettist of the day is Julian Sturgis. Why not write a grand opera with him? *My* work in that direction would be, deservedly or otherwise, generally pooh-poohed.

"Yours truly,
"W. S. Gilbert."

From the point of view of the partnership and its success, it was unquestionably the best argument, very carefully phrased, which a collaborator could put forward in the peculiar circumstances. Gilbert desired more Savoy triumphs; Sullivan did not. His reply to Gilbert a few days later must have suggested that the comic-opera partnership was over, and that never again would they stand side by side to receive the plaudits of a Savoy audience. He wrote:

Storm—and "The Gondoliers"

"*12th March*, 1889.

"My dear Gilbert,—

"I confess that the indifference of the public to the 'Yeomen of the Guard' has disappointed me greatly, as I looked upon its success as opening out a large field for works of a more serious and romantic character. If the result means a return to our former style of piece, I must say at once, and with deep regret that I cannot do it.

"I have lost the liking for writing comic opera, and entertain very grave doubts as to my power of doing it. You yourself have reproached me directly and indirectly with the seriousness of my music, fitted more for the Cathedral than the Comic Opera stage, and I cannot but feel that in very many cases the reproach is just. I have lost the necessary nerve for it, and it is not too much to say that it is distasteful to me. The types used over and over again (unavoidable in such a company as ours), the Grossmith part, the middle-aged woman with fading charms, cannot again be clothed with music by me. Nor can I again write to any wildly impossible plot in which there is not some human interest.

"And here I differ from your opinion that the most successful of our works have been those where the plot has been wild and irresponsible. 'Pinafore' (bar the changing of Capt. Corcoran and Rackstraw at the end, which is an episode of no dramatic importance to the piece) 'Patience' and 'Mikado,' these have been plots with a consistent story and mildly humorous, but worked out by human beings. (This by the way.)

"But now we must decide, not argue. You say that in a serious opera, *you* must more or less sacrifice yourself. I say that this is just what I have been doing in all our joint pieces, and, what is more, must continue to do in Comic Opera to make it successful. Business and syllabic setting assume an importance which, however much they fetter me, cannot be overlooked. I am bound, in the interests of the piece, to give way. Hence the reason of my wishing to do a work where the music is to be the first consideration—where words are to suggest music, not govern it, and where music will intensify and emphasize the emotional effect of the words.

"Now is there any 'modus vivendi' by which my requirements can be met, and which you can enter into willingly and without any detriment to your hearty interest in the piece? And will it not facilitate matters if you bear in mind that in Sept. there will be very little of the old Savoy Comp. left? Grossmith goes; Barrington has gone. Temple wants to go, and Miss Ulmar must go. . . . Here, then, we seem to be in an 'impasse,' and unless you can solve the difficulty I don't see my way out of it."

To this letter Gilbert replied on the day following:

"*19th March,* '89.

"DEAR SULLIVAN,—

"Your letter has filled me with amazement and regret.

"If you are really under the astounding impression that you have been effacing yourself during the last twelve years —and if you are in earnest when you say that you wish to write an opera with me in which 'the music shall be the first consideration' (by which I understand an opera in which the libretto, and consequently the librettist, must occupy a subordinate place) there is most certainly no 'modus vivendi' to be found that shall be satisfactory to both of us.

"You are an adept in your profession, and I am an adept in mine. If we meet, it must be as master and master—not as master and servant.

"Yours faithfully,
"W. S. GILBERT."

A few days later Sullivan wrote again:

"*27th March,* '89.

"MY DEAR GILBERT,—

"I was so annoyed at your abrupt letter to me that I thought it wiser not to answer it without a few days' delay. I wrote to Carte yesterday to mention some of the points on which I thought I had just grounds for dissatisfaction. As he will probably repeat them to you, I need not enter into particulars again. I write therefore only to say that it seems to me a silly and unnecessary thing for you and I to quarrel over a matter that can really be so easily arranged, and that I really don't think my requests are unreasonable.

"All I ask is that in the future, (1) my judgment and opinion should have some weight with you in the laying out of the *musical situation*, even to making important alterations after the work has been framed, because it is impossible sometimes to form a right judgment until one begins to work at the number or situation itself.

"(2) That I should have a more important share in arranging the attitudes and business in all the musical portions, and, (3) that the rehearsals should be arranged in such a way as not to weary the voices, and cause everyone to sing carelessly and without regard for tune, time or account.

"In no way do I trench on your ground, or demand anything but what has to do directly with the music and its efficient representation.

"It is to these matters (and more specially the first—that of the musical construction of the book) that I attach the greatest importance, and I cannot but feel that you will admit they are rational.

"If you will accept all this in the spirit in which I write, we can go on smoothly as if nothing had happened, and, I hope, successfully. If not, I shall regret it deeply, but, in any case, you will hear no more recrimination on my part.

"Yours sincerely,

"ARTHUR SULLIVAN."

On the same day Sullivan wrote in his diary:

"Wrote a long letter to Carte, stating my feelings on the subject of my position in the theatre as contrasted with Gilbert's, and also protesting against the manner the stage rehearsals were conducted by G. wasting everybody's time, and ruining my music. If Gilbert will make certain concessions to me in the construction and manner of producing the pieces, I will go on writing as merrily as ever."

Sullivan's letter, and his communication to Carte, did not terminate the difference. Fuel was added to the fire, for Gilbert replied with hot resentment:

Sir Arthur Sullivan

"31st *March*, '89.

"DEAR SULLIVAN,——

"The requirements contained in your letter of the 27th are just and reasonable in every way. They are requirements with which I have always unhesitatingly complied, and indeed I have always felt, and fully appreciated, the value of your suggestions whenever you have thought it advisable to make any. . . .

"If that letter stood alone there would be nothing to prevent me embarking at once, in a cheerful and friendly spirit, upon the work which (subject to your approval) I have been constructing during the last 10 days. But unhappily the letter does not stand alone. It was preceded by a letter to Carte (avowedly written that its contents might be communicated to me) which teems with unreasonable demands and utterly groundless accusations—the very least of which, if it had the smallest basis of truth, would suffice to disqualify me absolutely from collaboration with you. In that most cruelly unjust and ungenerous letter you say 'except during the vocal rehearsals and the two orchestral rehearsals, I am a cipher in the theatre.' Have you no recollection of 'business' arranged and re-arranged to meet your reasonable objectives? Have you no recollection of any expressed wish of yours that was not acted upon, without expostulation, argument or demur, upon the spot?

"You say that our operas are Gilbert's pieces with music added by you, and that Carte can hardly wonder that 12 years of this has a little tired you. I say that when you deliberately assert that for 12 years you, uncomparably the greatest English musician of the age—a man whose genius is a proverb wherever the English tongue is spoken—a man who can deal *en prince* with operatic managers, singers, music publishers and musical societies—when you, who hold this unparalleled position, deliberately state that you have submitted silently and uncomplainingly for 12 years to be extinguished, ignored, set aside, rebuffed, and generally effaced by your librettist, you grievously reflect, not upon him, but upon yourself and the noble Art of which you are so eminent a professor.

"Yours faithfully,
"W. S. GILBERT."

Storm—and "The Gondoliers"

Throughout April a stream of letters passed between them —letters which, if not untinctured with acrimony, nevertheless bore unmistakable signs of friendship, and a desire on both sides to preserve the partnership. Sullivan was conscious of the fact that he could work at a serious opera simultaneously with the preparation of a light work for the Savoy. As Gilbert reminded him, he·had done so before. But he desired more drama and romance for the next Savoy piece. Very well, Gilbert would give it to him. How complete was the accord ultimately arrived at between them is revealed in Sullivan's letter to his collaborator at the end of April.

"You admit that my requirements are just and reasonable," he wrote, "although holding to opinions they have always been met. Be this as it may, there should now be no difficulty in working harmoniously together in another piece, as we both thoroughly understand the position, and I am quite prepared to set to work at once upon a light or comic opera with you (provided of course that we are thoroughly agreed upon the subject).

"I am enabled to do this all the more willingly since I have now settled to write an opera on a large scale (Grand Opera is an offensive term) to be produced next Spring. I have my subject of my own choice,[1] and my collaborator; also an agreement with Carte to keep the new theatre for me for this purpose, and not to let it to anyone else before then. In this manner I can realize the great desire of my life, and at the same time continue a collaboration which I regard with a stronger sentiment than that of pecuniary advance. All this involves an immediate setting to work with the Savoy piece so as to get it finished by August or September. How will this fit in with your arrangements?"

The unhappy episode concluded with Sullivan's diary note on May 9th:

"Long and frank explanation with Gilbert; free and unspoken on both sides. Shook hands and buried the hatchet."

A little later he wrote to Gilbert:

[1] *Ivanhoe.*

"I understood from Carte some time ago that you had some subject connected with Venice and Venetian life, and this seemed to me to hold out great chances of bright colour and taking music. Can you not develop this with something we can both go into with warmth and enthusiasm, and thus give me a subject in which (like the 'Mikado' or 'Patience') we can both be interested?"

It was this letter that decided Gilbert on the plot of the opera now known as *The Gondoliers*.

During the months the argument had been in progress Sullivan had been out of London; the greater part of the time he was travelling on the Continent and Gilbert's letters were intermittent. Before leaving England he had paid a round of visits. His health had never been better; his spirits never higher. He stayed with the Prince and Princess of Wales at Sandringham.

"I was most cordially welcomed by the P. and Pcess and all the family," he pencilled in his diary. "All the five children were there, also the Empress of Germany and her 3 daughters. It was the first time I had seen Her Majesty since the Emperor's death. She looked so sad, and I was quite touched by her affectionate greeting of me. I really couldn't speak. Before dinner we had the phonograph." [1]

A few days later, he left for the Continent with the Prince of Wales:

"February 12.—Went by the Prince of Wales' special with H.R.H., Clarke and R. Sassoon in the saloon. Very cold. Special boat (Empress) brought us over to Calais (*very* smooth passage) in an hour and seven minutes. Supped with H.R.H. at Calais; excellent supper. Private room. Left by ordinary mail for Paris."

The Prince of Wales went on to Cannes; Sullivan to Monte Carlo. A diary note reads:

"February 21st.—P. of Wales came from Cannes to stay at 'Le Nid,' and wished me to go with him after the Casino to

[1] Sullivan had taken a phonograph—then a new invention—to Sandringham to amuse the Royal children.

Ciro's. Brought him into the Hotel to have a look at the ball."

A round of festivities followed until, at the end of March, Sullivan left for Venice, and here he found the atmosphere for *The Gondoliers*. The City entranced him, the churches, the Campanile with its wonderful views. These things were a continuous delight. Only the music at the Opera disappointed him. Night after night he sat at the Opera, but for all the Italian musical reputation, the performances failed utterly to impress him.

"Went to the 'Rossini' theatre to hear *Norma*," runs a diary note. "Norman and Adalliri, both about 40, with worn-out voices. Tenor like a butcher. Ovovess excellent. Band rough, chorus coarse."

He returned by Vienna and Paris, and at the beginning of June Gilbert brought him the outline of *The Gondoliers*.

"June 8—2.30. Gilbert came and read sketch plot of new piece. Bright, interesting, funny and very pretty," he wrote in his diary.

Gilbert did not complete the libretto until the beginning of October, but he sent the work piecemeal to Sullivan to set. In the middle of the month the Savoy principals were called together at the Savoy Hotel, and Gilbert read the play to them, then rehearsed them in a private room.

Throughout the later summer Sullivan had been working on the music spasmodically at Grove (now Bridge) House, Weybridge. He would compose a couple of numbers, then not touch the work again for a week or more. There was no reason for haste. *The Yeomen of the Guard*, which had started the year none too well, was drawing full houses throughout the summer. The scheming out of the grand opera was also a lure that kept him away from his Savoy work. At the end of July, Julian Sturgis brought him the scenario of *Ivanhoe*, so that he had grand opera and light opera to compose at the same time.

With the early days of August, Sullivan began to concentrate on his work for the Savoy. The piece would certainly be required before the end of the year, whereas there was no possibility of Carte having his new theatre for grand opera finished before the following year. Sullivan remained at Weybridge, rowed, walked and composed his songs. The Duke's song and the Grand Inquisitor's Song in Act I were written in a single morning. "Thank you, gallant Gondolieri," was composed and framed at a single sitting.

Except for the days spent at the Leeds Festival, which he conducted in October, the entire Autumn was devoted to the new Savoy opera. The Festival performance was a break in the regular routine of his work which he enjoyed, for his long association with the Festival was a privilege he cherished. The last day was devoted to a performance of *The Golden Legend*, and to the end of his life he always declared he had never heard the work sung better. His diary reflects his enthusiasm:

"October 12th.—Last concert. Superb performance of the 'Golden Legend.' Albani, Damian, Mills and Brereton. The finest I have ever heard. Afterwards the enthusiasm was indescribable—cheering and waving their handkerchiefs at me for minutes. All over at last. Saw the Band off by the 'Special,' then home to supper and quiet."

With the coming of November, Sullivan adopted his customary habit of working by night. The opera had not been given a name. Although it was eventually produced on December 7th, it was not until five days before the first performance that it received its title. Meanwhile, number by number went into rehearsal as it was written, and his diary records how the latter stages of the work were reached:

"November 2.—Wrote 'Here is a Fix' and Finale to 2nd Act.

"November 3.—Wrote out frame of 'Here is a Fix' and Finale 2nd Act. Finished at 4 a.m.

"November 4.—Too tired to go to rehearsal. G. had a preliminary sort of stage rehearsal of half of 1st Act; came here afterwards. . . . Dinner at 9. Began work about 11, wrote *four* numbers: 'Thy Cold Disdain,' 'O, buy, buy,' 'Rising Early' (rewritten) and Brandram's song in 2nd Act. Finished at 4; to bed 4.15.

"November 5.—Wrote Duet for Duke and Duchess.

"November 6.—First stage rehearsal 11.30 to 4.30. Home to work. Framed 'Thy Wintry Frown,' 'O, Buy, Buy,'—Recit. 'Ruthless my Heart,' and 'Rising Early.'

"November 7.—Framed 'Small titles and orders,' 'On the day that I was Wedded,' and end of 2nd Act Finale.

"November 8.—Rehearsal at 11.30 to 3. Home at 5.15. Rewrote 'Thy Cold Disdain,' and 'O, Buy, Buy.' Wrote 'There Lived a King,' and 'Take a Pair of Sparkling Eyes,' also completed No. 1. (1st Act.) Finished at 5 a.m. with 'Take a Pair!'

"November 9.—Began scoring. 23 pages.

"November 10.—Began at 11.30 to score. . . . Scored down to end of 'Buon Giorno'—18 pages. (2.30 a.m.)

"November 11.—Scoring all day. Finished down to beginning of 'Thank you gay and gallant.' 36 pages. 4.30 a.m.

"November 12.—Rehearsed all 2nd Act music at Savoy 12.15 to 4.30. Scored down to end of No. 1. (13 pages.)

"November 13.—Scoring all day. Rewrote and scored 'Thy Wintry Frown,' and scored Nos. 2, 3, 4 and 5. (24 pages.)

"November 14.—Long music rehearsal 11.30 to 4. Rewrote and scored Duet (No. 6) and scored 7, 8, and 9. (23 pages.)

"November 15.—Very seedy all day. Scored No. 10.

'November 16.—Scoring all day. No 11 and Finale down to beginning of Salterella ('For everyone who feels inclined'), 31 pages, 3 a.m.

"November 17.—Scored Salterello and Recit. following . . . 16 pages.

"November 18.—Scoring. Finished Finale 1st Act. 10.15 p.m. (14 pages.) Then 7 pages of No. 1. (2nd Act.) 21 pages.

"November 19.—Rehearsed 2nd Act 11.30 to 4.30. Home, slept 1½ hours. Finished No. 1.

"November 20.—Scoring all day, Nos. 2, 4 and 5 (4 pages). Framed No. 3. (35 pages.) Bed at 4.

"November 21.—Scoring all day. No. 5 (Cachnalia) and

6 (29 pages). Also the strings and references to end of Finale.

"November 22.—Rehearsal of 2nd Act. 11.30 to 4.30. Home very tired. Scored 7 and 8 (18 pages). To bed at 4. Only slept an hour.

"November 23.—Scored 9, 10 (16 pages). Very tired.

"November 24.—Scored 11, 12. Poor old Freddy died at Marlow.[1]

"November 25.—Rehearsed 11.30 to 4.30. Finished Finale 3 a.m. All the Opera Introduction and few pages excepted, finished.

"November 26.—Rehearsal on stage 11.30 till 4. Dined at home and went to the Haymarket Theatre to see 'A Man's Shadow'—I am out of prison at last!

"December 2nd.—1st band rehearsal (*all* the music) of the New Opera at the Prince's Hall. Very few errors. Beautiful effect. Home to dine. After dinner wrote, arranged and scored the Overture, finishing at 3 a.m. Gilbert came down after rehearsal at Savoy at 11.15. Finally settled title 'The Gondoliers' or 'The King of Barataria.' Good title I think. Also settled to cut out dangerous dialogues at end of the piece."

He had finished, and by some miracle had escaped a serious breakdown. None of the operas had been composed at such terrific pressure as this one. Take only one of these days— November 8th—when, in addition to a long rehearsal, he rewrote two songs, and composed two others, including that superb melody "Take a Pair of Sparkling Eyes." Carte, Gilbert—they all warned him that in working at this pace he was jeopardizing his health, possibly juggling with his life; indeed Gilbert urged that the piece should be postponed. Sullivan merely smiled, and all through the night the light in his study burned till dawn as regularly as before. It was as if the pressure opened some door in his brain through which melody poured like a tide. At times, after arduous rehearsals, the body rebelled, his eyes were heavy with fatigue, and sleep, which he had kept at a distance as if it had been some vicious

[1] Frederic Clay.

enemy that would break in and stop his work, reasserted its demands. But directly he sat before the music-paper on his table he changed. His brain leapt as a horse to the spur. Fatigue fell aside before a mastering will, a new-found vigour.

At rehearsals his demeanour was the same. There was no irritability; only extreme patience. When difficulties occurred, he appeared to sense the tribulation of the singer almost before the singer was aware of it, and gave only sympathy and consideration.

At one of these rehearsals he was driven to caustic comment by the action of a singer who relied too much on singing by ear, and was decidedly acrobatic in his tune. At first the man's self-confidence and meandering methods amused Sullivan. For a while he allowed the singer to have his way. But presently he exclaimed:

"Bravo! That is really a very good tune of yours—capital. And now, if you don't mind, I will trouble you to sing mine!"

On Saturday, December 7th, *The Gondoliers* was produced to a crowded house and Sullivan wrote in his diary:

"December 7th.—Quiet all day. Went to the theatre at 8. Began at 8.35. Of course crammed house—a great reception. Everything went splendidly with immense 'go' and spirit, right up to the end. Gilbert and I got a tremendous ovation —we have never had such a brilliant first night. It looks as if the Opera were going to have a long run, and be a great success."

His estimate of the piece was correct; one of the most profitable successes of the Savoy partnership had been launched. Full of enthusiasm Gilbert wrote to him the following day:

"I must thank you again for the magnificent work you have put into the piece. It gives one the chance of shining right through the twentieth century with a reflected light."

"Don't talk of reflected light," Sullivan wrote back. "In such a perfect book as 'The Gondoliers' you shine with an individual brilliancy which no other writer can hope to attain. If any thanks are due anywhere, they should be from me to you for the patience, willingness, and unfailing good nature with which you have received my suggestions, and your readiness to help me by according to them."

The Gondoliers had started a run of 554 consecutive performances at the Savoy, and peace and accord seemed to govern the partnership.

Unfortunately this was only the lull before the storm.

CHAPTER XVI

The Rift in the Lute

EARLY in January 1890 Sullivan left London for Monte Carlo to rest before settling down to the composition of *Ivanhoe*, but returned a few weeks later in order to go through the scenario of the opera with Julian Sturgis. This done, he wandered off again—Brussels, Monte Carlo, Milan. In the first-named city, he went to see *Salammbo*, by Ernest Reyer, which had just been produced. He confessed that, to him, it was a complete blank, "a feeble imitation of Wagner —no melody, rhythm, style or distinction—no invention."

When he reached London at the end of March he found that a quarrel had broken out between Gilbert and D'Oyly Carte over the preliminary expenses involved in producing *The Gondoliers*, and, as April passed, the situation became acute. Gilbert, Sullivan and D'Oyly Carte each had a third share in the profits of every piece, and it was from this arrangement that the trouble arose.

Gilbert wrote to Sullivan on April 22nd:

"I have had difficulty with Carte.

"I was appalled to learn from him that the preliminary expenses of the 'Gondoliers' amounted to the stupendous sum of £4,500!!! This seemed so utterly unaccountable that I asked to see the details, and last night I received a *résumé* of them. . . . The most surprising item was £500 for *new carpets for the front of the house*!

"I pointed out to Carte that we (you and I) were by our agreement liable only for 'repairs incidental to the perform- ance'—that new carpets could not possibly be 'repairs,' and that carpets in the lobbies and on the staircases in front could not, by any reasonable latitude of construction, be considered as 'incidental to the performances'—except in a sense that would include everything of every kind belonging to every part of the theatre."

At the very hour when the partnership appeared to be more secure than it had been for years the thunderbolt fell. At first the matter seemed one for easy adjustment, but, without wishing to take sides in the quarrel, Sullivan was compelled—since he was the owner of a third share, and therefore as interested as Gilbert in the charge for the carpets—to state his views. He felt that the carpets were a legitimate charge, and he told Gilbert so. He did more, he set down on paper his own statement of the case, and made the following entries in his diary:

"Saturday, April 26th.—Long interview between Gilbert and myself. He gave me an account of the interview between Carte and himself. I could not agree with him on some of the disputed points about which the quarrel arose, such as the question of the renewal of worn-out carpets, and the responsibility of the preliminary stage expenses. As a discussion of the accounts seemed advisable, and very much desired by Gilbert, I undertook to arrange a meeting at my house between Gilbert, Carte and myself for calm consideration of them, Gilbert himself suggesting that we should meet and discuss them on the condition that no reference whatever should be made on either side to the heated conversation which had taken place between himself and Carte.

"I undertook to arrange this, and proposed that it should stand over for a week as I was anxious to go out of town, and the delay would tend to smooth matters.

"Sunday, April 27.—Gilbert came to see me in the morning, and brought with him a paper containing the heads of a new agreement to be made between us three. These he read to me, and left the paper with me for consideration. . . . I again proposed to delay taking any active steps for a week. Gilbert agreed with me in this, quoting from the 'Gondoliers,' and giving me the impression that the breach should not be widened, but, on the contrary, that our mutual relations should be placed on our former amicable footing.

The Rift in the Lute

"Saturday, May 3rd.—Wrote to Gilbert. I cordially agreed with him that it would be better to have a new agreement which should be so drawn up to obviate the possibility of any dispute as to the construction to be put upon it. But I thought it might be better to let that stand over until the necessity or desirability of writing a new piece for the Savoy Theatre should arrive—that in consequence of the great success of the 'Gondoliers this contingency [not] to happen for some months."

That Sullivan agreed with D'Oyly Carte in the dispute over the carpets, and refused to enter at once into a new agreement angered Gilbert, who replied (May 5):

"The time for putting an end to our collaboration has at last arrived. In accordance, therefore, with the contents of my note to you of this morning, I am writing a letter to Carte (of which I enclose a copy) giving him notice that he is not to produce or perform any of my libretti after Christmas 1890. In point of fact after the withdrawal of the Gondoliers, our united work will be heard in public no more."

Once these words were written any chance of the partnership surviving disappeared. There was no course open to Sullivan but to send his agreement to the termination of the collaboration. "Over and over again," he wrote to Gilbert in one of his letters, "I have said laughingly but earnestly, 'I will write twenty more operas with Gilbert if he will always be so nice and ungrudging in his concessions, and as ready to help me as he has been from the beginning to end in this piece.'" (*Gondoliers*.)

As the weeks passed the breach widened. Meanwhile, the Savoy was filled to overflowing every night. Throughout the summer, while the dispute raged, all seats for the opera were sold out some days ahead of the performances. That something was amiss became common knowledge, and, when in August it became known that Gilbert, who had always poked fun at lawyers in his plays, had actually put his case into the hands of lawyers, it was realized that the dispute had reached serious proportions.

The storm that had arisen over the carpets had now smashed

a partnership which, for fourteen years, had not only delighted two continents with its productions, but also, as a business concern, had been highly profitable. There seemed no vestige of hope that the vitriolic letters which had been flying about like bullets could ever be forgotten. The Law had drawn its ugly and sordid trail of discord across a partnership which hitherto had only yielded harmony and success.

A few days after the case, Gilbert wrote to Sullivan and suggested a reconciliation with the Cartes, a letter to which Sullivan replied with frankness:

"You will, I am sure, readily understand the difficulty I feel in answering your letter," he said. "My old personal regard for you as a friend pleads as strongly to let the past five months be blotted out of our years of friendship as if they had never been lived through, as if the pain and suffering I (and I honestly believe you also) have endured had only been a nightmare. But I am only human, and I confess frankly that I am still smarting under a sense of the unjust and ungenerous treatment I have received at your hands.

"If there is to be a reconciliation let it be a thorough one with confidence restored all round, not merely a patched-up truce.

"But confidence cannot be restored whilst you still contend that no other course was open to you but to take the action which was an injury and humiliation to me. And you are doing yourself and your nature a gross injustice in pleading thus. I would much rather believe, as I now solemnly believe, that you plunged without forethought into these disastrous proceedings in a fit of uncontrolled anger greatly influenced by the bad health you were suffering from. . . .

"Don't think me exaggerating when I tell you that I am physically and mentally ill over this wretched business. I have not yet got over the shock of seeing our names coupled, not in brilliant collaboration over a work destined for world-wide celebrity, but in hostile antagonism over a few miserable pounds."

It was not until November that there was a sign of any cessation in hostilities. But on November 11th Sullivan wrote in his diary:

The Rift in the Lute

"Gilbert met Mr. and Mrs. Carte by appointment at Adelphi Terrace—discussed the disputes—admitted he had been wrong."

There was peace at the Savoy. The quarrel fell into the limbo of forgotten things, but it left its scars. The collaboration—when it was resumed at a later date—was never the same again. The spirit that had made it, the adventure, the prosperity that had shrouded it with romance, had departed for ever. The ill-fated carpet had virtually destroyed the greatest partnership in the history of the stage.

Meanwhile Sullivan plunged into the heavy work of composing his grand opera.

CHAPTER XVII

" Ivanhoe "

IVANHOE represents a distinct and separate chapter in Sullivan's life. It stands apart as a form of musical beauty without association with what had gone before. Whilst London was crowding to the *Gondoliers*, he sat in the quietude of Queen's Mansions engaged upon an opera so different from that at the Savoy that it is not easy to find the link of parentage between them.

He was tired of light opera. Had the *Gondoliers* failed in 1890, it is doubtful if the united pleas of Gilbert and D'Oyly Carte would have brought him back to it again until he had delivered himself of the more serious themes that were singing in his brain. He wanted human characters for his melodies, the colour and adventure of romance, and *Ivanhoe* gave them to him.

He began to compose *Ivanhoe* at Grove House, Weybridge, on May 17th, 1890. It was quite a casual beginning. "Took up 1st Act of new opera Ivanhoe and began it. Didn't do much," he wrote in his diary. He was disturbed by other things, chiefly the Savoy quarrel which kept him from his task and gave him moody hours. The violent letters that dropped with such regularity into his letter-box restrained his mind from roving back into the period of *Ivanhoe*.

He scarcely touched the work again till the coming of June. He was delighted with the scheme of the Opera which Sturgis had prepared, and, save for a few alterations, he set it eventually as Sturgis wrote it. The first composition he made for the opera was the Finale to Act I.

Throughout June he worked at *Ivanhoe* with such regularity as the perturbation of his mind would permit. But in the middle of the month he put away such of the first Act as he had written, because he was dissatisfied with it. He started in another place. He wrote the duet between Rebecca and the Templar in Act II. He left the work for a fortnight, then came back to it and wrote King Richard's song in Act II. Once again the opera was put in a drawer.

When September came, very little of the opera had been written. "Worked hard scoring;[1] only down to Cedric's song, 1st scene," he wrote in his diary on September 6th. "How awfully slowly it goes." He was blaming himself. He did not realize that the storm in a tea-cup over some carpets was battering upon a mind so sensitive that it ceased to yield the melodies it was accustomed to give off freely.

Sturgis visited him regularly. "Worked with him at all sorts of details in the opera," he wrote one day. "He is quick at seizing my meaning, and falls into it with kindly readiness."

Sullivan broke into the third Act before he had completed the second. Never before had he been such a creature of moods, never so highly-strung. So alive was his brain to the importance of the work he was doing that he became obsessed by nervous qualms. At Weybridge the lure of the river frequently kept him from the work. He rowed, he walked through the fields, attended village fairs, to write only in those calm intervals when he could shut up his thoughts, free from infringement by the wretched law case that had filled the newspapers. The usual careful notes of his composing and scoring which he kept in his diary regularly when at work on his operas became abridged, almost uninteresting in their brevity. Thus:

"September 27.—15 pages.
"September 30.—15 pages.
"October 1.—Seedy all day—4 pages.
"October 2.—Finished 1st scene and 8 pages of duet following. 28 pages.
"October 3.—Interrupted. 7 score.
"October 4.—J. Sturgis came in the morning, arr. some

---

[1] But a great deal had been composed.

alterations in last Act.   11, score (to end of duet) 9 pages following; strings only.   Didn't go out.

"October 5.—Scoring all day.   9 pages wind (heavy); 4 (8) score.   3 score and 1 of strings only.   Didn't go out.

"October 6.—Tired and much interrupted.   6 score. (pages).   Opening of 3rd scene recomposed.   Arr. strings of 6/8 movement.   4 pages.

"October 8.—Scoring slowly (3rd scene.   Act I.)   19 scoring.   12 heavy.

"October 9.—Began to work at 9.45, and did 13 pages.

"October 11.—Didn't do much work—only 13 pages.

"October 12.—16 pages.

"October 13.—Finished score of 1st Act.

"October 14.—Began 2nd Act score.   14 pages.

"October 17.—At work 1st scene, 2nd Act.   Didn't go out.

"October 18.—Trio 2nd Act.

"October 19.—Worked all day at Trio.   1st Sc., 2nd Act.

"October 20.—Worked hard and finished 1st Scene of Act II, including re-writing Templar's solo 'Its Southern Splendour,' 4 a.m.   Only 52 pages in 5 days!

"October 21.—Began Forest scene.   16 pages.

"October 22.—At work.   Contd. Forest Scene—12 pages score; then stuck at night, and had to recompose a good deal before 'King's' song.

"October 24.—At work all day up to 3 a.m.

"October 25.—At work all day.   Finished score to end of Richard's Song.

"October 26.—At work all day.   Forest Scene.   Wrote and scored 'Friar's song.'   Very good I think.   14 pages.

"October 27.—Wrote till 3.15 a.m.   Finished Forest Scene; much of it re-written.   16 pages."

During the next five days he scored for over twelve hours each day.   On November 5th, he worked till 5.20 a.m. and finished the 3rd scene in the 2nd Act.   Night followed night, without any cessation in the work of framing and scoring. Music, over which he had sat till daylight, was torn up ruthlessly as new ideas came to him.   He would send for Sturgis, together they would reconstruct a portion of the plot. It meant the destruction of pages of music, but he did not hesitate. He was brutal in his self-condemnation.

"November 17.—Wrote till 5 a.m.

"November 18.—Wrote till 2.45 a.m. Only 9 pages. Hope to get on better to-morrow.

"November 24.—Scoring hard. Finished 1st scene. 3rd Act at 4 a.m. (Friday morning). Awful business—about 97 pages of heavy scoring.

"November 30.—Scoring all day. Finished score of 2nd scene. 3rd Act at 5 a.m.! 76 pages.

"December 6.—Didn't sleep all night. Sturgis came at 12. Settled end of Opera. Took out present sombre ending and arranged to put in a brighter one.

"December 9th.—Began to compose end of Opera. Didn't go out.

"December 13.—Put the last note to score at 6 p.m. *Absolutely finished.* Thank God. Seven months' hard labour. 715 pages of score."

A few days later—on December 31st—Sullivan was thrown into great distress by the death of his favourite dog "Tommy." He wrote in his diary:

"*Poor old Tommy died during the night.* He came to me in Nov. 1882, from Edward Hall, from whom I claimed him as 'assets' for the £7,000 lost through his firm. Never will be seen such a dear, loving, intelligent dog again."

Ivanhoe went into active rehearsal, for it had been decided to produce it at the new Royal English Opera House on January 31st, 1891. Writing about the opera to a friend shortly before its production, Sullivan said:

"I must say that I look upon this opera—'Ivanhoe'—as the most important work I have yet written. Not only from its magnitude, but also from the strength of the musical work I have put into it. I have endeavoured to be, before all things, dramatic. . . .

"The opera is in three acts and nine scenes, each scene having a different set, and this, of course, makes it somewhat more difficult to work than other operas, but my friend, Mr.

Julian Sturgis and I could not compress it into less owing to the great number of incidents in the novel, all of which have a bearing on the story. Between the first and second scenes of the last act we shall have to drop the curtain for ten or twelve minutes owing to the heavy set required for both scenes. Practically this makes the opera in four acts. But I have a prejudice against four acts, and, therefore, call the opera in three acts.

"We have been rehearsing hard—sometimes two long rehearsals a day, morning and evening. . . . I need scarcely tell you, an old stager, what rehearsing a new opera with a double cast means, as I have endeavoured to mix up the artists at rehearsal just as they will be in the performance. . . .

"We have a splendid chorus and an equally superb orchestra, the latter mustering between 60 and 70 picked artists. That I am anxious about the result you will understand, as it is a very important epoch in my musical career, and, remember, that if it is successful it will open a great field for other English composers."

Throughout the rehearsals, which were held at the Prince's Hall, the utmost care was taken to prevent any knowledge of the music reaching the public. Sullivan declared, and probably rightly, that if *Ho Jolly Jenkin* were disclosed, people would be whistling it in the street before the opera could be produced. He therefore had all the music collected and locked away after each rehearsal.

D'Oyly Carte had built his theatre lavishly, and he furnished it as lavishly. He spared nothing over the mounting of the opera. *Ivanhoe* was an orgy of splendour. "Nothing that is asked for is refused in any department," Sullivan wrote during the rehearsals. "The only care he (Carte) seems to have is that everything should be of the best."

The first night of *Ivanhoe* was to Sullivan one of the greatest events of his life; perhaps he had never experienced the same elation since the first performance of the *Tempest* music. *Ivanhoe* had been the outlet for a form of music the range of which he had not hitherto attempted.

The theatre was crowded by an audience of Royalty and Society and London's lovers of music. And not only London.

"Ivanhoe"

People came from the far recesses of Scotland to be present at the performance. There was only one jarring note to Sullivan, and that was the absence of Gilbert. He had offered him stalls, but there were still some rumblings of the old thunder, and on the morning of the performance Gilbert wrote bluntly: "I· decline your stalls."

Sullivan described the first night in his diary:

"January 31st, 1891.—Lovely day. 3 letters from Gilbert, 2 answered. Went to the theatre (R.E.O.) at 7.40. Tremendous crowd outside. At 8 Prince and Princess of Wales with Pcss. Victoria and Maude and Duke and Duchess of Edinburgh entered their box. 'God save the Queen' played by orchestra, Cellier conducting. At 8.5 I entered. Tremendous reception by a brilliant and packed house. The night was really superb. Began 'Ivanhoe,' but the 1st 60 or 80 bars quite inaudible owing to the noise made by the pit on account of standers in the gangway—then they were removed and the opera went on and went splendidly, without a hitch from beginning to end. All sang well. . . . Went up after the 1st Act to the Prince's room; he and the Duke came and smoked cigarettes in my room afterwards. Great enthusiasm at the end; everyone called. I went on with Sturgis. I gave all the stage hands five shillings each afterwards. Home at 4."

The work was acclaimed throughout the Press and throughout the country. Congratulations poured in upon Sullivan. Count Hochberg cabled from Berlin for the right to produce *Ivanhoe* at the Hof Opera. Vienna and Paris began to inquire as to the chances of putting on a work so truly English in its story and its music.

In the course of a letter, which Sullivan received three days after the first performance, Princess Louise wrote:

"The Queen wishes me to write and tell you with what pleasure she sees in the papers of to-day that your opera met with such a great success on Saturday.

"It is a particular satisfaction to her, as she believes it is partly owing to her own instigation that you undertook this great work.

"What a joy it must be to you to feel that your work is so satisfactorily completed; pray let me congratulate you with all my heart on this your greatest triumph."[1]

Tosti, the song writer, always devout in his admiration of Sullivan's work, sent him warm words of praise:

"My dear Friend,—

"*Come un forte guerriero* [like to a strong warrior] you have won the great battle, and not only should musical art congratulate you on having given it a modern masterpiece, but your country should be proud of you, because you are one of the national glories.

"As for me, my dear friend, I am just expressing to you how happy that splendid evening on Saturday and your so-well-deserved success has made me. Ivanhoe was what we expected, a work which was great and worthy of you. I repeat that I spent an unforgettable evening. . . .

"Your old devoted friend,
"F. Paolo Tosti."

"You are most generous towards the English Nation," wrote another melodist, Jacques Blumenthal, "for, having already given it two composers of the name of Sullivan— viz.: the comic and the sacred—you now endow it with a third Sullivan, the highly dramatic—I am sure he will, if possible, be still more highly prized."

Ivanhoe, by the claim of merit, should have had a longer run, but it played no more than 160 performances.[2] The enthusiasm which had greeted it, both in the theatre and the Press, convinced Sullivan that it would run as long as any of the Savoy successes, but he was mistaken. He had given of his best and the public had been slow in responding. He was disappointed and nonplussed.

At the beginning of October Tom Chappell, the music publisher, saw Sullivan, and told him that Gilbert was desirous

---

[1] In his acknowledgment of the letter Sullivan stated that *Ivanhoe* had been directly inspired by Queen Victoria's remark to him, and the music was, by permission, dedicated to her.

[2] It should be remembered that heretofore no grand opera had ever been run for a continuous performance.

of a ' complete reconciliation" after the differences between
them had been submitted to arbitration.   Weary as Sullivan
was of the old quarrel, he felt that 'to draw the rake across a
heap of half-forgotten things was undesirable.   The pain ot
ancient discords was abating.   Gilbert remained in his mind
the collaborator he had so long esteemed, and he had lost
those grievances he had felt against him.   He accordingly
wrote to him:

"4th October, 1891.

"Dear Gilbert,—

"Tom Chappell tells me that you propose that you and I
should submit the matters which have been the cause of our
rupture to a third party, and, according to his decision, that
one or the other of us should confess himself in the wrong,
and thereupon we could renew our old friendly relations.

"The matters originally in dispute being really all settled
and forgotten, I feel that it would be a great mistake to reopen
them now, and a reference to a third party would only produce
interminable arguments and counter-arguments without either
side being convinced.

"I have no desire to rake up old grievances, or to enter
into a fresh discussion as to who was right and who wrong.
So far as I am concerned the past is no more thought of, and
I am quite ready to let bygones be bygones, and to meet you
at all times in the most friendly spirit, provided that the dis-
agreeable events of the past eighteen months are never alluded
to.   I say this in good faith, and I hope you will meet me
in the same spirit.

"Yours sincerely,

"Arthur Sullivan."

The letter evoked a lengthy reply from Gilbert in which
he again reiterated some of the points at issue, but the desire
for a *rapprochement* was as live in him as in Sullivan.   There
was no commercial bias in the mind of either.   Sullivan was
even now entering into an agreement with Sydney Grundy
for the libretto of *Haddon Hall*, and Gilbert was working on
two musical plays, one of which Alfred Cellier was to set,
and George Grossmith the other.   Any immediate renewal

of the collaboration was—whatever the result of these gestures towards a better feeling—out of the question. But the instincts on both sides were those of friendship alone.

"My proposition had its origin in a question put to me by Chappell as to whether there was any prospect or possibility of our working together again," wrote Gilbert. "I replied to the effect that, as matters stood—each of us honestly conceiving that he had been unjustly treated by the other— it appeared to me that such a cordial understanding as should exist between men, working together as we had worked for so many years, could not possibly exist. He seemed disappointed at my reply, and at a subsequent interview, two or three days later, I suggested that such an understanding might, perhaps, be arrived at if what I have always held to be the main question between us . . . were referred privately and in a friendly spirit to some intimate friend of both.

"Nothing is further from my wish than to enter upon any discussion which might involve recriminations, and perhaps intensify any feeling of unfair treatment which may exist in the mind of either or both—but I know you will agree with me that successful and cordial co-operation will be very difficult, if not impossible, if, when we meet, either of us has a living grievance up his sleeve. It is perhaps unnecessary to assure you that all feeling of bitterness has long since passed from my mind, but there remains a dull leaden feeling that I have been treated with inexplicable unfairness by an old and valued friend with whom I have been *en rapport* for many years, and with whose distinguished name I had had the good fortune to find my own indissolubly associated in a series of works which are known and valued wherever the English language is spoken. This is the present state of my mind as regards our relations towards each other, and if you can suggest any reasonable means whereby this cloud can be removed, it will give me infinite pleasure to adopt it."

By return of post Sullivan sent a brief note which healed the breach and brought about, not only a meeting, but an ultimate renewal of the partnership.

"Ivanhoe"

"*October* 6th, 1891.

"DEAR GILBERT,—

"Let us meet and shake hands. . . . We can dispel the clouds hanging over us by setting up a counter-irritant in the form of a cloud of smoke."

Honour was satisfied and recrimination dead. There was elation in the minds of both. That night Sullivan made a note in his diary:

"October 12th, 1891.—Gilbert came (by appointment) at 12—stayed till 2. Full reconciliation and shook hands."

CHAPTER XVIII

Illness and " Haddon Hall "

THE horizon, so far as Sullivan's Savoy work was concerned, appeared clear and unbroken with the passing of the Savoy storm. By the beginning of December Grundy had delivered to him the libretto of *Haddon Hall*, and it was his intention to winter abroad, and work at the opera whenever days of rain or his moods drove him to his desk.

But other things held him to London till after Christmas. At the request of Lord Tennyson he wrote the incidental music to *The Foresters* which Augustine Daly was prepared to produce, with Ada Rehan in the part of Maid Marian. Sullivan objected strongly to the title *The Foresters*; he said it was colourless. He implored Tennyson to change it to *Maid Marian*. But the ageing poet, unyielding as ever in his opinions, stuck to his guns.

"I have done the best I could with the music for Lord Tennyson's play, but it is after all not very satisfactory to have to write music which, whilst it is merely incidental to the play, at the same time requires proper and adequate interpretation," Sullivan wrote to Daly.

The scene with the Fairies bothered him a good deal, and he had lengthy correspondence with the poet urging certain modifications. "You can never get the chorus girls capable of singing a little solo each," he told Daly.

"I wish you could bring it out in England next season for poor old Lord Tennyson's sake," Sullivan wrote again. But *The Foresters* was put away in the common grave of failures. To-day it is unremembered; one may say almost unknown. But a few of the musical numbers from it, such as "O, Sleep," endure with the same vitality as Sullivan's moſt popular work. *The Foreſters* was a failure *d'eſtime*.

In the laſt days of *Ivanhoe*, D'Oyly Carte had endeavoured to persuade Sullivan to set a play by J. M. Barrie called *Jane Annie*. "There is one thing quite certain," Carte wrote to Sullivan when he sent him Barrie's scenario, "which is if you should go further into it and work with Mr. Barrie no one will say that you have taken up with an author who has not marked literary ability, and who is of a totally different type to the ordinary run of librettiſts of comic opera."

The scenario, however, did not appeal to Sullivan. *Jane Annie* was eventually set by Erneſt Ford, who was associated with Carte at the Royal English Opera House, but, when it was produced eighteen months later, it ran only fifty nights at the Savoy, then disappeared as completely as *The Foreſters*.

When Sullivan left for Monte Carlo at the end of December he was a sick man. An attack of the old kidney trouble during the previous summer had sent him to Contrexeville to drink the waters, but a month of the treatment only left him with a sense of uncertainty and insecurity. "Has Contrexeville done me good?" he wrote in his diary on the day he left it. "I can't say yet, for I ſtill have the same pains as before."

As the autumn advanced he knew that the enemy was waiting furtive and ready to return. He lived in continual dread. At times during his work, sharp passages of pain reminded him that if the malady were not actually gaining a closer grip, at leaſt it was not relinquishing its hold.

He reached Monte Carlo, where he had taken a villa, at the New Year, and settled down to *Haddon Hall*. The firſt day after his arrival he composed a song and chorus *Ribbons to Sell*; the following day he wrote two songs, *Oh, tell me what is a maid to say?* and *The Sun it is Set*, in addition to the firſt two pages of the Finale. A couple of days later he composed two more songs and sixteen pages of the Finale of Aĉt II. That night he was attacked with pain. He fought it with the fierce will he always exercised when suffering threatened to interfere with work in which he was intereſted. Getting up he dragged himself to his desk. Days of violent ſtruggle againſt the recurring onslaughts of pain succeeded each other.

H

Only courage kept him going. There was so much he had to do. And now after one of his worst nights, a new libretto, *The Happy Valley*, came to him from Gilbert, as if to remind him of the necessity for beating off the enemy.

Throughout January and February he worked in a state of continual suffering, but *Haddon Hall* slowly became a reality. Sometimes he would put away his work for days on end, revel in the sunshine, spend a few hours at the tables, sup at the "Paris," and strive to forget that a night of sleepless torture probably awaited him. He lived in moods of alternating elation and depression. The exhilaration was all too short lived. His nights became consistently sleepless and horrible. And yet, between the spasms of pain, he still worked.

At the end of the month he was seized with illness one morning just as he was about to sit down to his work. He was put to bed, and the pain kept in check by morphia injections. But he became rapidly worse. At times he lay as if in a coma, scarcely recognizing his housekeeper or his man-servant Louis, as they moved silently round his bed. Then his brain would spring afresh with quickening life. He would call for paper and pencil and scribble notes to people, gulp barley water and go on scribbling. Only for a short time he was given respite. A fresh attack of shivering would sweep over him, leaving him weak and nerveless, to be followed by intense pain, and morphia.

In England they said he was dying. The Queen telegraphed for news of him. The Prince of Wales, who had gone to Cannes in an attempt to assuage the grief caused by the death of the Duke of Clarence a few weeks before, sent a surgeon of high repute to confer with the doctor by the bedside. Letters, telegrams, came in an unending deluge. In a couple of months Sullivan would be fifty. But would he ever reach fifty? Such was the gravity of his state that they believed he would pass out in one of the vicious attacks. He could not live on morphia, and it seemed equally certain that pain would not permit him to live without it. They telegraphed for his nephew.

In the middle of April D'Oyly Carte came to see him, and

the presence of one so closely connected with his work brought back to his dreaming mind the desire to write. A day passed without morphia. He would have turtle soup! He was improving, so the doctor declared, and ere long the Savoy would open its doors upon his magic again. Then came the set-back. More pain—more morphia. It seemed as if it would be a case for the surgeon after all, and then anything might happen.

He was convinced that he was dying. He lay in bed, a wan figure who seemed to have been touched by the fingers of Death. When he spoke it was to give instructions for what was to take place after his demise. He arranged his affairs with the care and detail of one who knew that he had finished with the world. . . . A fresh paroxysm of agony ensued, and those by the bedside believed it must be the last. Then his nephew and the servants carried him from his bed and put him in a hot bath, an action that saved his life.

Two days more and the patient was well on the road to recovery. Then the bedroom door opened and Squire Bancroft came in. In the presence of his old friend life began to clamour in him again. Two days and no morphia! He grew stronger with the passage of hours until, at the end of the month, an attempt was made to take him back to London. At Calais four sailors carried him on board the steamer, and laid him out in a large cabin.

And so he came back to London, which had begun to fear that it had lost him for ever. He drove in Battersea Park, went to Lord's and sat in the sun watching the cricket, stayed with the Prince and Princess of Wales at Sandringham. When he tried to work it was to discover that the brain, always so agile, still hesitated to respond to the old activities; weakness still lingered tauntingly in his limbs.

July was on the wane when he returned to his opera, and, although he composed or scored daily, the rate of progress was slow. Only on two occasions did he work through the night on *Haddon Hall*. Perhaps the warning of the last few months had at last been accepted at its proper worth! But the poor progress he made irked him. "How slow it all is!" he wrote. At the end of August he reproached himself in his diary because he had only scored 88 pages in six days. And this from one who a few weeks previously had appeared to dice with Death as to whether he should pass through its door!

The *première* of *Haddon Hall* was fixed for Saturday, September 24th, but Sullivan did not complete the work until Saturday the 11th, when he made the following diary entry:

"In all day. Scored 18 and 19 (17 pages) before dinner, 14 and 15 Duet, Trio following (17 pages) after dinner. Finished at 11.40 p.m. The whole opera done. Thank God."

Never was a pious note written more seriously. *Haddon Hall* represented the struggle of a giant—a mental giant—against physical weakness. More than half of it had been wrung from him by the sheer ardour of his task while his body was in torment. But when the opera was produced on its appointed day, the vicissitudes that had beset its birth were unknown to those who crowded the Savoy Theatre. Only the locked black books—his diaries—recorded the story.

"Conducted first performance of new opera 'Haddon Hall,'" he wrote in his diary on September 24th. "Crammed House —reception immense—quite unnerved me. All went well— last Act enormous success. Called afterwards with Grundy. Gilbert came round to see me in my room. . . . Home, dead tired—to bed."

The critics, while acclaiming the beauty of Sullivan's music, condemned Grundy's libretto, a criticism which Sullivan always regarded as unjustified. Grundy was not a Gilbert, he was never the same lyrical master, a deficiency he willingly acknowledged. But the libretto of *Haddon Hall* was, because Sullivan had set it, judged from the standard Gilbert himself had established. It was only further proof—as a few critics sagely observed—that the Gilbert and Sullivan partnership stood by itself apart.

Haddon Hall, with its English atmosphere and charm, appeared to lack the essentials of success. The music score sold in thousands while the play was performed to thinning houses as the winter passed. Bands played *Haddon Hall* in the Kursaals, and with the coming summer it was heard on all the piers. In fashionable restaurants one dined to the strains of *Haddon Hall*. Vagrant barrel-organs shuffled down bye-ways and forgotten streets where music was an unknown quantity and gave *Haddon Hall*. It was played in school-halls and the organs rendered it as a product of English life.

Haddon Hall was a musical achievement; as an opera a comparative failure. Grundy had given of his best as had Sullivan, and D'Oyly Carte's mounting of the play was superb. But the London of 1892 did not want it. It was nobody's failure.

At the end of the year when Sullivan was about to leave London for Monte Carlo, Gilbert brought him the suggestion for a new piece which he had named *Utopia*. For four years they had worked apart. D'Oyly Carte had given up his scheme for running the Royal English Opera House, and had sold the theatre. Innumerable business meetings were called between the trio; at last it seemed that the partnership might be rebuilded. The Press began to scatter the news of a reconciliation; it described endless operas which the pair were going to write together, but of which Gilbert at Harrow and Sullivan at Queen's Mansions had never dreamed. At the end of 1892 the *entente* was complete.

On December 31st Sullivan wrote in his diary:

"Saw New Year in; hoped and prayed that it might be a happier one for me than this last, half of which was lost through my illness. *Health* is the secret of happiness."

CHAPTER XIX

The End of the Partnership

SULLIVAN remained at the villa he had taken for the winter on the Riviera till April, 1893, and at the end of January Gilbert went out to him with the sketched plot of the new piece. They took long coastal walks together, discussed their old triumphs, and were more closely in accord than they had ever been. The differences of the past few years seemed to have been completely healed. It was a brief visit of only three days' duration, and Gilbert then returned to London to work on the opera.

"I arrived here, all right, last night," he wrote from Harrow, "after a beastly passage, and three tiresome days in Paris. I send you Cook on Billiards—the study of that work *has made me what I am in Billiards*, and if you devote six or eight hours a day to it regularly, you may hope to play up to my form when you return."

"I am working hard at the piece," he wrote a month later —"but I find it very difficult to plot out Act I without being tedious. I have written seven or eight numbers (but some of them are alternatives) and a considerable amount of detached dialogue. I think the difficulties will all yield to treatment. I could send you a few numbers if you cared to have them, but I expect you would rather wait until Act I is completed."

Sullivan, however, had no desire to depart from his usual practice of composing his operas in London and in the quiet of his own room. All these works, with the exception of the Second Act of *The Pirates of Penzance*, which he had composed in New York, and the greater part of *Haddon Hall*, were conceived in London. When abroad, he made copious notes of themes which drifted into his mind and would depart

The End of the Partnership

as mysteriously if he did not set them down, but the distractions of foreign places and the demands of social engagements rendered serious work impossible for him. The kaleidoscope of Riviera life held too strong an attraction.

His first task on returning to London was to compose the March which he first called the "Surprise March," afterwards re-named the "Imperial March," for the state opening of the Imperial Institute by Queen Victoria. The work occupied him but three days, and at the ceremony on May 10th, he directed (in levee dress) the orchestra of ninety-eight performers who played it.

With the coming of June he began to think seriously about the new opera, for Barrie's *Jane Annie*, which Carte had produced three weeks previously, hoping thereby to keep the Savoy open during the summer, was dying a rapid death. Carte was anxious about the future. He had no wish to close the theatre, but the failure of the Barrie play had left him with no alternative. On June 19th Sullivan wrote in his diary: "Began new opera. Slow work."

D'Oyly Carte intended that the new Gilbert and Sullivan opera should be mounted in the most elaborate manner possible. He was a lover of his craft, an enthusiast to the smallest detail. The preliminary expenses of *Utopia Limited* were estimated at seven thousand pounds. Sullivan became alarmed, and in his turn alarmed Gilbert. Cuts were made, scenes re-arranged, but, even so, *Utopia Limited* was the most expensively produced opera of the partnership, and actually cost £7,200 to put on. A letter from Gilbert in August reveals the difficulties against which they were contending.

"DEAR S.,—

"I quite agree with you that it is highly desirable that the enormous estimated expense of production should be curtailed, if this can be done without cramping the piece. I confess I should be sorry to lose the Gents at Arms—who always stand two at the entrance and two at the exit of the Presence Chamber, to regulate the admission and exit of ladies presented—and I am afraid that, without them, the ladies will have the appearance of loafing on to the stage,

without any circumstance. Besides, you must remember that
these four people must be dressed *somehow*, they can't go
naked (unless you insist on it), and if they are put into good
uniforms they will cost at least £50 apiece. I think a little
economy might be effected by cutting out two or three of the
costly hussar and lancer uniforms, and substituting the plain
blue and gold dress that Hampshire wears—and which could
be obtained second-hand. One or two plain velvet court
dresses would not look amiss in the crowd—and these will
cost £10 instead of £50. Mind, I am as much for retrench-
ment as you are—the only question is, where can it be best
effected, and with least injury to the piece?

"I agree with you that the ladies' bouquets and diamonds
might well be curtailed. The merest paste (mixed with glass
emeralds and rubies) will do for the jewellery. As to the
pages, there must be boys to steer the trains of the three prin-
cesses and Lady Sophy when they come on for the Quartett.
Remember the Princess is in the position of the Queen. But
if they can be dispensed with, all the better.

"Very truly yours,
"W. S. GILBERT."

Whilst the composition was in progress Gilbert went to
Homburg. He was in the throes of an attack of gout. From
Homburg he wrote continuously about the work, and plied
Sullivan with suggestions for changes. Now and again, a
touch of the true Gilbertian humour would appear in these
letters.

"I am worse rather than better," he wrote. "My right
foot (which I call Labouchere) is troublesome, and I take a
vicious pleasure (not unalloyed with pain) in cramming him
into a boot which is much too small for him. My left foot
(known in Homburg as 'Clement Scott') is a milder nuisance,
but still tiresome, and would hurt me a good deal if he could."

He sent Sullivan a new song for the piece with this trite
remark:

" 'Court Reputations he'll revise.' This flashed on me in
a moment. Herein is the difference between a lyrical genius
and a mere literary mechanic."

The End of the Partnership

Sullivan completed Act I in a month, and when he met Gilbert at the end of July the latter read over the libretto of Act II. At the same time he complimented Sullivan on the Finale of Act I, which he declared was the best Finale he had ever written.

In its final stages the opera was hindered by differences of opinion between author and composer with regard to one of the characters in the piece. Sullivan protested strongly against there being an "old lady in love" in the piece, referring, of course, to Lady Sophy.

"It now appears," Gilbert replied, "as I gather from your letter of to-day, that you wish her to be in Act II, a grave and dignified lady, to be taken seriously and apart from any grotesque suggestion. But (to say nothing of the fact that by investing her with a pathetic interest, I should be laying myself open to the charge of repeating Mr. Grundy's treatment of the part in the last Act of Haddon Hall) I have in Act I committed her irrevocably to a more or less humorous fate, and in this you have aided and abetted me. Surely to make a sudden *volte face* and treat her at the end of Act II as a pathetic personage (there being no single serious note in the piece up to this point), would be to absolutely stultify myself in the face of the audience. Possibly I may have, even now, failed to grasp your intention in its completeness— possibly you may have failed to grasp mine—most assuredly it is not necessary that she should be so very old, ugly, raddled and grotesque. . . . Nor do I propose that she shall be 'seething with love and passion.' She is in love with the King (as a lady of 45 may well be with a man of 50) but her frenzy is not of a gross or animal type as you seem to imagine."

The collaborators then met, and the character of Lady Sophy was settled for all time. She would not offend against the canons of propriety; she was now endowed with the full measure of pathetic interest, and in the measure of her changing she became more dignified.

A fresh difficulty occurred over the Finale to Act II. Sullivan found that, after struggling with it for days on end without success, it was a metre almost impossible to set. Gilbert realized the difficulty, but as he had no other ending to the opera in mind, he suggested that Sullivan should compose the music first, and he would then write words to fit it. This was about the only occasion in which any music of one of their operas was set down before the words, and the music eventually puzzled Gilbert to almost the same extent as his words had puzzled Sullivan.

"I got up at seven this morning and polished off the new finale before breakfast," Gilbert wrote at last. "Here it is. It is mere doggerel—but words written to an existing tune are nearly sure to be that. I'm sorry to lose the other finale, but I quite see your difficulty, and that it can't be helped. You can chop this about just as you please. . . ."

Gilbert originally gave the name of Philarion to the monarch in Utopia; but the name bothered him. It was ill-sounding, and lacked the flow of the usual Gilbertian titles. When the opera was half written, he changed it.

"I have re-christened King Philarion—'King Paramount the First,'" he wrote to Sullivan. "This involves an occasional alteration of a word or two in one or two of the lyrics, but nothing that will affect the metre. I hope you like the change, Philarion is too like Hilarion—and means nothing—whereas King Paramount is a good *sounding* name for a despot—and affords an effective contrast with his subservient position."

Sullivan began the composition of Act II on August 6th, and he wrote in his diary:

"Began working at 2nd Act. First number—No. 12—(tenor song) impossible to set. Composed 13 (Duet Zara and Fitz) and 14 (King and Minstrels) 'As in England.'"

He had now returned to Weybridge for the summer. Usually he would work for a few hours, then row on the river and return to the house to work again. He played tennis, rode his tricycle, attended occasional race meetings during the blazing days of a wonderful summer which 1893 gave to England.

Then more diversion—his pet parrot disappeared. *Utopia* was discarded while he trudged over the countryside looking for it. "Lost and searched for in vain," he wrote in his diary. The gardener's boy saw Polly at Shepperton, but the bird, amorous of freedom, flew across the river. More vain searching. "Myself and servants all miserable at his loss." But the next day Polly appeared on the roof of the college at Woburn Park, Addlestone; a boy scrambled up after it, and, with the errant bird in his arms, returned in triumph to Weybridge. "Great rejoicings. Gave the boy the reward of £2," is the diary note.

The diary records the last stages of the opera.

"Aug. 8.—Wrote song in 2nd Act ('An English Girl'). Drove to Kempton.

"Aug. 10.—Working 2nd Act. On the River in the evening.

"Aug. 11.—Working 2nd Act.

"Aug. 12.—Worked all day. Framed trio (No. 17), 'A Capital Plot,' also No. 14 ('Society has quite forsaken').

"Aug. 13.—Framed No. 20 ('An English Girl') and re-wrote, framed No. 14 ('Society has quite forsaken').

"Aug. 14.—Terribly hot. Wrote Quartett 21 ('O Sweet Surprise').

"Aug. 15.—Heat awful; couldn't do much. Writing and framing.

"Aug. 16.—Terrible heat continued. Wrote and framed duet Lady S. and King, 2nd Act.

"Aug. 17.—Terrible heat, 90°. Impossible to work owing to Regatta and fair being held. Two large musical steam round-abouts outside house. So gave myself up to the Regatta and sports. Frank Cellier[1] arrived 5.30. Worked at opera with him at night.

"Aug. 18.—Working with Cellier till Gilbert arrived 12.30. After lunch G. and I worked at new opera, suggestions, alterations etc. Real good day's work. At 7 rowed him to Halliford and back. Heat awful; 93° in the shade.

"Aug. 23.—Pouring wet day. Re-wrote Duet (No. 3) Sca: and Phan: (1st Act); framed Trio No. 16 (King Sch. Phan); Re-wrote and framed Lady Sophy's song (No. 22) and framed Zara's song 'Youth is a Boon.' One hour's tricycling, but roads too heavy for pleasure.

---

[1] Younger brother of Alfred Cellier and conductor at the Savoy Theatre.

"Aug. 24.—Finished up alterations, etc.; framed duet 'Words of Love;' re-wrote many little bits. Lettered everything ready for copyist.

"Aug. 26.—Continued scoring.

"Sept. 1.—Began scoring 'Entrance of Zara.' Very tired, so went to Sandown.

"Sept. 12.—Wrote and framed King's song, 'First You're Born,' also little alterations. Worked hard at Duet, 'Oh, Admirable Plan'—impossible to get it into shape.

"Sept. 14.—Composed and framed No. 13 song for Fitz, 'A tenor, all singers above'; No. 26 Chorus, 'Down With Them,' and at night the duet, 'O Admirable Plan,' having received amended words of letter from G. at 8 p.m.

"Sept. 16.—Composed dance (in A) for drawing-room scene. Went to Kempton Races at 1.30.

"Sept. 20.—Began scoring again, having done Finale to 1st Act, and Nos. 7 and 8. Heavy job."

Four days scoring.

"Sept. 29.—Scoring all day; finished whole work at 2.30 a.m. Tremendous effort!"

During these latter days of composing and scoring Sullivan had also attended the long rehearsals at the Savoy. He completed his music only nine days before the opera was produced, but he had rehearsed the work continuously up to the numbers on which he was actually working.

On the day prior to the production a public rehearsal was held, to which critics, literary men and women—indeed any who had a legitimate interest in the drama—were admitted. Such a thing had never been done before at the Savoy. The new operas as they succeeded each other had been kept as secret as a Royal plot. It was Gilbert who was responsible for the innovation. His work had been attacked in the past, he declared, because his critics did not understand it; they had not had time to understand it before writing their criticisms. So he argued. Therefore he gave them now the opportunity of thoroughly understanding the play by seeing it twice.

The End of the Partnership

On the night of the first performance Sullivan wrote in his diary:

"October 7th.—Production of 'Utopia Limited' at the Savoy Theatre 8.15 p.m. I shockingly nervous as usual—more than usual. Went into the orchestra at 8.15 sharp. My ovation lasted 65 seconds! Piece went wonderfully well—not a hitch of any kind, and afterwards G. and I had a *double call*."

When the two appeared before the curtain there was rapturous enthusiasm which became a roar as the twain publicly shook hands. The old feud—the audience declared as it poured from the theatre into the night—had been laid aside for ever, leaving only the promise of a new era of successes. After the performance Gilbert, Sullivan and D'Oyly Carte—each taking with them about eight guests—adjourned to supper in the Savoy Hotel, and Miss Nancy McIntosh, the American soprano, who appeared for the first time in London in *Utopia*, occupied the post of honour.

The Press praised *Utopia*. Its wonderful setting and the atmosphere of romance which Gilbert had woven into the piece, was to some extent a departure from the operas that had preceded it. Moreover, it appeared to be better cast than several of the productions that reached greater heights of success than *Utopia* was to know. Walter Passmore, who had joined the Savoy Company in the ill-fated *Jane Annie*, now made his first appearance in a Gilbert and Sullivan opera, and whatever the company lost by the departure of George Grossmith it more than gained on the night that Passmore stepped into his shoes at the Savoy.

Sullivan was the only person concerned who was critical of the play, and it was his own work he criticized. The Finale displeased him. Two days after the launching of *Utopia*, he sat down and composed a new one which was introduced into the opera four nights later, the public being quite unaware that the change had taken place.

Utopia now settled down into what promised to be a prosperous run, and Sullivan made no plans for the future. He was still drawn towards grand opera, and if a suitable libretto

227

had come to hand at this time he probably would have set it. The modest success of *Ivanhoe* by no means convinced him that there was not a great triumph awaiting him somewhere in this form of composition. "All those who embark on grand opera throw their brains into the lap of the gods," he told a friend. "It is the greatest gamble in the world." *Utopia* had not revived his interest in comic opera; he still yearned for the human story which would give opportunity to the human appeal in his music.

In November he went to Berlin to superintend the preparations for the production of *Ivanhoe* by Count Hochberg at the Opera House. *The Gondoliers* was just concluding a successful run at Unter den Linden Theatre, but when Sullivan saw the German version he was perturbed by the manner in which the music was taken. "The tempi is all too slow. There is no 'go' in it," he wrote. What disturbed him still more was the announcement that, at the production of *The Mikado* at Unter den Linden Theatre the following week, a woman—Madame Ilka von Palmay—was to play the part of Nanki-Poo. An injunction was immediately issued against the theatre. Four years later, when *The Yeomen of the Guard* was revived at the Savoy, Madame von Palmay—who had made her *début* in the *Grand Duke*—played the part of Elsie Maynard.

Utopia occupied the Savoy stage for 245 performances. When it had to be withdrawn at the beginning of the summer at 1894, D'Oyly Carte had no piece with which to follow it. He had hoped that, with the recommencement of the collaboration, opera would have followed opera with the old energy and enthusiasm that had inspired both Gilbert and Sullivan. He was to be bitterly disappointed. Certainly Gilbert talked to Sullivan about a play dealing with the period of Henri III, but the proposal had gone no further than words. At the same time *Utopia* had failed in New York. It was produced on Easter Monday, 1894, and Sullivan was aware that it was doomed to failure for he recorded the fact in his diary the same day.

Apart from a song which he composed for Sydney Grundy's play *An Old Jew*—a play that failed—Sullivan wrote nothing

The End of the Partnership

during the first six months of 1894. The mood of uncertainty refused to be shaken off. He threw himself more deeply into social affairs, dined everywhere and visited all the best plays in town; went over to Ireland and appeared at a theatre in Belfast where they were playing *Utopia*, only to be recognized and acclaimed with a thunder of applause which made him hurriedly withdraw.

In May he was 52, and the anniversary was celebrated by a dinner at the Garrick Club. The Prince of Wales was there, the Duke of Coburg, Sir Frederick Leighton, Lord Russell of Killowen, Henry Irving, Charles Wyndham, John Hare, Beerbohm Tree, Augustus Harris, and many more eminent people in whose friendship he rejoiced. After dinner at the Club there was a gathering of about two hundred people, ambassadors and their wives, etc., at Queen's Mansions in a room that, in the usual way, was intended to hold one hundred. Not till half-past three in the morning did the Prince leave the party.

All through his later life Sullivan loved the Turf. When work pressed heavily upon him, a few days at Newmarket or Ascot would bring him back fresh and clear-headed to his manuscript. Or he would compose during a morning, leave his manuscript hurriedly like a schoolboy released from class, swallow a hasty lunch and rush off to an afternoon's racing, from which he would return and work through half the night.

During 1894 he owned a horse which was in charge of J. Jewitt at Bedford Cottage, Newmarket. His colours—cerise with violet sleeves and cap—appeared at many meetings, but seldom passed the post first. "Cranmer" was the best horse he owned, but when it was beaten by a head by "Blue Mark" at Newmarket in September, he promptly bought "Blue Mark" for £500. He ran it three times and won only once, then sold it to Blundell Maple a month later for a hundred pounds less than he gave for it.

With "Cranmer" he won a few races, but never enough to convince him that he was born to success as an owner. Another stroke of misfortune befell him when he and two friends[1] decided to buy the Duchess of Montrose's yearlings for ten

[1] The two friends were Captain Machel and Ernest Clay Ker Seymour.

thousand pounds. On the day following, the trio reconsidered the matter, and abandoned the deal. But among these yearlings was the famous "La Flêche!"

Sullivan made careful notes in his diaries about the races he attended, and described the horses which, at this period, were the talk of England. These notes, although they do not come within the purview of this volume, are sometimes of general interest, such as his entry on June 29th:

"Went to the Levee (left my cocked hat in the cab!) then to Sandown with the Prince of Wales to see the 'Clarence and Avondale' which Florizel II did *not* win, but Lady Minting did."

It was the zest of the race that he loved. If he had owned a Derby winner he would have been as proud of it as he was of his most successful opera. But, if the fortunes of the Turf were not to follow his colours, he was a sportsman who snatched what joy he could from the race and was content.

Less than three months after the production of *Utopia* it was obvious to D'Oyly Carte that the opera would not endure any length of time. He could no longer give six months' notice and require the collaborators to put up a new opera before those months had expired, for they had declined to be so bound when they entered into the new agreement after *The Gondoliers*.

The vast expenditure involved in the staging of *Utopia* had of course reduced the earnings of all the partners.

"With *Mikado* the shares of profit reached 15 per cent. each," D'Oyly Carte wrote to Gilbert in January; "with *Princess Ida* they came to between 7 and 8 per cent.; with *The Gondoliers* between 11 and 12 per cent.; and the preliminaries of that opera were of course a great deal less than those of the present opera [*Utopia*] seemed likely to be, and were. . . .

"Experience has shown that even with our greatest successes there is a drop of from £3,000 to £5,000 in the gross receipts of the third three months as compared with the second. With *The Gondoliers* the drop from the second to the third quarter was £3,400; with the *Yeomen* it was £4,800; with the

The End of the Partnership

Mikado £3,100, while with *Ruddigore* the drop reached nearly £7,000."

In a letter written to Gilbert the day following he said:

"I think that if the next production is to have a fair chance of being a successful commercial speculation, it is essential that the preliminary expenses should be something altogether different to those of *Utopia*. . . . The result of *Utopia* so far is that with a magnificent production, a cast selected to fit yours and Sullivan's requirements, with all the prestige of the renewal of your collaboration, the tremendous advertisement it has obtained, and enthusiastic first-night reception, most laudatory press notices (except two preposterous evening papers) and the largest advance booking at first and for a short time that we ever had, the piece is not, in its third month, drawing to any extent, and is obviously not going to have a long run. . . .

" There is no doubt in my mind that what the people want now is simply 'fun,' and little else. . . . I firmly believe that if you and Sullivan would write a frankly comic piece—say, a modern farcical comedy to music—that with your united genius, we might score at least as much success as is obtained by the drivelling stuff I have referred to. . . .[1] If the preliminary expenses of the next opera are reduced to, say, £2,000, and the salary list reduced to something like it was in the days of "Patience," etc., we could afford after the first flash of crowded business in the opening months, to play for six months to an average of £150 a night, and feel happy about it."

D'Oyly Carte's correspondence with Gilbert did not, however, produce the play that was to follow *Utopia*. When the latter came to an end in the late spring, Carte put on a piece called *Mirette* by Messager, which survived the summer and then perished of inanition.

Sullivan's next Savoy opera was the outcome of a chance dinner he had with F. C. Burnand in the late summer. They discussed the future of the Savoy which seemed obscure since D'Oyly Carte had no play in hand with which to follow

[1] He mentioned some plays of small cleverness that were drawing big houses at the time.

Mirette. Gilbert was hidden away in his retreat, none too happy about the short run of *Utopia*, an opera in which he had placed his faith as a rival to *Mikado* in longevity. Towards the end of the meal Burnand suggested that they should resurrect from the dust of 1867 the play *The Contrabandista*, which they had written together. He proposed to take the plot and turn it into a new play, leaving only the bare bones of their former collaboration.

Sullivan, anxious to help his friend, accepted the suggestion. He had put good work into *The Contrabandista*, but the piece had died too soon. Before they went out of the Garrick Club that night the arrangement was complete. Sullivan agreed to retain such music as he thought worth keeping from *The Contrabandista* and to rewrite the remainder.

Burnand very quickly supplied his partner with the libretto which they named *The Chieftain*, and D'Oyly Carte undertook to produce the opera at the end of the year. In October Sullivan set to work in earnest on the music, and spent his leisure in racing. He went to Kempton, Newmarket, Sandown, then again to Newmarket to see his former horse beaten by a head in the Cambridgeshire. A month previously he had, however, known the luck of the Turf, for his diary note for September 12th reads:

"Doncaster, St. Leger won by Throstle, about whom I had taken 1000 to 40!"

When *The Chieftain* was produced on December 12th, it became obvious at once that it had few chances of survival. The mustiness of the sixties pervaded the piece. Burnand as a successor to Gilbert had failed in his task, and failed the more because he had attempted to conjure life into an old plot instead of inventing a new one. One saw the skeleton of 1867 stalking through the piece, and heard the bones rattle under the modern trappings with which Burnand had attempted to adorn it.

Only sentiment and the warmth of his friendship for Burnand made Sullivan undertake *The Chieftain*. Though the music is tuneful, it has not the melodious qualities of some of the Savoy successes. His real interest was still towards serious music, and in July he had begun the music to *King*

Arthur which was to be produced at the Lyceum scarcely six weeks after *The Chieftain* at the Savoy.

There was no longer any need for Sullivan to work on themes that were irksome to him. He was making £20,000 a year, and when the *Mikado* revivals came on at the Savoy, and, later, that of *The Yeomen of the Guard*, the figure rose higher. His songs and cantatas were selling in greater numbers than ever, and he was turning away more work than any man, however gifted and swift in his composing, could undertake. He could have made an immense fortune by "pot-boiling," but he refused to "pot-boil." His art stood for him as some ever-burning lamp.

Moreover, he gave away money with the reckless generosity of a big human soul. His letters to his secretary, Smythe, are full of records of these secret gifts. "I met —— to-day —he is having a bad time. Send him thirty pounds," or, "I hear that —— is in financial trouble since his mother's death. Send him fifty pounds, and say there is no need to acknowledge as I have gone abroad."

To hear of a friend—a friend of artistic merit—being in financial trouble came to him as a personal grief, and he would give, and give again, often anonymously, till he felt that the first terrors of anxiety on the part of the friend had been assuaged. His human understanding figures in all his serious music; it steals, evasive and full of beauty, into his lighter works. Amidst the merriment of *Iolanthe* or *Mikado* one becomes suddenly aware of a piece of melody so haunting and often so sorrowful that, before the phase has passed into a fresh burst of joyous comedy, one realizes that it is a thought in music that has come from the human heart.

After the production of *The Chieftain*, Sullivan pressed forward with the incidental music for Comyns Carr's play *King Arthur*, and he completed it on January 7th at 4 in the morning. But he was dissatisfied with the Finale of the prologue, so, two days before the play was produced, he wrote and scored a new Finale in a single night. When the play was produced at the Lyceum on the 12th Sullivan conducted.

He then left London for his annual holiday on the Riviera. But news of thinning houses at the Savoy filled him with dismay. He then began to write new songs and dances for *The Chieftain* which were scored and sent home and embodied in the opera. It was a valiant but vain effort to stem the decline in the box-office receipts. "I never go to the rooms after dinner," he wrote in his diary, and the same night he wrote two new songs for the ill-fated opera and went to bed at 5.30 a.m. Even three months after the opera had begun its run, and when it was indeed on its last legs, he was still pouring new music into it. Some of the best numbers were written at Monte Carlo—numbers that only passed into popular favour after the opera was dead.

The theme of the opera was wrong; it was out of date by thirty years, and D'Oyly Carte knew that he was fighting a losing battle with it. It played to £1,400 the first week, £1,300 the second and third, £1,200 the fourth, £1,100 the fifth, then £800 and £700 before it was taken off. It ran for ninety-six performances, and was then withdrawn; and *Mikado*, full of unexpended vigour, occupied the Savoy stage in its stead.

Towards the end of 1895, Gilbert emerged from his seclusion with a new libretto which he had titled *The Grand Duke* or *The Statutory Duel*, and again the collaboration made a bid for a fresh triumph at the Savoy. Sullivan completed the music at the end of February, 1896, and, as had been the case with *Utopia*, a full-dress rehearsal was given in the presence of a crowded house on the night before the first performance, the rehearsal being carried through without a single stoppage.

On the following evening, March 7th, the opera was produced, with Ilka von Palmay in the soprano part, and Sullivan's diary note for that day is the best evidence of the impression left upon his mind:

"Began new opera 'Grand Duke' at ¼ past eight—usual reception. Opera went well; over at 11.15. Parts of it dragged a little, dialogue too redundant, but success great and genuine I think. Thank God opera is finished and out."

The Press received the piece well, and for some weeks it played to crowded houses. But the partnership was dying; indeed it was already dead. The brilliant staging and fine acting of one of the best companies ever engaged in Gilbert and Sullivan opera could not save a play for which London had no desire. It ran for 123 performances—the shortest run of any opera which the collaborators had produced—and was withdrawn. The first eight weeks it played to about £1,600 a week, then the receipts fell to £1,200; a fortnight later to £900 and so downwards till the curtain fell for the last time.

Fresh differences then arose between Sullivan and his collaborator, and it became evident that they had worked together for the last time. One after another, the operas which they had created in the hey-day of their collaboration were revived, and London crowded with a zeal that could not be satisfied to see them. *The Mikado* reached its thousandth performance—an occasion which D'Oyly Carte marked by giving each member of the audience a programme in the shape of a Japanese fan. *The Yeomen of the Guard* was revived, and ran with almost greater strength than it had done at its original production. The fortunes of the Savoy never seemed brighter.

But the creators of the most distinctive light operas in the history of the stage went their several ways. A few desultory letters passed between them, and presently these, too, ceased.

CHAPTER XX

Royal Meetings and Wagnerian Nights

SULLIVAN was 54. He spent his birthday at Newmarket. Feeling desperately ill he had gone to the
course in time to see his horse lose the race. "An unlucky
day for me in every respect," the shaky scrawl in pencil
records in the diary.

His health was again troubling him. In June a chill
compelled him to take to his bed, a victim to influenza. When
he got up his one desire was to travel. He had lost the
inclination to work. *The Grand Duke*, now in rapid decline,
gave him no impetus to begin another light opera. He had
frequently told Gilbert that he felt he had reached the end
of his powers as a creator of light-opera music. He repeated
the assertion now, and believed in it. But he had yet to write
The Rose of Persia, which contains some of the most beautiful
music of his imagining.

He decided to write another grand opera, and sought for
a libretto. Ultimately he chose King Arthur as the theme.
He wanted romance, and his incidental music for the play
at the Lyceum had convinced him that the period was rich
in possibilities for a work on an elaborate scale. Then he
changed his mind. He would compose a play for Yvette
Guilbert; he even made arrangements for the libretto. But
he did neither of these things. Instead, he entered into an
agreement to write the music for a ballet entitled *Victoria and
Merrie England* which was to be produced in the spring of
1897, the Diamond Jubilee year of the Queen.

When at the end of the summer of 1896 he went to the
Engadine, he had no commitments beyond the ballet music.
Even if he had been disposed to compose a new light opera

there was no prospect of a libretto. He would never work with Gilbert again. And there was no other Gilbert.

The Engadine at the end of August was crowded with English Society. Mayfair had migrated into Switzerland. Members of the British royal family were there: the Duchess of York and her mother the Duchess of Teck. Sullivan's notes on the days that followed are of interest.

"Walked out with the royal party all the afternoon. In the evening I had a dinner party at the hotel: Duchess of York, Du. of Teck, Mr. and Mrs. Leo Rothschild, Prince Francis of Battenberg. After dinner all adjourned to my sitting-room—a little music till 12."

And a day later.

"Walked all the morning with the Royal party—lunched with them upstairs. Gave Princess May three combs, and Duchess of Teck two. Princess May gave me a beautiful photo of herself and the children."

He went on to Munich, to Vienna. The capital had changed since those days in the sixties when, on his musical pilgrimage with George Grove in search of the lost Schubert manuscripts, they had trodden its cobbles together. The old *cafés* they had known, tucked away beneath ageing roofs, had disappeared. The atmosphere of Beethoven and Schubert that had clung about these places also had disappeared, for now great buildings had arisen to reflect a commercial prosperity. Even the resting-places of the two masters had changed with the City, since in 1888 the skeletons had been exhumed and reburied in the Central Friedhof.

At Nauheim on the way home he received a telegram from the Empress Frederick of Germany inviting him to stay at the Friedrichof (Cronberg), and he accepted it with alacrity. Memories of other years must have passed across his mind, as a slow train, meandering across a dusty Germany, bore him thither. The late Emperor, "croaking chokingly" in the final months of his martyrdom of cancer—the Empress and the last meeting at Sandringham soon after she entered into her widowhood—and the Empress now—a lonely Englishwoman in Germany who found in Sullivan some link with her country and its art.

Sir Arthur Sullivan

His diary briefly records the visit:

"Very warmly welcomed by the Empress who is in excellent health and spirits. With her were her two daughters, Princess Adolph of Schaumberg-Lippe (Princess Victoria) and Princess Louis of Hesse (Pcs. Sophie). Sat down ten to dinner. After dinner I sat at the piano and played all sorts of scraps to please Her Majesty."

He came home by Paris, and reached London in the last days of September. He had intended to complete the ballet music by Christmas, but when Christmas came he had scarcely begun it. He was still weak and ill. London had been choked with fog; the sun for weeks on end had failed to glimmer on the London roofs. He therefore decided to compose this music abroad.

He took a villa for the season at Beaulieu—the Villa Mathilde. It was a new house, compact, and on the border of the sea. It had a large garden, and Sullivan always loved gardens. Here he began the ballet music; indeed the first day after he had moved in he spent ten hours in composing.

Victoria and Merrie England was intended to reflect the life of Britain. Its atmosphere was to be national, and Sullivan made his music national. His melodies seemed to wander through the centuries which had been the centuries of England. Of all his composing none is so truly national as that which came from him for this ballet.

All through January, 1897, he worked continuously at the music by day. He would compose till the afternoon and afterwards entertain his friends, take long drives, visit the tables at Monte Carlo. He would sup late, then, with the mood upon him, return to his manuscript in the room overlooking the sea, and, with curtains drawn, work till dawn disturbed him and urged him to bed. There are fragmentary entries in his diary which record how he worked:

"Sunday, March 7th.—Got up wonderfully fresh after having had *four* nights of hard work until 5 a.m. each morning. Sent off end of 3rd scene (Maypole).

"Wednesday, March 17th.—Much worried about 'Union

March.' Couldn't get it right. Sent off P.F. arr. of part of 3rd Scene.

"Thursday, March 18.—Began scoring last (7th) scene. Beastly lot of notes to write. Solved the 'Union March' difficulty by cutting out the Welsh!

"Tuesday, March 23rd.—Finished the 7th Scene (and complete work) at 5.30 a.m. Very difficult business.

"Thursday, March 25th.—Sent off (registered) Score 7th Scene to Bendall [1]—all done now thank God! Wired 'Finished.' "

Queen Victoria was at Cimiez. From Cimiez in the spring and Balmoral in the autumn she drew that health sustenance which enabled her to bear the increasing burdens of State. The Diamond Jubilee celebrations were to take place in June, and already the far corners of the Empire were preparing their contingents, the statesmen their speeches. The ageing Queen herself was nursing her strength in the sun of France for the uprising of an Empire to acclaim the sixtieth year of her reign. The nation lived in an atmosphere of expectation and preparation. Even an unknown singer at Koraput wrote to Sullivan that he would come over from India and sing whatever the composer produced in honour of the occasion—if Sullivan would send him five hundred pounds for his expenses!

That Sullivan would produce some work for the occasion was certain—indeed the Prince of Wales had already made the suggestion to the Queen—and his diary note on April 6th describes the beginning of his Jubilee hymn.

"Went to Cimiez to see Sir Arthur Bigge [2] about a 'command' hymn for the Jubilee. He told me that the Queen thought it desirable to have well-known tunes sung at the service outside St. Paul's, so that people could join in them if they liked, but that, as the real Thanksgiving service would be on the 20th June, it would be better that I should write a special tune for that day, which might be sung in every

[1] Wilfred Bendall, his secretary. His former secretary, Walter Smythe, who had been with him all through the years of the Savoy operas, died shortly before this date.

[2] The Queen's private secretary.

Church of the Empire. I suggested that Bishop Walsham Howe[1] should be commanded to write a special hymn for the occasion, and Sir A. Bigge said he would tell the Queen. I stayed by the Queen's invitation to lunch with the Household and left at 3.30."

Nine days later—on Easter Thursday—he wrote in his diary:

"Drove to Cimiez to see Bigge. Duke of Coburg came in whilst I was there—told him it was exactly 43 years since I (practically) joined the Chapel Royal. I entered on Tuesday the 12th April, 1854, but made my first appearance in the chapel and sang a solo on Maundy Thursday following.

"Told him I should like to play the organ on Easter Day for the Queen. I think he must have gone and told the Queen for I got a telegram from her the next day asking me to play. Said good-bye to the Duke, who left for Coburg that night."

On Easter Sunday he wrote:

"Lovely morning. Drove to Regina Hotel, Cimiez, to play the organ (Harmonium) at Service in the Chapel by the Queen's invitation. Saw Princess Beatrice for a few minutes before service to arrange about hymns. Queen came into the Chapel at 11 (whilst I played a Voluntary) accompanied by Princess Beatrice, Princess Victoria of Schleswig-Holstein, Pcess. Beatrice's three children, the suite and servants. Self and Lord Rowton only outsiders. . . . Queen sent me a lovely pocket-book as a souvenir of the day."

As the spring warmed to incoming summer, preparations for the royal celebrations quickened throughout the country. The sixty wonderful years were to be blazed in beacons from the hilltops, the acclamations of respect to roll with unanimity of sound from the churches, the cathedrals, the little Bethels. The Poet Laureate, Alfred Austin, with some sense of the whimsical duty that devolved upon him to produce a poem worthy of the occasion, hurried into verse. He sent Sullivan a song which Sullivan frankly refused to set.

"You say we cannot supplant the National Anthem," he wrote to Austin. "Certainly not. I, for my part, don't wish

[1] The Bishop of Wakefield.

A cartoon of Arthur Sullivan drawn by Linley Sambourne for *Punch*

to, even if I could! But my idea was to have a few shining lines (3 verses at the utmost) with strong rhythmical accents, and a 'burden' to each verse—the 'burden' to be the same each time of course. Then, if I could find a good swinging *tune* (an absolute necessity) the thing would be sung by solo, by chorus, played by military bands—at theatres, at music halls, meetings of every description, and on the march. Simple words and simple tune. . . . I am not writing songs, *qua* songs, any more, therefore, dainty and full of charm as your song is, it would never enter my head to set it to music.

"I need scarcely tell you that I have had piles of words voluntarily sent to me with urgent requests that I would set them, in view of the 'forthcoming glorious celebrations,' etc., etc.; but unless I can get something that appeals to me instantaneously I shall do nothing, and leave the celebration to my younger brethren."

Sullivan's suggestion to the Queen's private secretary that the Bishop of Wakefield should write the Jubilee Hymn was adopted. The Bishop wrote and told him that the Prince of Wales had asked him to write the hymn. Probably the Bishop never knew from whom the suggestion came. But he set his ecclesiastical brain working; he wrestled with the mighty work with which he had been entrusted. He visioned, no doubt, millions of his fellow subjects in the crowded pews on Jubilee Sunday singing these words that were intended to stir a nation.

Sullivan set the words for the Queen had approved them; that was enough. What she thought of them never percolated through that eternal silence that can surround a throne. It is the privilege of the throne to be severely non-committal in silence.

Less than a month before the Jubilee, *Victoria and Merrie England* was produced at the Alhambra.

"Tuesday, May 25th.—Full dress rehearsal (private) of Ballet at 1," says the diary. "First performance at night. Magnificent house—all the *élite* of London present, including Princess Louise, Duke of Cambridge and the Adolphus Tecks. Great enthusiasm. Conducted the performance myself. Genuine success."

He wrote truly. The piece was the most attractive production of Jubilee year, and made a lot of money.

Directly the Jubilee celebrations were at an end, Queen Victoria sent for Sullivan. She had always recognized him as the premier British musician of her reign. Had he not, by the delight of his melodies, driven the Mendelssohn music from her Broadwood at Windsor in favour of his own? She recognized, too, how completely national had been his composing during the Jubilee preparations; he had caught the history of England and charmed it into notes. At the beginning of July Sullivan went to Windsor.

"Monday, July 5th.—Invited to Windsor. Went about 6. Nice little room. Dined at 8.30 with the Household. After dinner was received by the Queen in the Long Corridor. Had twenty minutes' conversation with Her Majesty who was most kind and gracious. After I retired, she sent me the Jubilee Medal by Miss Phipps. Played billiards and smoked with the Household till bedtime."

A month later he departed to Bayreuth for the Wagner celebration. He criticized Wagner very frankly in his diary. He always admired the genius of Wagner, but he could not bring himself to complete agreement with him. The majesty and dramatic power of Wagner when it was genuine appealed to him and drew his admiration. But, with his musical knowledge, he could detect the real Wagner from the sham. He could detect the laziness in Wagner when, sitting in luxurious ease, Wagner sought to deceive his disciples by pieces of work that should have been condemned as lowering his towering banner. Sullivan never openly criticized Wagner or any musician. He had written failures himself, but they had been sincere failures. He had at least believed in them at the time.

He reached Bayreuth at the beginning of August.

"Put on light clothes and went to the performance of 'Parsifal,'" he wrote. "Although many points open to severe criticism, the work and performance impressed me immensely. Theatre, which holds over 1,600, quite full. Saw many,

English friends, Prince and Princess of Wales, Lady de Grey, Arthur Balfour, etc."

Three days later he heard *Rheingold* and the frankness of the artist judging a fellow artist in the secret judgment-chamber of his diary is marked:

"Beginning of 'Ring' performance, 'Rheingold,' commenced at 5, and went on without break till 7.30. Then home to dinner. Much disappointed in the performance; *all* of them. Orchestra rough and ragged, conducted by Siegfried Wagner. Vocalists beneath contempt. Sometimes stage management is good, but much is conventional and childish. It is difficult to know how Wagner could have got up any enthusiasm or interest in such a lying, thieving, blackguardly set of low creatures as all the characters in his Opera prove themselves to be."

And a day later:

"Performance of 'Walküric.' (House party, Lady de Grey, Emily Yzuago, A. J. Balfour, etc., Prince and Princess of Wales.) Very pleasant party—good lunch. Back at 3.15. Unfortunately fell asleep and didn't wake till 5, and so missed last act. Much that is beautiful in the Opera—less dreary padding than in the others."

His disappointment with Wagner increased at each performance. The diary began to record not only disappointment but vituperation. He praised, he blamed with cutting sarcasm:

"August 16th.—Performance of 'Siegfried.' I think it intolerably dull and heavy, and so undramatic—nothing but 'conversations,' and I am weary of Leit Motiven. Burgskater (Tenor) is young and good-looking and has a pretty voice, but he will kill it if he sings Siegfried and similar rôles much more. He was dead beat at the end of the Opera. What a curious mixture of sublimity and absolute puerile drivel are all these Wagner operas. Sometimes the story and action would disgrace even a Surrey [1] pantomime."

The following evening he wrote:

"Last 'Ring' performance 'Götterdämmerung.' 1st Act

[1] The Surrey Theatre—the home of cheap melodrama of the period.

4 to 6. Dull and dreary. 2nd Act 6.30 to 8. Just as dull and dreary. 3rd Act 8.45 to 10. Very fine and impressive. The Leit Motiven seemed all natural and not dragged in, and the whole act is much more dramatic, and musically finer than any of the others."

He packed and came home. Europe now was searching for a new thinker in music. There had been a weary procession of the unformed who gave promise which they could not fulfil. Hardly had the first Press acclamations been forgotten than they disappeared like flashing stars into the murk. Sullivan was always searching for new genius that might be borne forward to success, and no musician ever spent more time and trouble to discover a rival to himself.

The new star for which he sought appeared in the firmament a year later. It was Coleridge-Taylor. The new-comer was but a boy, a youth who had struggled. When Sullivan first heard *Hiawatha* in November, 1898, he realized what that youth would mean to music. He acclaimed him with a full measure of praise unstintingly given. He told musical London about this young man who played the organ and composed new themes in music in the scant leisure of a driven life. It may have been that when he first heard *Hiawatha* he remembered his own ambitions with his *Tempest* music. Or, maybe, he recalled its first performance at the Crystal Palace, and Charles Dickens shaking his hand.

What he thought about Coleridge-Taylor he wrote in his diary on the day that he heard *Hiawatha*.

"November 11th, 1898.—Dined at home and went to Roy: Coll: Music Concert to hear Coleridge-Taylor's 'Hiawatha.' Much impressed by the lad's genius. He is a *composer*—not a music-maker. The music is fresh and original —he has melody and harmony in abundance, and his scoring is brilliant and full of colour—at times luscious, rich and sensual. The work was very well done."

His faith in Coleridge-Taylor was justified. He had merely foreseen the judgment of Time.

CHAPTER XXI

The Final Operas

THE Diamond Jubilee with its crowds and its clamour passed with the blaze of a June sun to its place in history. The last flags were pulled down from their staffs, and the reign of Victoria went on. She would, some declared, live for ever.

When September came, Sullivan began to think about his next opera. Comyns Carr called and discussed a piece which he proposed to write with Arthur Pinero. He said that he was going away with Pinero to shape out the work, and would return with the scenario of the first Act the following week. When in the middle of October Carr read the scenario of the complete opera to Sullivan, the composer was delighted with it. "I like it immensely," he wrote. "It is original and fanciful. I don't know whether it is *too* serious."

The opera, which was eventually given the title of *The Beauty Stone*, proved to be one of the most difficult tasks of Sullivan's life. The libretto was too wordy, and was from beginning to end a constant source of trouble to him. By the middle of December something of a deadlock had arisen between the collaborators. "Dined at Joe Carr's with Pinero —long talk after dinner. First signs of difficulties likely to arise," he wrote. "Both Pinero and Carr, gifted and brilliant men, with *no* experience in writing for music, and yet obstinately declining to accept any suggestions from me, as to form and construction. Told them that the musical construction of the piece is capable of great improvement, but they decline to alter. 'Quod scripsi, scripsi,' they both say."

A partial agreement was arrived at, but the difficulties

with the libretto took the zest out of Sullivan. Much of the composition was done on the Riviera, and his diary is littered with references to the difficulties that beset him.

"It is heartbreaking," he wrote, "to have to try and make a musical piece out of such a badly constructed (for music) mass of involved sentences."

He struggled with the music, he laid it aside, he took it up again. There was no rift in the lute of friendship, but he felt that he was fighting an impossible battle. When the work was complete he disliked it. The spirit of light opera seemed elusive and absent. It was as if he had tried to build a square house to an architectural plan which ordained that the building should be round.

After much tribulation *The Beauty Stone* was completed in time for production at the end of May, 1898. It was foredoomed to failure; its life flickered from the start, and it survived but seven weeks. It contained some good numbers, even if, in the main, the fire of the old Sullivan operas was missing. But the story clove its way through a forest of words. The music seemed merely an appendage that helped the cleaving, and would have brought about no dire result by its absence. *The Beauty Stone* was a play, merely illustrated by music; in no sense was it a light opera. But because of the difficulties which he tried vainly to surmount, Sullivan put in more work upon it than he did upon the *Mikado*.

When the autumn came he conducted the Leeds Festival for the last time. His association with the Festival had been unbroken since 1878. In that year, when the invitation came to him, he was so ill and worn out that he at once wrote declining the honour, but kept the letter back in case a renewal of health and strength should occur, as it happily did. For twenty years it was his *bâton* that carried the Festival to success. During twenty years in the changing music of England the Leeds Festival had grown in prestige and importance, and Sullivan seemed to have become a part of it.

But the frequent breaks in his health had been disturbing to the Committee—so disturbing that, when Sullivan went to conduct the Festival in 1898, Frederick Cowen and Charles Stanford were actually retained in Leeds during the whole function so that they might take up the conducting in the event of his collapse.

"There was," he wrote to Mr. Spark, the Festival secretary, at a later date, "no need for such action at the last Festival, because, except for the nervous apprehension of approaching pain, I was quite well, with a clean bill of health from my doctor. Since the Festival the much-dreaded attack has come, and I am now, I am grateful to say, strong and well, and in better health than I have been since my long and dangerous illness of 1892."

It was on Saturday, October 8th, that he conducted the Festival for the last time. Perhaps some there foresaw that he would never come again. It may have been that the augury of Death, often present yet undefined—an atmosphere of doubt that sometimes seems to hover about life at the very moment when life seems so secure—was subconsciously evident. Or it may have been that the Festival bore a richer beauty and sincerity in its performance than it had ever known before. But when he laid down his *bâton* on the last note the ovation he received was remarkable. No audience, no choir, had hitherto been so completely in accord. His life was hurrying to its close, yet who would have said that they were bidding him a last farewell? It seemed to be the hour of his greatest triumph in Leeds.

He wrote in his diary:

"Saturday, October 8th, 1898.—*Leeds*. Last day of Festival. After last performance, the Chorus cheered me so tremendously, that I suddenly broke down, and ran off the orchestra crying like a child. When I came out of my room again, *all* the Chorus was waiting for me, and I shook hands with all! Then went and had a light supper at Albani's, and at 11.10 saw the Band off in their Special. Red and blue fire, and cheering as usual. When at supper was surprised by a serenade (by about 30 of the male chorus). I invited them in, gave them champagne and cigars, and they sang half a dozen pieces, retiring at 1 a.m. Went to bed tired—rather a trying day.

"On the whole, the best performances we have had. The

chorus better balanced than ever, and of beautiful tone. Orchestra superb, and playing with more delicacy and subdued tone than usual."

He did not believe that he had been to Leeds for the last time, for he confidently expected to conduct the Festival of 1901. He looked forward to it with the old enthusiasm, and at a later date wrote to Mr. Spark: "In 1901 I shall have been 40 years before the public (as I date my career from the time I returned from Leipzig in 1861), and I intend making the Festival an occasion of publicly retiring from the active pursuit of my profession, and to do this with *éclat* I mean to produce a work (which I am engaged upon now) which would be, I hope, a worthy successor to the 'Golden Legend,' and form a dignified close to my personal public appearances. The words are from one of the (in my humble opinion) greatest poems in the English language, and it has taken a strong hold upon me."

He had been in correspondence with Rudyard Kipling about the setting of *Recessional*, but the difficulties offered by the metre of the poem eventually seemed insuperable. Sullivan had to confess that the measure of the lines baffled him.

Death claimed him before the Festival in question took place, and the work he had intended for it was never composed.[1]

Meanwhile the old Gilbert and Sullivan operas were in constant revival at the Savoy. *The Gondoliers* came on in March, 1898, and had been withdrawn to make way for *The Beauty Stone*, but, when the latter failed, *The Gondoliers* came back and kept the theatre open. Towards the end of the year D'Oyly Carte decided to revive *The Sorcerer*. Twenty-one years to the day after it had been originally produced it was seen at the Savoy. Sullivan went down to take the rehearsal on the morning of the revival, and said that he found he knew "precious little about the piece." The diary entry concluded:

"Dined at home and went to the Savoy to conduct the 21st anniversary of the production of the 'Sorcerer'—originally

---

[1] No record of the identity of this poem exists.

produced at the Op. Comique 17th November, 1877. Tremendous house—ditto reception. Opera went very well. Call for Gilbert and self—we went on together, but did not speak to each other."

This was the last occasion on which they met. That this final meeting should have taken place in the very theatre associated with their name, and on the stage that had witnessed their greatest triumphs, was one of Life's bitterest ironies. They had come as strangers from their several ways to take their call on this 21st anniversary, only to pass out of the theatre door estranged as they had entered it.

Less than a week before this unhappy episode a beginning was made on what was to be the last opera Sullivan completed. Through his secretary, Wilfred Bendall, he had been introduced to Basil Hood, a young dramatist who had achieved a high average of successes. Hood had threatened to invade that territory of sentiment which Barrie held so closely as his own. It was on November 11th that he first talked over a play with Sullivan.

"Basil Hood came; talked over possibility of doing a new piece together," the diary reads. "I know of no one so good now (putting Gilbert out of the question, of course). He has promised to think over some of our suggestions."

They met almost daily, and the opera soon began to take definite shape. At the beginning of October, Hood brought Sullivan the Finale. Two days later he arrived with all the lyrics of Act 1. The piece had an Eastern atmosphere, and they entitled it at once *Hassan*. "The Finale," Sullivan wrote, "is very good and only wants compressing and change of metre."

The opera might have been rapidly composed had not events at the Savoy delayed progress. The theme pleased Sullivan; the Eastern atmosphere, the thread of romance throughout the play gave opportunity to his music. Hood, he found to be an excellent collaborator. "He is such a nice fellow and so pleasant to work with," he wrote.

But on January 7th, 1899, the Cartes produced a musical adaptation of a French piece under the title of *The Lucky Star* —a play with an Eastern setting. To follow such a piece with another, the atmosphere of which was Oriental, was obviously impossible. Though he had almost completed the libretto of *Hassan*, Basil Hood put it away and searched for a new theme. Three days after *The Lucky Star* was produced at the Savoy, he returned to Sullivan with the idea for a piece called *The Miners*, which Sullivan declared "excellent and very funny."

Still the collaboration was delayed. Sullivan was stricken with influenza, and as soon as he could travel he went to the Riviera. All desire to work left him. He learned to play golf. He walked, drove from one beauty spot to another. He watched the season wane till he was the last visitor left in the hotel, like a single migrant remaining when summer had fled. Then out of sheer loneliness he went on to Switzerland.

He disliked work when the holiday mood was upon him, but he tired of idleness as rapidly. Before he had been in Switzerland very long, he wired to Basil Hood to come out to him, and, as the result of some days spent in walking the mountain paths together, they decided to abandon *The Miners* and take up *Hassan* again. July arrived. *The Lucky Star*, after a moderately successful run at the Savoy of a hundred and forty-three performances, had been taken off in the late spring, and *H.M.S. Pinafore* revived to keep the theatre open.

The "Persian Opera," as Sullivan called *Hassan* in his diary, was begun in Switzerland. He sent to London for music-paper with the intention of composing the major part of the opera before returning to England. But progress was slow. The Swiss atmosphere disturbed him; the extreme heat of the nights kept him from sleep. Moreover, he was constantly in pain. His strength, he said, seemed to be failing, the old vitality to have departed unawares. He became nervous and fidgety. Small things, which in normal times would not have worried him, assumed sufficient importance to be entered in the diary. *The Times* had not come that morning. The papers which should have come on Wednesday did not arrive till Thursday. All these *minutiæ* went into the diary. Some agents offered him a house which he desired to rent for a couple of months, and, when he wrote to take it, they told him it was let. "What brutes these house agents are!" was the entry he made, convinced that he set down the truth.

All the plans for composing the opera at first came to little. He destroyed as much as he retained.

"Began No. 1 Chor. and song Hassan. Began Finale 1st Act (de novo)," he wrote on July 27th. And three days later: "At work. Getting on better." The next day: "At work, pretty good."

His spirits, and consequently his power to work, rose and fell without apparent cause. On some days he worked freely; on others only with the greatest difficulty.

"Working—but slowly," he wrote on August 8th, and two days later: "I worked—but very bad day—still at this wretched Trio 'Harum Scarum.'

"Working still at Trio. Managed to finish it, but must still alter a good deal," he wrote on the following day.

"Working at 'Musical Maidens.' *Cannot* get it right," was the entry on August 14th.

"Worked at 'What Will Become of Them,' and Priest's Song (with police) 'We have come to invade' with introduction. Then again at 'The Musical Maidens.' Seems hopeless."

He decided to return to England immediately, and in a house he had taken at Wokingham the work progressed more rapidly. D'Oyly Carte decided to produce the opera at the end of November, but Sullivan's score was not completed until the 18th of the month, when he wrote in his diary:

"Finished last bit of score of new opera to be called 'The Rose of Persia.' Have been rather longer than usual over the scoring, but a good many changes and alterations made during progress may account for it."

But other events had placed a staying hand upon him. The South African War broke out with a suddenness that took by surprise a nation long steeped in peace. The ageing monarch at Windsor prayed incessantly for a people plunged into battle again. Did she—or anyone else—know how the war had happened? Many of her people had never heard of Kruger. Who was Kruger? It needed the newspapers to explain him.

Of all epidemics the passion of War moves the most rapidly. London became a place of waving flags—whoever would have conceived that so many Union Jacks had been manufactured? The enthusiasm for a war somewhere thousands of miles away against someone who had offended the British dignity spread from town to village as a flame.

It was then that Kipling wrote "The Absent-Minded Beggar," and Sullivan was asked by the *Daily Mail* to set it. Many stories have been told of how Sullivan was unable to set the odd metre, walked, raved, gave it up, took the work on again. Most of them are untrue. That Sullivan found the metre of the poem the most difficult with which he had ever had to contend, remains a fact. It was not until November 1st that he decided to set the poem, and on the 5th his diary reads:

"Finished and wrote out 'Absent-Minded Beggar.'"

The song that was to stir the nation as no other song had done since "We don't want to fight, but, by Jingo, if we do," was first heard by the public at the Alhambra Theatre on November 13th. Sullivan's record of the event is interesting:

"Went to Alhambra to rehearse 'Ab. M. Beg.' with Coates and Orchestra. Then to Savoy to rehearse new opera.

"Conducted 'Ab. M. Beg.' at the Alhambra in the evening—Packed house—wild enthusiasm. All sang chorus! I stood on the stage and conducted the *encore*—funny sight!"

A few days later he wrote to Kipling:

"Dear Mr. Kipling,—

"Your splendid words went, and still go every night with a swing and enthusiasm which even my music cannot stifle. It has been a great pleasure to me to set words of yours."

The song took England by storm; it drove all other songs from the barrel-organs; tens of thousands of copies were rushed from the presses and sold for the benefit of soldiers' dependants, a fund the *Daily Mail* started and carried to a very successful conclusion. The Queen wrote to Sullivan for a copy; troops marched away to the troopships singing it. . . . The "Pay! Pay! Pay!" piled up a rich chest for the War charity.

The work on this song had been an interlude—a successful if irksome interlude—in Sullivan's work on *The Rose of Persia*, as *Hassan* had been re-titled. When the opera went into rehearsal he was dissatisfied with it. There were large portions he would have re-scored, but Time was unfriendly. The opera had been billed for production on November 29th.

"Full rehearsal (band, dresses, etc.) at theatre," he wrote on the 27th. "Everything went smoothly, but it seemed *dull* as ditchwater—all depressed."

The day before the production he wrote:

"Full dress rehearsal of 'Rose of Persia'—2 o'clock. No stoppages. Made a speech to Stage afterwards. Things seemed brighter, but I don't anticipate very great success."

Before many hours had passed he was to alter his opinion. He had under-estimated his own work. His depression suggests that he did not know, or was not able to judge the lure of the atmosphere he had put into his music. The Savoy had been none too successful for him of late years—indeed he had written to Mrs. D'Oyly Carte saying that he felt that fortune had for the time being left the house. His health, which was now giving him almost continuous trouble, was, perhaps, a contributory cause to his mental malaise. He foresaw little success for the opera, but, to his surprise, he found it.

London needed more than ever a play that would tend to remove the gloom that had settled over the capital like a pall as the result of events in South Africa. No one knew what was happening in South Africa, except that everything seemed to be going wrong. Even as the crowds were pouring into the Savoy for the first performance, the wounded were lying in heaps after the battle of Modder River a few hours before.

Sullivan recorded in his diary that night a few dramatic lines which reveal his own impressions of the performance:

"November 29th, Wednesday.—1st performance of 'Rose of Persia' at Savoy Theatre. I conducted as usual. Hideously nervous as usual—great reception as usual—great house

253

as usual—excellent performance as usual—everything as usual—except that the piece is really a great success I think, which is *unusual* lately."

Walter Passmore as Hassan was "the soul of the opera," said Sullivan. All the pick of the Savoy players figured in the piece. The production was a work of Art, albeit it cost some thousands less than the ill-fated *Utopia*. There was a possibility of everybody making money, and everybody did make money, for the *Rose* blossomed for more than two hundred performances.

Sullivan had imagined that luck had left the Savoy, but his new opera—his last completed opera—was to put the luck back into it. When *The Rose of Persia* had run its course, *The Pirates of Penzance* was revived, and, after a successful season, gave way to *Patience*.

Sullivan always had a fad for inventing things. He invented many novelties which somehow never got beyond the stage of drawings and models. One of his schemes was a blind which would roll itself up directly the button was pressed.

It was at this period that he invented a safety device for a carriage whereby, if the horse ran away, one could release the shafts by pulling a lever so that the horse was freed from the carriage. A model was made which he took to Marlborough House for the inspection of the Prince of Wales. He recorded the event in his diary:

"Took my model at 11.30 to Marlboro House to shew it to P. of Wales. He was thoroughly delighted with it, and shewed·keen interest. Sent for Lord Suffield, who was in the house, to shew it to him. S. also thought well of it, but thought it should be worked from *inside* by the occupant. Both H.R.H. and myself combatted this, as giving too much facility for nervous people. H.R.H. promised to let me apply it to one of his carriages."

A month later he wrote:

"Went to Holmes' who had carriage ready with my S.S.S.[1] attached. Drove it about Portland Place. *Very* successful."

---

[1] Sullivan's Safety Shafts.

The Final Operas

Whether owners of carriages were of opinion that their horses ran away so seldom that the invention was an unnecessary precaution cannot be said. The invention was certainly fitted to the Prince of Wales's carriage. Then it seemed to disappear. Probably the fresh demands of Sullivan's music drove his hobby out of his head.

At Christmas he decided to set to work immediately on a composition similar in character to *The Golden Legend*. Themes followed each other across his mind only to be dismissed after many of them had been jotted into note-books. His imagination was never more active, though the vitality of his body was drifting away like the slow and gradual sinking of a tide—so slow—so gradual—as to be unobserved. Pain would recur at intervals, sharp and swift, and, after spasms of agony and nervousness that drew the perspiration from every pore, his mind would seem to be released, and soar like a bird delivered from the narrow cage of suffering. The last Christmas he was to know, with a wonderful Christmas tree, recalled the ecstasies of his youth. Social affairs had their old appeal; the play of life about him yielded continual delight and interest. "I thought I was growing old," he wrote. "But does one grow old if there is always something to interest?"

He fully believed that at 57 his mental powers were as great as they had been at 27. He was unquestionably right. It was only his body that was failing.

CHAPTER XXII

The Last Phase

THE new century dawned with a clamminess that wrapped London in a wet cloak. And yet, as the murk increased, Sullivan clung with a fierce passion to his home at Queen's Mansions. There was nothing to keep him in London, but London had never held him more closely to itself. He was full of projects, yet, except for the fact that he agreed to write another light opera with Basil Hood, he committed himself to none of them. D'Oyly Carte wanted him to take over the Savoy Theatre, and at first he was inclined to agree. He might have entered into theatrical ownership but for a caprice which made him change his mind.

On January 2nd he went down to the Crystal Palace to attend a meeting. He watched the diving horses that were performing there, stepped on to the train to return, and, falling between the platform and the footboard, was nearly killed. When he reached home he said he had been involved in a "dangerous accident." He was quite sure of the fact that he had had a wonderful adventure!

The future appeared before him now as a gaily shining road. He would compose what he wished; his mood should direct the measure of his notes. It so often happens that, in its final stages, the body deceives the mind with assurance as to an inexhaustible store of vitality and power it does not possess. Sullivan was not conscious of failing powers, only of a restlessness that interested him in manifold schemes.

At the end of February he decided suddenly to go to Monte Carlo, but in a month he tired of the place. The tables no longer possessed their old attraction, and he seldom played. He walked, usually alone; he visited friends—Melba, Haddon

256

Chambers the playwright, some Continental acquaintances who migrated to the Riviera every year as regularly as the swallows sought the sun. He ate sparsely. He wrote copious letters. To Mrs. Ronalds—with whom he had communicated almost daily for many years when absent from London—he now frequently wrote twice a day, and supplemented his letters with telegrams. At length, unable to work or collect his ideas abroad, he returned hurriedly to Paris, where he stayed for some days feeling too weak to complete the journey.

Yet this weakness did not surprise him, or give him warning. He was perhaps unconscious of the significance of his diary notes, of the elation he there expressed at returning to the comfort of his flat. If his thoughts brought premonitions, they were lost in the absorption of his work.

"Sir George Martin and Colonel Arthur Collins came to see me," he wrote in his diary on May 26th, "former invited me on behalf of Dean and Chapter to write a Te Deum for Grand Peace Service when War is over. Consented to try and see what I could do."

He went to Epsom to see the Prince of Wales win the Derby with Diamond Jubilee. It was on the course that he heard that Roberts was at Johannesburg. The significance of the event hastened him with his *Te Deum*. The war was as good as over; he shared the common optimism of the man in the street who declared this to be so.

But, hardly had he begun the composition of the *Te Deum* than a telegram from Berlin urged him to set out for that City, at the request of the Emperor, to conduct one of his own operas. It was an unfortunate visit. He disliked the manner in which the opera was produced, and he was besieged every moment of the day by reporters, British and German. On one occasion after he had had a long talk with the Kaiser, the representative of a London daily paper succeeded in breaking down that reserve which he had always exercised when talking to the Press. The Emperor's remarks were telegraphed to London and duly published, and, coming at a time when London was embroiled with Berlin over the Kaiser's attitude towards Paul Kruger, they created a flame of contro-

257

versy. His indiscretion, though innocent in intention, filled him with rancour. He wrote in his diary on June 17th:

"Brooding all day long over unfortunate interview. Curse the press and its correspondents. I cannot get over the fact that after all these years of care and avoidance of disclosing anything—even the most ordinary incidents about the Royal Family—I should have let my enthusiasm run away with my discretion, and related before professional reporters what had passed between H. Majesty and myself."

It was no more than a two days' sensation, but it annoyed the Prince of Wales, and gave Sullivan many weeks of worry.

Towards the end of June, Basil Hood brought him the scenario of a new opera which he called *The Emerald Isle*. "Delightful, new and free," Sullivan noted in his diary. "Also some lyrics of 1st Act. Good, and up to the mark."

But he was not prepared to embark on the opera at once. He took a house at Shepperton for the summer and worked on the *Te Deum*, only to be continuously displeased with what he had done. In truth, many things were disturbing his sensitive mind. The Berlin episode, the necessity of composing the whole of *The Emerald Isle* so that it could be produced in November as D'Oyly Carte had planned, were factors that worried him. Nor did the appearance of "Ben" at his house at Shepperton help matters. Sullivan had a passion for animals, and he wanted a new dog which in due course came from Manchester.

"July 3.—'Ben,' a handsome young collie, arrived from Manchester on approval," records the diary. "Thorough-bred and nice-tempered and playful. He slept in my room this night—at least, he was supposed to sleep, but he was so restless and excited, and kept me awake *all night*. At 5.15 I took him downstairs and let him out, but I couldn't tie him up anywhere, so I had to take him back into my bedroom— then I hit him with my slipper till he lay down quietly under the bed till he was let out early. O what a night!"

"Ben" enjoyed two wonderful days with Sullivan. He stopped the *Te Deum*, he turned the house into turmoil and disorder, he dragged bones about over carpets. Then, with a label round his neck, and looking angelic, he was escorted to the railway station *en route* for Manchester, and the *Te Deum* went on as before.

On the 11th of July Sullivan wrote:

"Worked and finished construction of the last movement of 'Te Deum;' really satisfactory I think."

And three days later:

"Finished complete frame of 'Te Deum,' words and all."

On the completion of this work he made up his mind to go abroad, and, contrary to his accustomed method, to compose the greater part of *The Emerald Isle* before returning to London. But two events delayed him. On July 30th the Duke of Saxe-Coburg (Alfred, Duke of Edinburgh), the friend of his youth upward, died suddenly.

"July 31st.—Received terrible news of the Duke of Saxe-Coburg last night—upset me dreadfully—another of my oldest and best friends gone."

Following swiftly upon this blow, came the death of Lord Russell of Killowen within a fortnight.

"August 10.—My old friend Lord Russell of Killowen, Lord Chief Justice of England, died in London at Cromwell House, aged 68—after a few days' illness. Another friend gone! They go with cruel rapidity."

The clouds seemed to be gathering about Sullivan. He yielded to moods of depression. Earlier in the year the death of Sir George Grove had severed one of the longest and closest ties with his life. One after the other the associates of his best years passed out.

He went off to Switzerland to begin the opera, but the hotel was full of "howling and shrieking Germans." He moved on to Thusis, and there on August 23rd he composed the first number of *The Emerald Isle*. But composition was slow, and, even shut up as he was from acquaintances and noisy visitors, inspiration seemed evasive. Some of his diary notes detail his work on *The Emerald Isle*:

"August 26.—Worked at Quintett 'Their Courage High' (poor stuff) and March following.

"August 27.—Worked fairly well—did Devonshire song and Chorus preceding. Still goes slowly.

"August 30.—Worked like a horse and finished *Finale* as far as words go. Very good too.

"September 3.—Began *framing*. Commenced with Finale. Wired home for scoring paper. Bendall is a genius; thinks others like himself; packed me up about 20 sheets of paper to write the Opera on!

"September 5.—At work shaping and framing Nos. 1, 2 and 3. Very tiresome work. I seem very short of ideas. I wired home 'No paper arrived, am absolutely at a standstill.' Received packet from Hood with some numbers of 2nd Act.

"September 6.—Worked all day—got No. 3 (No. 2 cut out) into shape at last, and framed. I think it is paltry stuff, but worried me all the same.

"September 9.—Worked at Trio 'Multiplication,' finished and framed it. Neuralgic pains lessening.

"September 10.—Lovely day. Worked hard. Rewrote and framed song 'Da Luan,' framed recit. between 1 and 2. Composed entrance of Lord Lieut. and party.

"September 12.—Recomposed and framed Quintett 'If I were you.'

"September 13.—At work framing. Finished Chorus of Soldiers."

A few days later, in going to call upon the Duchess of York, he was caught in a rain-storm and drenched. A chill settled in his throat which became inflamed, extremely painful, and almost robbed him of the power of speech. He packed up all he had written of *The Emerald Isle* and set out quickly for Paris. Some augury of his impending death may have come to him, for he declared that he would never see his English home again. But he reached London on September 19th, and the music he carried in his bag was the last he was to compose. At the end of September he made an effort to work again. Sick and weak he dragged himself to his desk.

"Tried to work—no result," he wrote in his diary.

The Last Phase

He went to Tunbridge Wells. On the day of his journey he wrote:

"Felt very seedy all day—pain from kidney trouble ... Awfully nervous and in terror about myself. Very low. ... After dinner, while having coffee, felt old pain coming on; in half an hour I was *writhing*, and bathed in sweat. I couldn't stand it any longer, and sent for a doctor, and in my note told him what the trouble was. He came and got me in bed and injected something—I don't know what, but certainly not morphine, which relieved me directly and gave me a good night's rest."

The day following he got up at midday "feeling shaken to pieces and very weak after the attack," and lay down till night time. He struggled up and tried to work, but without success. When a few hours later the doctor overhauled him and gave him an encouraging report, his mind responded at once to a new burst of energy. "Had a good walk and began to think I could work again," he wrote.

A week passed. He had alternating moods of confidence and depression, but always the desire to work. In the quiet of his room he would sit at his table, pen in hand, but the inspiration had left him for ever. In a fresh mood of despair he would go out and walk a little, return to the table and sit with the unscored sheets before him for hours on end.

It was the inability to work that frightened him, and closed the curtains of gloom about his mind. His entry in his diary on October 14th—the day before he left Tunbridge Wells—reflects his mental suffering:

"Have been here just a fortnight, and what have I done? Little more than nothing, first from illness and physical incapability, secondly from *brooding* and nervous terror about myself. Practically I have done nothing *for a month*. Have now finished and framed 1st Act, and they are rehearsing it."

The day following came the last entry he was ever to make in his diary:

"October 15th.—*Lovely day*. ... I am sorry to leave such a lovely day."

"I am sorry to leave such a lovely day." It was the cry

of a heart, as poignant as some of the most beautiful phrases of his composing. He returned to London, but the power to work had been driven from him.

Meanwhile, the Savoy had been kept open by revivals. In June D'Oyly Carte had re-staged *The Pirates of Penzance*, and ran it with success through to the beginning of November. On November 7th *Patience* was to be revived, for it was now obvious that *The Emerald Isle* must be postponed indefinitely. Sullivan had promised to conduct the first night of the revival. Until three days before the curtain went up he was firm in the belief that he would do so. It was a night of great enthusiasm, and, at the end of it, only Gilbert and D'Oyly Carte took the call.

For Sullivan, his career had ended. His *Te Deum*, which he had completed in readiness for the coming of peace, he was never to hear. His opera, of which he had sketched fifteen numbers, was to be completed by another hand.

Soon after the revival of *Patience*, Gilbert was taken ill, and, as the month wore on, grew rapidly worse. He had been clay-puddling the new lake he had made at his home, Grims Dyke—the lake in which ultimately he was to perish—and he contracted rheumatic fever. But hearing of Sullivan's dangerous illness the old wounds were forgotten, and only the long friendship and triumphs remained in his memory. The kindliness of a nature that could be courtly and generous in kindness glowed like a flame. He took up his pen and wrote this letter to Sullivan who received it ten days before his death:

"MY DEAR SULLIVAN,—

"I would be glad to come up to town to see you before I go, but unfortunately in my present enfeebled condition a carriage journey to London involves my lying down a couple of hours before I am fit for anything, besides stopping all night in town. The railway journey is still more fatiguing. I have lost sixty pounds in weight, and my arms and legs are of the consistency of cotton-wool. I sincerely hope to find you all right again on my return, and the new opera running merrily.

"Yours very truly,

"W. S. GILBERT."

The Last Phase

Late in the afternoon of November 21st a curious change occurred in Sullivan's condition which, though serious, did not seem to premise the coming of death. He had had these bouts with death before, and had always triumphed. His mind was clear, but when he spoke the trouble in his throat —which had only partially subsided—prevented his voice from rising above a whisper. He complained of no pain, but as a precautionary measure it was arranged that Sir Thomas Barlow, the Royal Physician, should be called in for consultation in the morning.

He became drowsy, then he seemed to sleep. About six o'clock the next morning his bell was heard ringing violently, and when his housekeeper, Clothilde Raquet, and his valet, Louis Jager, hurried into his room, dissolution had begun.

"My heart!" he exclaimed. "My heart!"

He lay quietly, breathing intermittently and with difficulty. His life appeared to slip away as his nephew held him in his arms. Presently his breathing ceased. . . .

During his last hour of life a woman, frantic with fear, waited vainly for a cab. At the first warning that the end was approaching Mrs. Ronalds had risen and dressed quickly. The street was empty; no vehicle could be obtained to bear her to the death-chamber. When at last one was procured and she arrived at Queen's Mansions, the heavier footstep of Sir Thomas Barlow followed her up the stairs.

But both had come too late. Arthur Sullivan was dead.

London scarcely believed that it had lost Sullivan. Vague rumours of illness, of a half-completed opera, had held no bodings of his death. He was to have conducted *Patience*, to have given a concert at Bristol. And he had died almost before London was aware that he was ill.

A wave of grief swept through the Empire—through the world. The Queen telegraphed her condolences; a dozen countries laid their tributes at the feet of genius.

Sullivan had for many years expressed the wish to be buried beside his parents in Brompton Cemetery. Indeed he had written (eighteen years before) full instructions for his burial, which he sealed in an envelope marked "Directions for my

funeral, etc. To be opened immediately after my death."
This document read as follows:

DIRECTIONS

1. I wish my body to be embalmed before burial. Let nothing prevent this being done.
2. My funeral is to be conducted in the same manner as that of my dear Mother, and if possible, by the same undertaker.
3. My body to be buried in the same grave with my Father, Mother and brother in Brompton Cemetery.
4. If it can be conveniently arranged, I should like the Quartett from "The Light of the World" ("Yea, though I Walk") or the Funeral Hymn from the "Martyr of Antioch" to be sung at my funeral, the latter if there is a chorus.

ARTHUR SULLIVAN,
18 *August*, 1882.

It was, however, the wish of the Dean and Chapter of St. Paul's that the place of burial should be changed, and the decision was only arrived at after the grave in Brompton Cemetery had actually been opened to receive him. Sullivan had been a Chapel Royal Chorister, and the Queen ordained that the first part of the service should be held at the Chapel Royal. Apart from this, the wish was expressed that Sullivan should be buried in the crypt of St. Paul's Cathedral.[1] The other directions were carried out as he had written them.

As it chanced, the funeral procession passed to St. Paul's by way of the Embankment. D'Oyly Carte was then lying seriously ill at his house in Adelphi Terrace, and only a few months were to pass before he, too, joined the Master Company.

And the last scene in St. Paul's: the coffin on its purple trestles—the Archdeacon droning the Committal in his deep bass voice—the mountains of flowers—and the Savoy Chorus,

[1] The Dean and Chapter of St. Paul's asked that he should be buried in the Cathedral, hence the two services.

the tears streaming down their faces, as they strove to sing the farewell: "Brother, Thou art gone before Us."

Two days later vandals stole all the cards, bearing Royal and celebrated autographs, from the floral gifts in the Crypt. They could not leave him his honours, even in a sanctuary he had so often made beautiful with his music.

Apart from family bequests, Sullivan left in his will, dated March 4th, 1899, his portrait by Millais to the National Portrait Gallery, and his autograph scores of *The Mikado* and *The Martyr of Antioch* to the Royal Academy of Music. To the Royal College of Music he left his autograph score of *The Golden Legend* and *The Yeomen of the Guard*. To the Prince of Wales he bequeathed his tortoiseshell and silver cardbox; to the Duke of York a carved coconut mounted in silver.[1] To the Duke of Saxe-Coburg and Gotha his autograph score of *The Light of the World*.[2] To François Cellier he bequeathed the autograph scores of *The Pirates of Penzance* and *Patience*.[3] And, finally, to Mrs. Ronalds he bequeathed an autograph score of *The Lost Chord*, a dinner and dessert service (the latter marked "Louis Phillippe Tuileries") and a quantity of silver.

To Arthur Sullivan's nephew W. S. Gilbert wrote from Helouan in December:

"MY DEAR SULLIVAN,—

"I did not hear of your uncle's terribly sudden death until three days since, or I should have written to express my personal sorrow, and my sympathy with you in the great loss you have sustained. It is a satisfaction to me to feel that I was impelled, shortly before his death, to write to him to propose to shake hands over our recent differences, and even a greater satisfaction to learn, through you, that my offer of reconciliation was cordially accepted. I wish I had been in England that I might have had an opportunity of joining the mourners at his funeral."

[1] Said to have belonged to Captain Cook, the circumnavigator.
[2] Now the property of H.R.H. the Princess Louise.
[3] Both since purchased by his nephew.

Sir Arthur Sullivan

At a later date, in 1905, when the Sullivan bust was about to be placed in the Savoy Gardens, Gilbert wrote to his nephew:

"Marshall[1] tells me that you want a quotation from one of the libretti to inscribe on your uncle's bust. What do you say to this (from *The Yeomen*):

> "Is life a boon?
> If so, it must befall
> That Death, whene'er he call,
> Must call too soon!

"It is difficult to find anything quite fitted to so sad an occasion, but I think this might do.

"Yours truly,
"W. S. GILBERT."

In this final word of affection lies proof of the fact that there was no real quarrel between Gilbert and Sullivan. All that the sensation-mongers have magnified into a quarrel was the differing in temperament of two artistic men. The fidelities of friendship, the debt they owed each other, were bonds too strong and binding for them to be severed utterly. Quibble and temper, difference and hurt, drive no separating wedge between those who have built their careers, their lives together. The tributes of Gilbert to his friend in those last days, in those later days when Sullivan was sealed away beneath the stones of St. Paul's, leave no uncertain knowledge of the strength of that friendship. In equal measure did Sullivan yield the laurels to Gilbert in the years after a historic carpet —a most historic carpet and one shorn of magical effect— tore them asunder. Moreover, all through the years of difference, Sullivan's nephew was always welcomed at Grims Dyke and treated by Gilbert with unvarying kindness.

It is now half a century that has passed over the dust of Sullivan. His music goes on, a lasting pillar in the whole structure of English composing. He created a form of English light music which the years have vainly striven to copy, and, just as the lapidary may strive to imitate a gem in vain, so will those who strive to imitate Sullivan eternally fail.

---

[1] Captain Robert Marshall, the playwright.

The Last Phase

Music of real creative genius can never be successfully copied; there is never a counterfeit strain in music which can be mistaken for the real. He represents a school—his school—as distinct as that of Wagner and Handel. It has become the standard school of English light music.

His versatility hindered the development of his serious work. *The Golden Legend,* one of his most popular composition was the stepping-stone—and only the stepping-stone—to what might have been far mightier things. For in all his works Sullivan was a melodist; it was the first lesson he learned of his craft. Melody followed him throughout his life. He sang of life—the heart of life—without the need of monumental and impressive chords. He gave back to life in his notes what he had derived from it—the understanding of Mankind, and the sympathy of the Human Race.

LIST OF WORKS

Compiled by WILLIAM C. SMITH, late of the British Museum

The Works are given as far as possible in chronological order. A date preceding the name of the publisher indicates the year of composition when it differs from that of publication. In cases where the date of publication does not appear on the Work an approximate date is supplied in brackets [ ].

Only the earliest or most important editions are mentioned. In a few cases the works still remain in manuscript, or if they were published no details are available.

When Hymn Tunes have more than one title, the Hymn Books in which the variations occur are given as well as the original sources. No attempt has been made to trace the Tunes through the many Hymn Books of the period.

In compiling this list every possible care has been taken to make it more complete and accurate than any list that has been hitherto available. In every case where copies of the works have been accessible for examination they have been checked for particulars of date and publisher, and nothing has been included on second-hand evidence where it was possible to obtain better information at first hand.

Sing unto the Lord and praise His Name. Anthem. 1855.
> Sung in the Chapel Royal during Sullivan's choristership.

O Israel! Sacred Song. *Novello*, 1855.

It was a Lover and his Lass. Duet and Chorus. 1857.
> Performed at Royal Academy, July 14th, 1857.

Overture in C Minor, " Timon of Athens." 1857.

Choral and Orchestral Fugue, " Cum Sancto Spiritu." 1857.

Seaside Thoughts. Four-part Song for men's voices. 1857.
> *Novello*, 1904. (Orpheus, No. 368.)

Sonata for Piano. ⎱[1857?]
Songs and Part Songs. ⎰
> Early works in manuscript, referred to in Sir A. C. Mackenzie's

article "The Life-Work of Sullivan." (*Sammelbände der Inter-nationalen-Musik Gesellschaft.* Jahr. III, Heft 3. 1902.)

Overture in D Minor. 1858. (Dedicated to John Goss.)

Psalm for Chorus and Orchestra. 1858. (In German.)

The two preceding works appear as one in some authorities.

Romance for String Quartet. 1859.

Overture, " Feast of Roses." 1859.

Cadenza to Mozart's Concerto in A. 1859.

Performed at Leipzig.

The Music to Shakespeare's Tempest. Op. 1. 1860–61. *Cramer*, [1862–64.] Vocal score [?], some excerpts and chorus parts. *Novello*, [1875.] Vocal score (accompaniment for piano duet and piano) arranged by Franklin Taylor. *Novello*, 1891. Full score.

Played in Leipzig, April 11th, 1861, and with several added numbers, Crystal Palace, April 5th, 1862.

Thoughts, for the Pianoforte. Op. 2. No. 1. Allegretto con grazia. No. 2. Allegro grazioso. *Cramer*, [1862.]

Afterwards republished as **Reverie in A,** and **Melody in D.** *Phillips & Page.* [date?] Piano solo and violin and piano.

Procession March. Orchestral work. *Cramer*, [1863.] Piano solo and duet.

Princess of Wales' March. Orchestral work. *Cramer*, [1863.] Piano solo and duet.

Bride from the North. Song. *Cramer*, 1863.

I heard the Nightingale. Song. *Chappell*, [1863.]

The Last Night of the Year. Four-part Song. *Novello*, 1863. (*Musical Times*, Dec.) Another edition, [1864.]

When Love and Beauty. Madrigal. 1863. *See* "The Sapphire Necklace." 1863–64.

Orpheus with his Lute.
O Mistress mine.
Sigh no more, Ladies. ⎫ Five Songs, words from Shakespeare. 1863–
The Willow Song. ⎬ 64. *Metzler*, [1866.]
Rosalind. ⎭

The Sapphire Necklace. An unfinished opera. 1863–64. Two numbers were published:

"**Over the Roof.**" Song. *Cramer*, 1866. *Cramer*, [1885.]

"**When Love and Beauty.**" Madrigal. *Novello*, 1898.

The Overture was played at St. James's Hall, July 11th, 1866.

L'Ile enchantée. Ballet. 1864.

Produced, Covent Garden, May 14th, 1864.

Kenilworth. Masque Op. 4. 1864. *Chappell*, [1865.] Vocal score.
> Produced, Birmingham Festival, Sept. 8th, 1864.

O love the Lord. Anthem. *Novello*, [1864.] (Novello's Collection of thirty-one Anthems.)

Sweet Day, so cool. Song. *Metzler*, 1864. *Ashdown & Parry*, [1881.]

We have heard with our Ears. Anthem. *Novello*, [1865.]

Thou art lost to me. Song. *Boosey*, [1865.]

Will he come? Song. *Boosey*, [1865.]

Symphony in E, the Irish, for Orchestra. 1866. *Novello*, 1915. Full score.
> First performance, Crystal Palace, March 10th, 1866.

Concerto for Violoncello. 1866.
> Played by Piatti at Crystal Palace, Nov. 24th, 1866.

Overture in C, "In Memoriam," for Orchestra. 1866. *Novello*, [1885.] Full score, piano solo and duet.
> First performance, Norwich Festival, Oct. 30th, 1866.

Te Deum, Jubilate and Kyrie, in D. *Novello*, [1866.] Te Deum. *Novello*, [1872.] Jubilate and Kyrie.

Arabian Love Song. Song. *Chappell*, [1866.]

A weary Lot is thine. Song. *Chappell*, [1866.]

Over the Roof. Song. 1866. [1885.] *See* "The Sapphire Necklace." 1863–64.

If doughty Deeds. Song. *Chappell*, [1866.]

She is not fair to outward View. Song. *Boosey*, [1866.]

O taste and see. Anthem. *Novello*, [1867.]
> Also published in *Musical Times*, Oct., 1867.

Cox and Box. Comic Operetta. 1867. *Boosey*, [1871.] Vocal score with dialogue. Libretto (Morton and Burnand) *Lacy*, [1874.]
> Privately produced, London, April 27th, 1867; also played for charitable purposes at Manchester, at the Adelphi, London, May 11th, and at the Gallery of Illustration, Regent Street, May 18th, 1867.

The Rainy Day. Part Song. *Novello*, [1867.] *Novello*, [1868.] As No. 1 of "Six Four-Part Songs."

O hush thee, my Babie. Part Song. *Novello*, [1867.] *Novello*, [1868.] As No. 2 of "Six Four-Part Songs."

O God, Thou art worthy. Anthem. 1867. *Novello*, [1871.]

Marmion. Overture. 1867.
> First performance, Philharmonic Society, June 3rd, 1867.

List of Works

County Guy. Song. *Ashdown,* [1867.]

The Maiden's Story. Song. *Chappell,* [1867.]

Give. Song. *Boosey,* 1867.

In the Summers long ago. Song. 1867. *Metzler,* [1877.] As "My Love beyond the Sea."

What does little Birdie say ? " Song. *Ashdown,* [1867.]

Hymn of the Homeland. Hymn Tune. *Strahan,* 1867. (Good Words.) *Boosey,* 1868.

Thou God of Love. Hymn Tune. 1867. *Macmillan,* 1868. (Book of Praise Hymnal, No. 306.)

Of Thy Love. (St. Lucian.) Hymn Tune. 1867. *Macmillan,* 1868. (Book of Praise Hymnal, No. 320.) *Novello,* 1902. (Hymn Tunes, No. 36.)

Mount Zion. Hymn Tune. *Nisbet,* 1867. (Psalms and Hymns for Divine Worship, No. 221.) Another edition, 1872.

Collected edition of the "Hymn Tunes" assigns this tune to "Church Praise," No. 272 (1883). This work was published by Nisbet and was based on "Psalms and Hymns for Divine Worship."

Formosa. (Falfield.) Hymn Tune. *Nisbet,* 1867. (Psalms and Hymns for Divine Worship, No. 273.) Another edition, 1872.

In "The Hymnary" (*Novello,* 1872) the tune appears as "Formosa" three times. (Nos. 114, 544 and 601.)

In "Church Hymns with Tunes" (*S.P.C.K.,* 1874) it appears twice as "Falfield." (Nos. 294 and 430.)

In "Church Praise" (*Nisbet,* 1883) it is called "Falfield or Formosa," and is given to Hymns Nos. 34, 64 and 188.

St. Luke. (St. Nathaniel.) Hymn Tune. *Nisbet,* 1867. (Psalms and Hymns for Divine Worship, No. 285.) Another edition, 1872.

Appears in "Church Hymns with Tunes" (*S.P.C.K.,* 1874, Nos. 257, 272, 443) as "St. Nathaniel," the name being thus changed because the collection includes Jeremiah Clarke's "St. Luke." Sullivan's tune is included as "St. Nathaniel" in "Church Praise" (*Nisbet,* 1883, No. 13) and also in the collected edition of "Hymn Tunes" (*Novello,* 1902).

Day Dreams. Six pieces for piano solo. *Boosey,* 1867.

A German edition by Kistner, Leipzig, appeared as Op. 14.

The Contrabandista. Comic Opera. Libretto by F. C. Burnand. 1867. *Boosey,* [1871.] Vocal score and piano solo.

Produced at St. George's Hall, Dec. 18th, 1867. An enlarged version as "The Chieftain," produced Dec. 12th, 1894.

Rejoice in the Lord. Anthem. *Boosey,* 1868.

Evening. Part Song. *Novello*, [1868.] Published separately, and as No. 3 of "Six Four-Part Songs."

Joy to the Victors. Part Song. *Novello*, [1868.] Published separately, and as No. 4 of "Six Four-Part Songs."

Parting Gleams. Part Song. *Novello*, [1868.] Published separately, and as No. 5 of "Six Four-Part Songs."

Echoes. Part Song. *Novello*, [1868.] Published separately, and as No. 6 of "Six Four-Part Songs."

Song of Peace. Part Song from the Cantata "On Shore and Sea." *Boosey*, 1868.

> The Cantata was performed at the opening of the International Exhibition, Albert Hall, May 1st, 1871.

I sing the Birth. Sacred Part Song. *Boosey*, 1868.

The Long Day closes. Part Song. *Novello*, 1868.

The Beleaguered. Part Song. *Novello*, 1868.

The Moon in silent Brightness. Song. *Metzler*, 1868.

O fair Dove, O fond Dove. Song. *Ashdown*, [1868.]

O sweet and fair. Song. *Boosey*, 1868.

I wish to tune my quiv'ring Lyre. Song. *Boosey*, [1868.]

The Snow lies white. Song. *Boosey*, [1868.]

The Mother's Dream. Song. *Boosey*, 1868.

Twilight. Piano Solo. *Chappell*, [1868.]

> A German edition by Kistner, Leipzig, appeared as Op. 12.

Duo Concertante, for Violoncello and Pianoforte. Op. 2. *Lamborn Cock, Addison & Co.*, [1868.]

Additional Accompaniments to Handel's " Jephtha." 1869.

The Prodigal Son. Oratorio. *Boosey*, [1869.] Vocal score.

> Produced, Worcester Festival, Sept. 8th, 1869.

Sing, O Heavens. Anthem. *Boosey*, 1869.

The Troubadour. Song. *Boosey*, 1869.

Birds in the Night. Song from "Cox and Box," with different words. *Boosey*, [1869.]

Sad Memories. Song. *Metzler*, [1869.]

Dove Song. Song. *Boosey*, 1869.

The Strain upraise. Hymn Tune. *Novello*, 1869. (Brown Borthwick's Supplemental Hymn and Tune Book. Third edition. No. 68.)

The Son of God. (St. Ann's.) Hymn Tune. [An arrangement.] *Novello*, 1869. (Brown Borthwick's Supplemental Hymn and Tune Book. Third edition. No. 74.)

Gennesareth. (Heber.) Hymn Tune. *Aylward: Salisbury*, 1869. (Sarum Hymnal, No. 288.) *Novello*, 1872. (Hymnary, No. 515.)

List of Works

Appears as "Succour" in "The Congregational Psalmist," No. 481. (*Hodder & Stoughton,* 1875.)

Overture di Ballo. 1870. *Novello,* 1889. Full score. *Stanley Lucas, Weber & Co.,* [1882.] Piano duet arranged by A. O'Leary. *Novello,* 1909. Pianoforte solo, by J. E. West.

    First performed, Birmingham Festival, Aug. 31st, 1870.

A Life that lives for you. Song. *Boosey,* 1870.

The Village Chimes. Song. *Boosey,* 1870.

Looking back. Song. *Boosey,* 1870.

All this Night. Carol. *Novello,* [1870.] (Christmas Carols, new and old, No. 41.)

On Shore and Sea. Cantata. *Boosey,* [1871.] Vocal score.

    Produced at the opening of the International Exhibition, Albert Hall, May 1st, 1871.

I will worship. Anthem. *Boosey,* [1871.]

It came upon the Midnight clear. Sacred Part Song. *Boosey,* 1871.

    No copy traced. Sullivan's arrangement of the traditional air to these words was published in "Church Hymns," 1874, and later by Novello.

Lead, kindly Light. Sacred Part Song. *Boosey,* 1871.

Through Sorrow's Path. Sacred Part Song. *Boosey,* 1871.

Watchman, what of the Night? Sacred Part Song. *Boosey,* 1871

The Way is long and drear. Sacred Part Song. *Boosey,* 1871.

The Window : or The Songs of the Wrens. A cycle of twelve songs (by Tennyson). *Strahan,* 1871.

The Merchant of Venice. Incidental Music. 1871. *Cramer,* [1873.] Piano duet. *Cramer,* [1877.] Piano solo by J. Rummel. *Bosworth; Leipzig,* [1898.] Full score and piano solo.

    Produced, Prince's Theatre, Manchester, Sept. 19th, 1871.

Nel ciel seren. Serenata from the music to "The Merchant of Venice." Words by F. Rizzelli. 1871. *Cramer,* [1873.] Also known as **"Venetian Serenade."**

Marche Danoise. *Weippert & Co.,* [1871.] Piano solo. *Stanley Lucas, Weber & Co.,* [1874.] Piano solo.

Onward, Christian Soldiers. (St. Gertrude.) *Novello,* 1871. (*Musical Times,* Dec.) *Novello,* [1872.] (Hymnary, No. 476.)

Thespis. Comic Opera. 1871. Libretto, Gilbert, Original Plays, Fourth Series. 1911.

    Produced, Gaiety, Dec. 23rd, 1871.

Courage, Brother. Hymn Tune. *Strahan,* 1872. (Good Words, pp. 25–27.)

Te Deum laudamus and Domine salvam fac Reginam . . . for the Festival . . . May 1, 1872, in celebration of the recovery of H.R.H. the Prince of Wales. *Novello*, [1872.] Vocal score. [1887.] Full score.

Once again. Song. *Boosey*, [1872.]

Golden Days. Song. *Boosey*, [1872.]

None but I can say. Song. *Boosey*, [1872.]

Guinevere. Song. *Cramer*, [1872.]

The Sailor's Grave. Song. *Cramer*, [1872.]

Little Maid of Arcadee. (From "Thespis.") *Cramer*, [1872.]

Lacrymæ. Hymn Tune. *Novello*, [1872.] (Hymnary, No. 222.)

Lux Mundi. Hymn Tune. *Novello*, [1872.] (Hymnary, No. 225.)

Saviour, when in Dust to Thee. (St. Mary Magdalene.) Hymn Tune. *Novello*, [1872.] (Hymnary, No. 249.)
> As "St. Mary Magdalene," *S.P.C.K.*, 1874. (Church Hymns with Tunes, No. 494.)

Welcome, happy Morning. (Fortunatus.) Hymn Tune. *Novello*, [1872.] (Hymnary, No. 284.) *Novello*, 1902. (Hymn Tunes, No. 54.)

St. Kevin. Hymn Tune. *Novello*, [1872.] (Hymnary, No. 285.)

Safe Home. Hymn Tune. *Novello*, [1872.] (Hymnary, No. 507.)

Gentle Shepherd. (The Long Home.) Hymn Tune. *Novello*, [1872.] (Hymnary, No. 509.)
> As "Tender Shepherd" *Novello*, 1902. (Hymn Tunes, No. 26.)

Angel Voices. Hymn Tune. *Novello*, [1872.] (Hymnary, No. 532.)

Propior Deo. (Aspiration.) Hymn Tune. *Novello*, [1872.] (Hymnary, No. 570.)
> Occurs as "Aspiration" in "The Congregational Psalmist," No. 422. (*Hodder & Stoughton*, 1875.)

Venite. (Rest.) Hymn Tune. *Novello*, [1872.] (Hymnary, No. 597.)

St. Edmund. (Fatherland.) Hymn Tune. *Novello*, [1872.] (Hymnary, No. 646.) *Novello*, 1902. (Hymn Tunes, No. 8.)

The White Plume. Song. *Weippert*, [1872.]

Oh! ma charmante. Romance. *Cramer*, [1872.]
> Italian version, "Oh! bella mia." *Cramer*, [1873.]
> English version, "Sweet Dreamer." *Cramer*, [1874.]

Coming Home. Duet. *Boosey*, [1873.]

The Light of the World. Oratorio. *Cramer*, [1873.] Vocal score.
> First performance, Birmingham Festival, Aug. 27th, 1873.

List of Works

There sits a Bird. Song. *Cramer*, [1873.]

Looking forward. Song. *Boosey*, 1873.

The Young Mother. Three simple Songs. 1873.

> No. 1. "Cradle Song." (The days are cold.) *Cramer*, [1874.] Another edition with the title, "**Little Darling, sleep again.**" *Metzler*, [1876.]

> No. 2. "**Ay de mi, my Bird.**" *Cramer*, [1874.] Another edition. *Metzler*, [1876.]

> No. 3. "**The First Departure.**" *Cramer*, [1874.] Another edition with different words entitled "**The Chorister.**" *Metzler*, [1876.]

The Marquis de Mincepie.
Care is all fiddle-de-dee. (Finale.) } 1873.

> Two Songs from "The Miller and his Man," Drawing-room Extravaganza written by F. C. Burnand with songs by Sullivan and incidental music composed and arranged by James F. Simpson. *Cramer*, [1874.] Vocal score with libretto, and also separate editions of the Sullivan songs.

Turn Thee again. Chorus adapted from Russian Church Music. *Novello*, [1874.] [1899.]

Mercy and Truth. Chorus adapted from Russian Church Music. *Novello*, [1874.] [1899.]

Sleep, my Love, sleep. Song. *Boosey*, [1874.]

Mary Morison. Song. *Boosey*, [1874.]

The Distant Shore. Song. *Chappell*, [1874.]

Thou art weary. Song. *Chappell*, [1874.]

My dear and only Love. Song. *Boosey*, [1874.]

Living Poems. Song. *Boosey*, [1874.]

Tender and true. Song. *Chappell*, [1874.]

Church Hymns, with Tunes. Edited by Arthur Sullivan. *S.P.C.K.*, 1874.

> Besides editing the collection, Sullivan harmonized or arranged sixty-nine of the tunes, contributed fourteen of his own which had previously appeared elsewhere, and also supplied the following twenty-four new ones:

> **Christus.** No. 496.

> **Clarence.** No. 64.

> **Cœna Domini.** No. 207.

> **Coronæ.** No. 354.

> **Dulci sonantia.** (Dulce sonans.) No. 316.

> **Ever faithful.** No. 414.

> **Evelyn.** No. 390.

Golden Sheaves. Nos. 281, 556.
Hanford. Nos. 400, 531.
Holy City. No. 497.
Hushed was the Evening Hymn. No. 572.
Lux eoi. Nos. 67, 174.
Lux in tenebræ. (Lux in tenebris.) No. 409.
Paradise. No. 473.
Pilgrimage. No. 367
Resurrexit. No. 132.
St. Francis. No. 220.
St. Millicent. No. 248
St. Patrick. No. 144.
St. Theresa. No. 566.
Saints of God. No. 191.
Ultor omnipotens. No. 262.
Valete. No. 30.
Veni Creator. No. 346.

Of these "Lux eoi" and "Lux in tenebræ" are not indicated in the collection as new tunes, although earlier editions cannot be traced.

Bendall's list of Sullivan's works includes "St. Luke" and "St. Mary Magdalene" as original tunes in "Church Hymns." "St. Luke" ("St. Nathaniel") appeared earlier in "Psalms and Hymns for Divine Worship," 1867, and "St. Mary Magdalene" as "Saviour, when in Dust" was first published in "The Hymnary," 1872.

Two other editions of "Church Hymns, with Tunes" were published [1875 and 1881] differing in some few respects from the first edition. In these later issues "Clarence" is given as an arrangement by Sullivan, and "St. Millicent," "St. Patrick" and "St. Theresa" are not indicated as having been specially composed for the collection.

Two Litany tunes, ascribed to Sullivan, are included in the [1875] edition:—"Litany, No. 585" (Jesu, we are far away), and "Litany, No. 592" (Jesu, Life of those who die). These tunes replace those by C. C. Scholefield and F. Clay which are given to the same words in the first edition of "Church Hymns." The two Sullivan Litanies also occur in the [1881] edition, although No. 592 appears there as anonymous.

Litany No. 1. (Jesu, we are far away.) [1874?] *S.P.C.K.*, [1875.] (Church Hymns with Tunes, No. 585.) *Novello*, 1902. (Hymn Tunes, No. 19.)
  See note on "Church Hymns."

List of Works

Litany No. 2. (Jesu, Life of those who die.) [1874?] *S.P.C.K.,* [1875.] (Church Hymns with Tunes, No. 592.) *Novello,* 1902. (Hymn Tunes, No. 20.)
    See note on "Church Hymns."

Litany No. 3. (Jesu, in Thy dying Woes.) *S.P.C.K.,* 1874. (Church Hymns with Tunes, No. 123.)
    The tune is an arrangement by Sullivan of a traditional melody. It was also published in "Hymns, Ancient and Modern" (Revised edition, 1875, No. 466) with words "God the Father," and also occurs in the collected edition of Sullivan's "Hymn Tunes," 1902, as an original work to the words "Be Thou with us." It is not given in Bendall's list.

Audite audientes me. (I heard the Voice of Jesus say.) Hymn Tune. *Shaw,* [1874.] (New Church Hymn Book, No. 408.)

Constance. Hymn Tune. *Shaw,* [1874.] (New Church Hymn Book, No. 511.)
    No words are given to the first edition of the tune, but it appears in "Hymn Tunes" (*Novello,* 1902) as "Who trusts in God."

Ecclesia. (The Church has waited long.) Hymn Tune. *Shaw,* [1874.] (New Church Hymn Book, No. 64.)
    As "O where shall Rest be found" in "Hymn Tunes." (*Novello,* 1902.)

Promissio Patris. (Our blest Redeemer.) *Shaw,* [1874.] (New Church Hymn Book, No. 167.)

Merry Wives of Windsor. Incidental music. 1874.
    Produced, Gaiety, Dec. 19th, 1874.

Love laid his sleepless Head. Song. 1874. *Boosey,* [1875.]
    Words by Swinburne, sung in the Gaiety production of "The Merry Wives of Windsor," Dec. 19th, 1874.

Trial by Jury. Dramatic Cantata. *Chappell,* [1875.] Vocal score with dialogue. Libretto, Gilbert, Original Plays, Series 1. 1876.
    Produced, New Royalty, March 25th, 1875.

The Zoo. Musical Folly. [Comic Opera.] Words by B. Rowe [i.e. B. C. Stephenson]. 1875.
    Produced, St. James's Theatre, June 5th, 1875.

I will mention. Anthem. *Novello,* [1875.]

Christmas Bells at Sea. Song. *Novello,* 1875.

The Love that loves me not. Song. *Novello,* 1875.

Let me dream again. Song. *Boosey,* [1875.]

Thou'rt passing hence. Song. *Chappell,* [1875.]

Sweethearts. Song. *Chappell,* [1875.]

Sir Arthur Sullivan

The River. Song. *Routledge; Novello,* 1875. From "The Sunlight of Song," a collection of poems with original music by various composers.

We've ploughed our Land. Song. *Routledge; Novello,* 1875. From "The Sunlight of Song," a collection of poems with original music by various composers.

Carrow. (My God I thank Thee.) Hymn Tune. *Hodder & Stoughton,* 1875. (Congregational Psalmist, No. 496.)

Upon the snow-clad Earth. Carol. *Metzler,* 1876.

My dearest Heart. Song. *Boosey,* 1876.

I will sing of Thy Power. Anthem. *Novello,* 1877. (*Musical Times,* Jan.)

Sometimes. Song. *Boosey,* 1877.

The Lost Chord. Song. *Boosey,* [1877.]

When thou art near. Song. *Boosey,* 1877.

Henry VIII. Incidental music. 1877. *Metzler,* [1879.] Piano score.

    Metzler also published an Orchestral Score [? date] and various excerpts, including:

        King Henry's Song. (Youth will needs have Dalliance.) 1877.

        Graceful Dance. 1878, etc.

        Processional March, 1893, etc.

    Produced, Theatre Royal, Manchester, Aug. 29th, 1877.

The Sorcerer. Comic Opera. *Metzler,* [1877.] Vocal score and piano solo. New edition, revised, [1884.] Libretto, Gilbert, [1877.]

    Produced, Opera Comique, Nov. 17th, 1877.

Hearken unto Me. Anthem. *Novello,* 1877. (*Musical Times,* Nov.)

Turn Thy Face. Anthem. *Novello,* 1878. (*Musical Times,* Jan.)

H.M.S. Pinafore. Comic Opera. *Metzler,* [1878.] Vocal score and piano solo.

    Amor am Bord. German version. *Litolff,* [1882.] Vocal score and piano solo. *Litolff,* [1883.] Vocal score. *Litolff,* [1884.] Piano solo.

    Bendall's list includes a "Full score" by Litolff, but the issue of this cannot be traced.

    Libretto, Gilbert, [1878.]

    Produced, Opera Comique, May 25th, 1878.

I would I were a King. Song. *Boosey,* 1878.

Morn, happy Morn. Trio in the play "Olivia," by W. G. Wills. *Metzler,* 1878.

List of Works

Old Love Letters. Song. *Boosey*, [1879.]

St. Agnes' Eve. Song. *Boosey*, [1879.]

The Pirates of Penzance. Comic Opera. 1879. *Chappell*, [1880.] Vocal score and piano solo. Libretto, Gilbert, Original Plays, Series 2. 1881.

First performance, Royal Bijou Theatre, Paignton, Dec. 30th, 1879.

American production, Fifth Avenue Theatre, New York, Dec. 31st, 1879.

First London performance, Opera Comique, April 3rd, 1880.

Edward Gray. Song. *Stanley Lucas, Weber & Co.*, [1880.]

Dominion Hymn. (**God bless our wide Dominion.**) *Chappell*, [1880.]

The Martyr of Antioch. Sacred Musical Drama. *Chappell*, [1880.] Vocal score. New edition, *Chappell*, [1898.] Vocal score. *Chappell*, [1899.] Full score.

First performance, Leeds Musical Festival, Oct. 15th, 1880.

Patience. Aesthetic Opera. *Chappell*, [1881.] Vocal score and piano solo. Libretto, Gilbert, [1881.]

Produced, Opera Comique, April 23rd, 1881.

The Sisters. Duet. *Leisure Hour*, 1881, pp. 230–35. *Stanley Lucas, Weber & Co.*, [1881.]

In the Twilight of our Love. Song from "Patience," with different words. *Chappell*, [1881.]

Iolanthe. Fairy Opera. 1882. *Chappell*, [1883.] Vocal score and piano solo. Libretto, Gilbert, [1883?]

Produced, Savoy, Nov. 25th, 1882.

There is none like unto the God of Jeshurun. Anthem. Composed by Sir John Goss, completed by Sir Arthur Sullivan. *Novello*, [1882.]

Hark! What mean those holy Voices? Carol. *Patey & Willis*, 1883. (*The Lute*, No. 12.)

Who is like unto Thee? Anthem. *Novello*, [1883.]

Princess Ida. Comic Opera. *Chappell*, [1884.] Vocal score and piano solo. Libretto, Gilbert, [1884.]

Produced, Savoy, Jan. 5th, 1884.

The Mikado. Comic Opera. *Chappell*, [1885.] Vocal score and piano solo. *Forberg*; *Chappell*, [1889.] Vocal score with German words, and piano solo. *Bosworth*, 1900. Full score with English words, vocal score with German words, and piano solo. Libretto, Gilbert, [1885.]

Produced, Savoy, March 14th, 1885.

A Shadow. Song. 1885. *Patey & Willis*, [1886.]

An Ode written for the Opening of the Colonial and Indian Exhibition, 1886. *Novello*, 1886. Vocal score.
> Performed, Albert Hall, May 4th, 1886.

The Golden Legend. Cantata. *Novello*, 1886. Vocal score. [1887.] Full score.
> Produced, Leeds Festival, Oct. 16th, 1886.

Ruddigore. Comic Opera. *Chappell*, [1887.] Vocal score and piano solo. Libretto, Gilbert, [1887.]
> Produced, Savoy, Jan. 22nd, 1887.

Ode written and composed for the Occasion of Laying the Foundation Stone of The Imperial Institute by Her Majesty the Queen. [July 4th, 1887.] *Chappell*, [1887.] Vocal score.

Ever. Song. *Chappell*, [1887.]

The Yeomen of the Guard. Comic Opera. *Chappell*, [1888.] Vocal score and piano solo. Libretto, Gilbert, [1888.]
> Produced, Savoy, Oct. 3rd, 1888.

Macbeth. Incidental music. *Chappell*, 1888. [Piano solo?] Overture. *Chappell*, [1893.] Full score.
> Produced, Lyceum, Dec. 29th, 1888.

Hymns for Children [Words] by Sarah Wilson. *Eyre & Spottiswoode*, [1888.]
> Contains eleven children's hymns arranged from previously published hymn tunes.

E tu nol sai. (You sleep.) Serenata. Sung in "The Profligate." [Play by Sir A. W. Pinero.] *Chappell*, [1889.]
> Two editions, Italian (G. Mazzacato) and English (B. C. Stephenson).

The Gondoliers. Comic Opera. 1889. *Chappell*, [1890.] Vocal score and piano solo. Libretto, Gilbert, [1889.]
> Produced, Savoy, Dec. 7th, 1889.

Ivanhoe. Romantic Opera. *Chappell*, [1891.] Full score, vocal score and piano solo. Libretto, Julian Sturgis from Sir Walter Scott, [1891.]
> Produced, Royal English Opera, Cambridge Circus, Jan. 31st, 1891.

The Foresters. Incidental music. *Chappell*, 1892. Vocal score.
> Produced, Daly's, New York, March 25th, 1892.

Haddon Hall. Light Opera. *Chappell*, 1892. Vocal score and piano solo. Libretto, Sydney Grundy, 1892.
> Produced, Savoy, Sept. 24th, 1892.

List of Works

Songs of two Savoyards. Words and illustrations by W. S. Gilbert. *Routledge; Chappell,* 1892.

A collected edition of songs from the operas, including choruses and concerted pieces arranged for a single voice by C. King Hall.

Utopia Limited. Comic Opera. *Chappell,* 1893. Vocal score and piano solo. Libretto, Gilbert, 1893.

Produced, Savoy, Oct. 7th, 1893.

Imperial March composed for the Opening of The Imperial Institute. *Chappell,* 1893. Piano solo and arrangements by King Hall and Berthold Tours. Orchestral and military band parts.

Bid me at least good-bye! Song. [From the play of "An Old Jew" by Sydney Grundy.] *Chappell,* 1894.

The Chieftain. Comic Opera. [Enlarged version of "The Contrabandista."] 1894. *Boosey,* 1895. Vocal score and piano solo. Libretto, Burnand, 1894.

Produced, Savoy, Dec. 12th, 1894.

"The Contrabandista" was produced Dec. 18th, 1867.

King Arthur. Incidental music. 1894. *Novello,* 1903. Edition arranged for concert performance by W Bendall. *Novello,* 1904. String parts.

Produced, Lyceum, Jan. 12th, 1895.

The Grand Duke. Comic Opera. *Chappell,* 1896. Vocal score and piano solo. Libretto, Gilbert, 1896.

Produced, Savoy, March 7th, 1896.

Victoria and Merrie England. Ballet. *Metzler,* 1897 Piano solo, arrangement by W. Bendall.

Produced, Alhambra, May 25th, 1897

O King of Kings. [Queen's Jubilee Hymn to the tune **"Bishopgarth."**] *Eyre & Spottiswoode,* 1897. *Novello,* [1897.] As "Bishopgarth," tune only.

In "Hymn Tunes," 1902, as **"O God, the Ruler of our Race."**

Wreaths for our Graves. Choral Song. 1897. *Novello,* 1898.

The Beauty Stone. Romantic Musical Drama. *Chappell,* 1898 Vocal score and piano solo. Libretto, Pinero and Comyns Carr, 1898.

Produced, Savoy, May 28th, 1898

The Rose of Persia. Comic Opera. 1899. *Chappell,* 1900. Vocal score and piano solo. *Bosworth,* [1901.] Full score. German edition with English words. Libretto, Basil Hood, 1899.

Produced, Savoy, Nov. 29th, 1899

Sir Arthur Sullivan

The Absent-minded Beggar. Song. *Enoch, for "The Daily Mail,"* 1899.

Victoria. (**To mourn our Dead we gather here.**) Hymn tune. 1899. *Novello,* 1902. (Hymn Tunes, No. 33.)

    The manuscript is dated June 16th, 1899, and has the words "My Times are in Thy Hand."

O Swallow, Swallow. Song. *J. Church Co.,* 1900.

Tears, idle Tears. Song. *J. Church Co.,* 1900.

Te Deum laudamus. A Thanksgiving for Victory. 1900. *Novello,* 1902. Full score and vocal score.

    Posthumous publication.

    Performed, St. Paul's, June 8th, 1902, at the close of the South African War.

The Emerald Isle. Comic Opera. Completed by Edward German. *Chappell,* 1901. Vocal score and piano solo. Libretto, Basil Hood, 1901.

    Produced, Savoy, April 27th, 1901.

My Child and I. Song. *Boosey,* 1901.

The Roseate Hues. Hymn Tune. *Novello,* 1901. (Parish Choir Book, No. 553.)

    According to the preface to "Hymn Tunes," 1902, originally composed for "The Hymnary" [1872.]

Bolwell. (**Thou to whom the sick and dying.**) Hymn Tune. *Novello,* 1902. (Hymn Tunes, No. 35.)

    In Novello's Parish Choir Book (No. 596) as a Coronation Hymn with the words, "Lord of Might, our Land's Defender."

Chapel Royal. (**O Love that wilt not let me go.**) Hymn Tune. *Novello,* 1902. (Hymn Tunes, No. 44.)

Hymn Tunes. Composed by Arthur Sullivan. *Novello,* 1902.

    Contains fifty-six tunes by Sullivan and twelve arrangements by him of other tunes. The collection is not complete.

Fair Daffodils. Four-part Song. *Novello,* 1903. (*Musical Times,* Oct.)

To one in Paradise. Song. *Novello,* 1904.

Longing for Home. Song. *Novello,* 1904.

My Heart is like a silent Lute. Song. *Novello,* 1904.

I will lay me down in Peace. Anthem. *Novello,* 1910.

In addition to the librettos mentioned in the above list, the following collected editions of Gilbert's works have been issued:

    Original Plays. 4 series. 1876, 1881, 1895, 1911.

    Original Comic Operas. [1891.]

List of Works

Savoy Operas . . . with illustrations by W. Russell Flint. 1909.
Iolanthe and other Operas . . . with illustrations by W. Russell Flint.
  1910.
[Comic Operas.] With coloured illustrations by W. Russell Flint.
  8 vols. 1911–12.
The Savoy Operas. Being the complete text of the Gilbert and
  Sullivan Operas, etc. 1926.

INDEX

INDEX

A

Adèle, Sullivan's housekeeper in Paris, 131

Adelphi Theatre, benefit performance of *Cox and Box* at, 63

Ages Ago, Clay and Gilbert's, 68

Albani, Mdme., replaces Pattini in second performance of *Golden Legend* in Berlin, 169, 170
   sings in *Golden Legend*, 162, 194
   sings in *Martyr of Antioch*, 127
   Sullivan's tribute to, 170

Albany, Duke of, Sullivan as chorister at christening of, 11
   Royal command to Sullivan at wedding of, 11 (note)

Albert, Prince Consort, present to Sullivan, 11

Albert Edward, Prince of Wales, and Mrs. Ronalds's rendering of *The Lost Chord*, 84
   and Sullivan's illness at Monte Carlo, 216
   at Sullivan's birthday dinners, 133, 229
   at Wagner celebration, 243
   attends, with Princess of Wales, first night of *Ivanhoe*, 209
   congratulates Sullivan on a "great honour in store," 133
   discusses question of Sullivan becoming Principal of National Training School, 78
   hears *The Martyr of Antioch*, 113
   in Berlin, 168, 169
   listens to play by telephone, 134
   model of Sullivan's safety device submitted to, 254
   Patience company presented to, 118
   signed photograph and autographed letter from, 109
   Sullivan visits the Continent with, 192
   Sullivan's bequest to, 265
   thanks Sullivan for Ode music, 172

Albert Hall, *Golden Legend* rendered at, 163, 176–7
   Martyr of Antioch given at, 113
   Wagner's *Parsifal* produced at, 147

Alexandria, Sullivan conducts concert at, 120

"Alice in Wonderland," Lewis Carroll's request to Sullivan *re*, 85–6

All this Night (carol), 273

Allingham introduced to Sullivan, 45

America, adventures in, 98 *et seq.,* 150 *et seq.*
   copyright of *Patience* infringed in, 124
   law regarding copyright in, 104, 124, 125, 150, 151

Amor am Bord (German version of *H.M.S. Pinafore*), 278

Amsterdam, Moscheles at, 22

"Angel Voices" (hymn tune), 274

Arab music, Sullivan's interest in, 119–20

Arabian Love Song, 270

"Aspiration" (hymn tune), 274

"Audite audientes me" (hymn tune), 277

Austin, Alfred, Sullivan and, 240–1

Ay de mi, my Bird (song), 275

B

Baden, visit to Mdme. Schumann at, 52

Baird, George (and son), Sullivan's copyists, 160 (note)

Balfe, meeting with, in Paris, 61
   writes operetta for St. George's Hall, 64

Balfour, Rt. Hon. A. J., attends Wagner celebration, 243

Baltimore, concert to Sullivan at, 104

Bancroft, Squire, visits Sullivan while ill at Monte Carlo, 217

Barlow, Sir Thomas, 263

Barnby, Joseph, conducts Wagner's *Parsifal*, 147

Index

Barnby, Joseph, congratulations on
   Martyr of Antioch from, 111
ties with Sullivan for Mendelssohn
   Scholarship, 15
Barrie, J. M., his play *Jane Annie*, 215
Battersea, solo singing in *Judas* at, 11
Bayswater, Sullivan's schooldays at, 8
Beatrice, Princess, 240
Beaulieu, Sullivan at, 238
Beauty Stone, The (romantic musical
   drama), 281
   short run of, 246
   Sullivan and libretto of, 245, 246
Beefeater, The, title changed to *Yeomen
   of the Guard*, 173 (and note)
Beefsteak Club, Sullivan at, 126
Beethoven, Döppler's memories of, 54, 55
   exhumation and reburial of body of,
   237
   portrait of (by Kriehuher), 54
Beleaguered, The (part song), 272
Belfast, Sullivan recognized and ac-
   claimed at, 229
Bendall, Wilfred (Sullivan's secretary),
   239 (note)
   introduces Basil Hood to Sullivan, 249
Bennett, Joseph, his libretto of *Golden
   Legend*, 159
   musical critic of *Daily Telegraph*, 146
   on changes made by Sullivan in *Golden
   Legend* music, 161
   (*see also under* Spark, Fred. R.)
Bennett, Prof. (afterwards Sir William
   Sterndale), pianoforte lessons under,
   16
Berlin, an injunction issued against
   Unter den Linden Theatre, 228
   Golden Legend produced in, 168, 170
   performance (in English) of *Mikado* in,
   156
Bid me at least good-bye! (song, from
   Grundy's *An Old Jew*), 281
Bigge, Sir Arthur (private secretary to
   Queen Victoria), 239, 240
Birds in the Night (song from *Cox and
   Box*), 272
Birmingham, Sullivan's *bon mot* on, 146
Birmingham Festival (1864), *Kenilworth*
   produced at, 46
Birmingham Festival (1884), conductor-
   ship of, falls to Richter, 146
"Bishopgarth" (hymn tune), 281

Bismarck, Herbert, supper with, 168
Blumenthal, Jacques, congratulations
   from, 210
Blunt, Wilfrid (and wife), visit to, 121
Boer War, outbreak of, 251 *et seq.*
"Bolwell" (hymn tune), 282
Bolwell Terrace (No. 8), birth of Sullivan
   at, 2
Brereton sings in *Golden Legend*, 194
Bride from the North (song), 269
Bridgman, C. V., reminiscences of
   Sullivan, 11, 13, 16
Bromley, Nellie, as plaintiff in *Trial by
   Jury*, 76
Browne, Walter, his part in *Patience*, 114
Browning, Robert, introduces Alling-
   ham to Sullivan, 45
Bruce, Lord Ernest, 11
Buffalo, a new company for *Pirates*
   launched at, 107
Bunn, Governor, meeting with, 156
Burgskater sings in *Siegfried* at Bay-
   reuth, 243
Burlesque, popularity of, 63
Burnand, F. C., at Sullivan's birthday
   party, 133
   burlesque of *Box and Cox* by, 63
   chance meeting with, turns Sullivan
   towards light opera, 63
   suggests enlarged version of *Contra-
   bandista*, 232
Butt, Clara, hears phonograph record of
   The Lost Chord, 84
By the Waters of Babylon (anthem), 8
Byng, Rev. the Hon. Francis, vicar of
   St. Michael's, Chester Square, 38
Byron, H. J., a witty reply to Palgrave
   Simpson, 69

C

Cairo, Sullivan in, 118 *et seq.*
Calvert, *Henry VIII* music for, 110
Cambridge University offers Sullivan
   Mus.Doc. degree, 80
Care is all fiddle-de-dee (song), 275
"Carpet" procession, described by Sulli-
   van, 121
Carpets, a dispute about, terminates
   Gilbert–Sullivan partnership, 199
   et seq.
Carr, J. Comyns, *King Arthur* by, 233
   libretto of *The Beauty Stone* by, 245

Index

"Carroll, Lewis" (C. L. Dodgson), asks
   Sullivan to set songs for "Alice in
   Wonderland," 85–6
"Carrow" (hymn tune), 278
Carte, R. D'Oyly, builds Royal English
   Opera House, 185 (note)
   builds Savoy Theatre, 117
   career of, 75
   death of, 264
   decides to go into management on his
     own account, 87
   harassed by co-directors of Opera
     Comique, 88, 90, 92, 94
   holds Sullivan to his agreement, 138–9
   lavish expenditure for producing *Ivan-
     hoe*, 208
   lawsuit against plagiarists of *Mikado*
     fails, 151
   letter to Gilbert on profits and gross
     receipts of several operas, 230
   quarrel with Gilbert, 199
   sells Royal English Opera House, 219
   suggests partnership between Gilbert
     and Sullivan, 75
   superb mounting of *Haddon Hall*, 219
   the Gilbert-Sullivan partnership in
     jeopardy, 138 *et seq.*
   tries to persuade Sullivan to set a play
     by Barrie, 215
   visits America, 94
   visits Sullivan while ill at Monte
     Carlo, 216
Cellier, Alfred, as fellow-chorister of
   Sullivan, 14
   failure of *Mrs. Jarramie's Genie* at
     Savoy, 176
   offers help on *The Sorcerer*, 87
   produces *Mikado* in Australia, 156
   sails for America, 97
Cellier, François, Sullivan's bequest to,
   265
Cellier, Frank, and Sullivan's illness on
   first night of *Princess Ida*, 137
Chapel Royal, age limit for choristers at,
   10
   anthem by Sullivan praised by Sir G.
     Smart, 17 (note)
   customary gifts to choristers on leaving,
     19
   distinguished visitors hear Sullivan
     sing at, 11
   fellow-choristers at, 14

Chapel Royal, first part of Sullivan's
   burial service at, 264
   Sullivan admitted to, 10
   Sullivan as teacher at, 37
"Chapel Royal" (hymn tune), 282
Chappell, Tom, a festive supper with,
   128, 129
   acquaints Sullivan of Gilbert's desire
     for "complete reconciliation," 210–
     11
   and sales of *Iolanthe* music, 130
Chieftain, The (enlarged version of *The
   Contrabandista*), produced, 232, 281
   music from *Contrabandista* used in, 65
   Sullivan's efforts to stem decline in
     box-office receipts, 234
Chinatown, a detective accompanies
   Sullivan through, 151
Chopin, Moscheles' opinion of music of,
   21
Choral and Orchestral Fugue, "Cum
   Sancto Spiritu," 268
Chorister, The (song), 10, 275
Chorley, accompanies Sullivan to Paris,
   42
   at second performance of *Tempest*
     music, 38
   libretto of *Kenilworth*, 46, 47
   libretto of *The Sapphire Necklace*, 46
Christian, Prince, proposes Sullivan for
   Marlborough Club, 126
Christmas, the German, influence on
   Sullivan, 30
Christmas Bells at Sea (song), 277
"Christus" (hymn tune), 275
"Church Hymns, with Tunes," Sullivan
   as editor of, 70, 275–6
Cimiez, Queen Victoria at, 239
   Sullivan plays at Easter Day service
     at, 240
Cirque Napoleon, Paris, 61
Civil Service Orchestral Society, founda-
   tion of, 60
"Clarence" (hymn tune), 275
Clarence, Duke of, arrives in Cairo, 122
   death of, 216
Claverton Terrace, Pimlico, the Sullivans
   at, 44
Claxton, Captain, compliment to Sulli-
   van, 11–12
Clay, Frederic, *bonhomie* of, 40
   celebrated songs composed by, 40

289

Index

Clay, Frederic, collaborates with W. S.
    Gilbert, 67, 68
death of, 196
introduces Sullivan to Gilbert, 40
stricken with paralysis, 136
studies with Hauptmann at Leipzig, 39
Coburg, Duke of, and Easter Day service at Cimiez, 240
    at Sullivan's birthday dinner, 229
"Cœna Domini" (hymn tune), 275
Coghlan, Miss Maria Clementina, marriage of, 3
    (see also Sullivan, Mrs. Thomas)
Coleridge-Taylor, Sullivan and, 244
Collins, Colonel Arthur, 257
Colonial and Indian Exhibition, opening of, Ode for, 159
Comedy Opera Company, formation of, 87
in liquidation, 113
lawsuit against, 113
    (see also under Opera Comique)
Coming Home (duet), 274
Concerto for Violoncello, 270
Conneau, Mdme., lady-in-waiting to Empress Eugénie, 66
Conscription in France, 79 (note)
"Constance" (hymn tune), 277
Contrabandista, The (comic opera), 60, 271
production and failure of, 64, 65
resurrection of, as The Chieftain, 232, 234
Contrexeville, Sullivan drinks waters at, 215
Cook, Captain (circumnavigator), reputed belonging of, bequeathed by Sullivan, 265
Copenhagen, reception at, 115–16
Copyright, lax law in America regarding, 104, 124, 125, 150, 151
"Coronæ" (hymn tune), 275
Costa, Sir Michael, his control at Covent Garden, 44
praises Sullivan, 11
County Guy (song), 271
"Courage, Brother" (hymn tune), 273
Courtenay visits Rossini, 43
Covent Garden, Île Enchantée produced at, 44–5
Promenade Concerts at, 93
Cowen, Frederick, as reserve conductor for Leeds Festival (1898), 246

Cox and Box (comic operetta), 60, 270
produced at the Adelphi, 63
Cradle Song, 275
Cronstadt, H.M.S. Hercules arrives at, 116
Crystal Palace, decline in popularity of concerts at, 73
first Handel Festival at, 12
Golden Legend given at, 163
Grove produces Schumann's First Symphony in B Flat at, 35
Tempest music performed at, 38
Crystal Palace School of Art, Sullivan's post at, 37
"Cum Sancto Spiritu" (fugue), 268
Curtin, ex-Governor, meeting with, 156
Czerny, 54

D

Daily Mail asks Sullivan to set Kipling's Absent-Minded Beggar, 252
fund for benefit of soldiers' dependents, 252
Dalany, Miss, introduction, by letter, to Sullivan, 79
Daly, Augustine, produces The Foresters in New York, 214
Damian sings in Golden Legend, 194
David, Ferdinand, how he helped his pupils, 24
instructs Sullivan in orchestral work and conducting, 23
member of committee appointed for publication of Mendelssohn MSS., 23 (note)
Mendelssohn's tribute to, 24
powers as conductor, 23
Day Dreams (six pieces for piano solo), 271
De Grey, Lady, at Wagner celebration, 243
Delle at Rossini's reception, 43
Denmark, King of, welcomes Duke of Edinburgh and Sullivan, 115–16
De Staäl, Russian Ambassador, 146
Devonshire, holiday work in, 13
Dicey, Edward, friend and executor of Sullivan, 120
Dickens, Charles, as guide in Paris, 42
hears Tempest music, 38
Dickens, Miss, 41
Dilke, Sir Charles, 146

Index

Distant Shore, The (song), 275
Dodgson, C. L. (*see* "Carroll, Lewis")
Dominion Hymn, 279
Döppler, V., reminiscences of Beethoven and Schubert, 54, 55
Dorothy, Cellier's, long run of, 174, 175
Dove Song (song), 272
Dubois décries *The Zoo*, 79
Duff, theatrical manager, 150, 151
"Dulci sonantis" (or "Dulce sonans") (hymn tune), 275
Du Maurier, George, plays leading part in *Cox and Box*, 64
Duo Concertante, for Violoncello and Pianoforte, 272

E

Earthquake shocks at Monte Carlo: a panic-stricken lady, 165–6
"Ecclesia" (hymn tune), 277
Echoes (part song), 272
Edinburgh, Duke of, and Royal Amateur Orchestral Society, 159
at Sullivan's birthday party, 133
calls on Sullivan, 113
death of, 259
declares *Light of the World* a triumph, 73–4
forwards Sullivan decoration from Sultan, 181–2
invites Sullivan and Clay to go as his guests to Russia, 115
letter from, after operation on Sullivan, 95
Sullivan's bequest to, 265
Sullivan's friendship with, 71
urges Sullivan to become head of National Training School of Music, 78
(with Duchess) attends first night of *Ivanhoe*, 209
Edward Gray, 97 (and note), 279
Egypt, three months in, 118 *et seq.*
Emerald Isle, The (comic opera), interrupted by illness and death, completed by another hand, 259 *et seq.*, 282
Engadine, the, diary notes on visit to, 237
England, foundation and spread of Schumann cult in, 35, 36
E tu nol sai (serenata, sung in *The Profligate*), 280

Eugénie, Empress, at Farnborough, 178
visits to, at Chiselhurst, 66
"Evelyn" (hymn tune), 275
Evening (part song), 272
Ever (song), 165, 280
"Ever faithful" (hymn tune), 275

F

Fair Daffodils (four-part song), 282
"Falfield" (hymn tune), 271
"Fatherland" (hymn tune), 274
Feast of Roses, The (Overture), 29, 269
Fildes, Luke, 172
First Departure, The (song), 275
Ford, Ernest, sets *Jane Annie*, 215
(*see also under* Wyndham, H. Saxe)
Foresters, The, incidental music to, 214, 280
Foriani, Signorina, 121
"Formosa" (hymn tune), 271
Forster, W. E., Sullivan's tirade against educational schemes of, 72
"Fortunatus" (hymn tune), 274
France, conscription in, after Franco-German War, 79 (note)
Franco-German War of 1870, 66
Frederick of Germany, Emperor, death of, 178
Frederick of Germany, Empress, 192
Sullivan's stay at the Friedrichof with, 237, 238
Fuller-Maitland, J. A. (*see* Maitland)

G

Gallery of Illustration, Regent Street, the German Reeds at, 64
Gambetta, death of, 131–2
Garcia, Mdme., visit to, 52
Garrick Club, Sullivan elected member of, 58 (note), 126
Gatti Brothers, inaugurate Promenade Concerts, 93
Geinson, Mr., 16
"Gennesareth" (hymn tune), 272
"Gentle Shepherd" (hymn tune), 274
George II, King, and Handel, 36
George, Prince (King George V), meeting with, in Cairo, 122
German, Edward, completes *The Emerald Isle*, 282
Germany, fresh trend of musical thought in, 21

Index

Gewandhaus Concerts, Leipzig, 21, 57

Gilbert, William Schwenck, and Frederic
Sullivan, 82

and Sullivan's resolve to write no more
Savoy operas, 139 et seq.

as billiard player, 220

at Sullivan's birthday party, 133

attacked by gout, goes to Homburg,
222

bibliography of standard works on,
284 et seq.

breach with Sullivan temporarily
healed, 145, 146, 203

collected editions of works of, 282-3

considers Yeomen libretto best of all
Savoy operas, 174

correspondence on suggested collaboration in grand opera, 185 et seq.

curt refusal to attend first performance
of Ivanhoe, 209

describes raid on Opera Comique, 95

desire for rapprochement with Sullivan
gratified, 212, 213

disappointed in a deal with Carl Rosa,
75

dissatisfied with first libretto of Patience, 111

dramatizes The Elixir of Love, 87

end of partnership with Sullivan, 235
et seq.

failure to distinguish the two forms of
Sullivan's genius, 175

fêted in America, 98

final meeting with Sullivan, 249

generous suggestion regarding deadlock with Sullivan from, 141-2

gives notice of termination of collaboration with Sullivan, 201

his association with The Martyr of
Antioch, 110, 111

kidnapped by Italian brigands, 67

last letter to Sullivan, 262

lawsuit with Carte, 201-2

luck at Monte Carlo tables, 175-6

parodies Tennyson's Princess, 69

partnership with Sullivan, 74

proof of his friendship with Sullivan,
266

quarrels with Carte, 199

recurring difficulties with Sullivan,
140 et seq., 157, 172, 173, 180, 184
et seq., 199 et seq., 223, 235

Gilbert, William Schwenck, serious
illness of, 262

suggests air of a popular song in
Yeomen, 178-9

suggests quotation for bust to Sullivan
in Savoy Gardens, 266

Sullivan's first meeting with, 68

the "lozenge plot," 157, 170, 171

visits America re pirating of Pinafore,
97

Gillott, Messrs., supply pens to Sullivan,
178

Give (song), 271

Gladstone, Rt. Hon. W. E., defies a
popular superstition, 146

informs Sullivan of his proposed
knighthood, 133

joins Civil Service Orchestral Society,
60

sees Iolanthe and congratulates Sullivan,
130-1

God bless our wide Dominion, 279

Golden Days (song), 274

Golden Legend, The (cantata), 280

autograph score bequeathed to Royal
College of Music, 265

diary entries regarding composition of,
159-61

Gilbert's congratulations on success of,
162

Press criticisms, 162

produced: an enthusiastic scene, 162

"Golden Sheaves" (hymn tune), 276

Goldschmidt, Mdme. (see Lind, Jenny)

Goldschmidt, Otto, Sullivan spends
Christmas of 1862 with, 39

Gondoliers, The, or The King of Barataria (romantic opera), 280

first night reception, 197

plot decided on, 192

preliminary expenses of, 199

rapid composition of, 194 et seq.

revival, 248

run of, 198

Goss, Sir John, appreciation of Sullivan's
Symphony in E Flat, 48-9

criticizes Prodigal Son, 62

harmony lessons under, 16

influence on Sullivan, 48

Sullivan's opinion of an anthem by,
13

Götterdämmerung, Sullivan on, 244

Index

Gounod comes to London to hear *The Light of the World*, 74

Grand Duke, The, or The Statutory Duel (comic opera), 281
full-dress rehearsal and production of, 234
short run of, 235

Grand opera viewed by Sullivan as "the greatest gamble in the world," 228

Graves, Charles L., "Life and Letters of Sir George Grove" by, 52 (note), 53 (note), 56 (note)

Grey, R. (*see under* Dark, S.)

Grossmith, George, as "Jack Point" in *Yeomen*, 181
as Sir Joseph Porter in *Pinafore*, 90
engaged for *The Sorcerer*, 88
his part in *Pirates of Penzance*, 107

Grove, Sir George and Schubert discoveries, 52 *et seq.*
and Sullivan's sale of copyright, 41
first meeting with, 35
knighthood for, 133
produces *Tempest* music at Crystal Palace, 38

Grundy, Sydney, libretto of *Haddon Hall* by, 211, 214, 218

Guinevere (song), 274

Gunn, Michael, decides to continue *Pinafore*, 94

H

Haddon Hall (light opera), 280
composition of, interrupted by illness, 215 *et seq.*
finished and produced, 218
popularity of music of, 218–19
the critics and, 218

Handel, George II and, 36

Handel Festival, Sullivan in chorus at, 12

"Hanford" (hymn tune), 276

Happy Valley, The, Gilbert's libretto of, sent to Sullivan, 216

Harcourt, Sir William, 146

Hardinge, Lord, 11

Hare John, 114
at Sullivan's birthday dinner, 229
consulted by Gilbert on title for a new libretto, 173 (and note)

Hark! What mean those holy Voices? (carol), 132, 279

Harris, Augustus, at Sullivan's birthday dinner, 229

Hartington, Marquis of, at Sullivan's birthday party, 133

Hassan renamed *The Rose of Persia* [*q.v.*]

Hauptmann, professor at Leipzig, 23, 39, 40

Hearken unto Me (anthem), 278

"Heber" (hymn tune), 272

Helmore, Thomas, accepts Sullivan as chorister at Chapel Royal, 10
conducts funeral service of Sullivan's mother, 123
his pride in Sullivan, 39
interest in his choristers, 12
method of dealing with choristers, 11
opinion of anthem (*We have heard with our ears*) by Sullivan, 26
tribute to Sullivan's singing, i. 12
tries Sullivan's voice, 9

Henry of Prussia, Prince, 117

Henry VIII, incidental music to, 110, 278

Hercules, tour with Duke of Edinburgh on, 115

H.M.S. Pinafore or The Lass that loved a Sailor (comic opera), 89, 278
authorized version produced in New York, 98 *et seq.*
distressing conditions under which music was written, 91, 92
effect of a tropical summer on, 92
Hamilton Clarke's arrangement of, produced at Promenade Concerts, 93
pirated versions of, 93
première of, 92
produced at Opera Comique, 90
revival of, 250

Hochberg, Count, cables for right to produce *Ivanhoe* in Berlin, 209

Holland, *Het Mikado* fills theatres in, 156

Hollingshead, John, and the first collaboration of Gilbert and Sullivan, 68

"Holy City" (hymn tune), 276

Hood, Basil (librettist of *The Emerald Isle*), 258
joins Sullivan in Switzerland, 250
libretto of *Hassan* (re-titled *Rose of Persia*) by, 249
submits libretto of *The Miners* to Sullivan, 249
Sullivan's tribute to, 249

Index

Household Words, verses in, set to music by Sullivan as *The Lost Chord*, 82

Howe, Bishop Walsham, writes Jubilee Hymn, 240, 241

Howling Dervishes, the, visit to, 118–19

"Hushed was the Evening Hymn" (hymn tune), 276

Hutchinson, B. C., marriage of, 136

"Hymn of the Homeland" (hymn tune), 271

Hymn Tunes, incomplete collection of, 282

Hymns composed and written by Sullivan in 1874, 70

Hymns for Children, 280

I

I heard the Nightingale (song), 269

"I heard the Voice of Jesus say" (hymn tune), 277

I sing the Birth (sacred part song), 272

I will lay me down in peace (anthem), 282

I will mention (anthem), 277

I will sing of Thy Power (anthem), 278

I will worship (anthem), 273

I wish to tune my quiv'ring Lyre (song), 272

I would I were a King (song), 278

If doughty Deeds (song), 41, 270

Île Enchantée, ballet music, produced at Covent Garden, 44, 45, 269

Imperial Institute, foundation-stone laid, 171

  state opening of, 221

Imperial March composed for opening of Imperial Institute, 221, 281

Imperial Theatre, Westminster, unauthorized version of *Pinafore* at, 96

In Memoriam, Overture in C to, 44, 270

  conditions under which written, 50–1

In the Summers long ago (song), 271

In the Twilight of our Love (song from *Patience*, with different words), 279

International Exhibition (1871), opening of, 272, 273

Interviewers, American, their persistency, 150, 151

Iolanthe or The Peer and the Peri (fairy opera), 279

  advance bookings for, 130

  arrangements made to prevent infringement of copyright, 125, 128

Iolanthe or The Peer and the Peri, composition of, proceeds during stay in Cornwall, 125

  inauspicious news reaches Sullivan on night of first performance of, 129

  large sale of vocal and pianoforte scores of, 130

  reconstruction of Act I, 126

  Sullivan begins music of, 124

  why called *Periola* at rehearsals, 128

Ireland, visit to, 45

Irish Symphony, origin of, 46

Irving, Henry, 113

  appreciation of *Mikado* by, 158

  asks Sullivan to write incidental music to *Macbeth*, 182

  at Sullivan's birthday dinner, 229

It came upon the Midnight clear (sacred part song), 273

It was a Lover and his Lass (duet and chorus), 268

Italy, Sullivan in, 112

Ivanhoe (romantic opera), 280

  in Berlin, 228

  inspired by and dedicated to Queen Victoria, 176, 177, 209, 210 (note)

  precautions against knowledge of music reaching the public before production, 208

  production of, 208, 209

  run of, 210 (and note)

  Sullivan's record of "seven months' hard labour" on, 205–7

J

Jager, Louis (valet to Sullivan), 263

Japanese, ground of their objection to *Mikado*, 156, 158

Jephtha, additional accompaniments to, 70, 272

Jesu, in Thy dying woes (Litany), 277

Jesu, Life of those who die (Litany), 277

Jesus, we are far away (Litany), 276

Joachim, musical career in Germany, 40 (note)

Joy to the Victors (part song), 272

K

"Kanoun" (Arab musical instrument), 119

Kenilworth (masque), 44, 270

  production and success of, 46

Index

Kenmare, Earl of, at Sullivan's birthday party, 133
Kiel, *Hercules* arrives at, 117
King Arthur, incidental music to, 233, 281
produced at the Lyceum, 233
Kipling, Rudyard, *Recessional* of, 248
writes *The Absent-Minded Beggar*, 252
Klingemann, C., informs Sullivan of his election as Mendelssohn Scholar, 15
last drilling by, before course at Leipzig, 20, 21
Klingemann, Mrs., offers to teach Sullivan German, 19
Kneller Hall, opened as training centre for military musicians, 7
Kriehuher's portrait of Beethoven, 54

L

Lacource at Rossini's reception, 43
"Lacrymæ" (hymn tune), 274
Lacy, Charlotte, marries Frederic Sullivan, 43
Lake Como, holiday on, 77
Last Night of the Year, The (four-part song), 269
Lead, kindly Light (sacred part song), 273
Leeds Festival (1880), *Martyr of Antioch* produced at, 110
Leeds Festival (1883), an amusing incident at, 135
Leeds Festival (1886), *Golden Legend* produced at, 162
Leeds Festival (1889), *Golden Legend* at, 195
Leeds Festival (1898), ovation to Sullivan at, 247
Committee, alarmed at Sullivan's health, retains other conductors, 246
Lehmann, Mrs. Frederic, Sullivan's friendship with, 40, 42
Leighton, Lord, 146
at Sullivan's birthday dinner, 229
Leipzig, description of great storm in (Aug. 1860), 30–1
In Memoriam produced at, 57
musical reputation of, 21
summer of 1860 in, 29
Leipzig Conservatoire, an act of grace by, 33
Sullivan at, 21 *et seq.*
teachers at, 23

Lenoir, Miss Helen, 138, 142
Léonie, Mdlle., and death of Gambetta, 130–1
Let me dream again (song), 41, 277
large sale of, 77
Life that lives for you, A (song), 273
Light of the World, The (oratorio), 70, 274
an event which inspired composition of, 72
hastily scored by Sullivan, 74
produced at Birmingham, 73
Sullivan's bequest of autograph score of, 265 (and note)
Lind, Jenny (Mdme. Goldschmidt), and *Tempest* music, 39
letter to Sullivan after failure of *The Contrabandista*, 65–6
regrets inability to attend first production of *The Prodigal Son*, 61
sings in Sullivan's Symphony in E Flat, 49
Sullivan's friendship with, 37
takes Sullivan to task for overworking, 37–8
Lindsay, Sir Coutts and Lady, 77
Liszt at smoking concert of Royal Amateur Orchestral Society, 159
Litanies by Sullivan, 276, 277
Little Darling, sleep again (song), 275
Little Maid of Arcadee (from *Thespis*), 274
Liverpool offers Sullivan directorship of its music, 70
Living Poems (song), 275
Lloyd, Edward, sings in *Golden Legend*, 162
sings in *Martyr of Antioch* at Brighton, 127
London, Moscheles' concerts in, 22
the Mendelssohn cult in, 34
Long Day closes, The (part song), 60, 272
"Long Home, The" (hymn tune), 274
Longing for Home (song), 282
Looking back (song), 41, 273
Looking forward (song), 275
Lorne, Marquess of, a stay with, 107
Los Angeles, death of sister-in-law at, 148
Sullivan takes his sister-in-law's family for a tour, 151
Lost Chord, The (song), 278
authoress of words of, 83

Index

Lost Chord, The, autographed score of, bequeathed to Mrs. Ronalds, 265
enormous sale of, 83
parody of, and Sullivan's disgust, 83
phonograph record of, 84
written at bedside of dying brother, 82, 83
Louise, Princess, 265 (note)
congratulates Sullivan on success of *Ivanhoe,* 209–10
hostess at Government House, 107
Love laid his sleepless Head (song), 277
Love that loves me not, The (song), 277
Lucky Star, The, atmosphere of, delays progress of *Hassan* (re-titled *Rose of Persia*), 249–50
"Lux eoi" (hymn tune), 276
"Lux in tenebræ" (or "Lux in tenebris") (hymn tune), 276
"Lux Mundi" (hymn tune), 274
Lyceum Theatre, *Macbeth* produced at, 182

M

Macbeth, Sullivan's incidental music to, 182–3, 280
McCarty, Gen., meeting with, 156
McCaul, Mr., entertains Sullivan at supper, 156
Macfarren Prof. G. A., acquaints Sullivan of offer of Mus.Doc., 80
knighthood for, 133
McGuckin, sings in *The Martyr of Antioch,* 127
Machel, Captain, 229 (note)
McIntosh, Miss Nancy, first appearance in London, 227
Mackenzie, Sir A. C., article on "Life-Work of Sullivan" by, 268–9
Maiden's Story, The (song), 271
Malet, Sir Edward, 122
Manchester, Sullivan's night drive to a cemetery at, 49, 50
Manns, August, produces *Tempest* music at Crystal Palace, 38
Maple, Blundell, purchases one of Sullivan's horses, 229
Marche Danoise (piano solo), 273
Mario, farewell tour of, 75
Marmion overture produced at Philharmonic, 60, 270
Marquis de Mincepie, The (song), 275

Marshall, Captain Robert, and the inscription to Savoy Gardens bust of Sullivan, 266
Martin, Sir George, invites Sullivan to write a Te Deum, 257
Martyr of Antioch, The (sacred musical drama), 279
autograph score of, bequeathed to Royal Academy of Music, 265
Gilbert's association with, 110
production of, 110
Sullivan conducts performance of, at Brighton, 127
Mary Morison (song), 275
Massenet congratulates Sullivan on *Mikado,* 158
Matthews, Charles, 69
Matthews, Miss, allows Sullivan use of her piano, 8
Maude, Princess, at first night of *Ivanhoe,* 209
Melody in D, 269
Mendelssohn, influence of, on the wane, 21
London faithful to music of, 34
organizes musical reception to Moscheles, 22
tribute to David, 24
Mendelssohn Committee resolve to send Sullivan to Leipzig, 18
Mendelssohn, Madame, appoints committee of selection of Mendelssohn MSS., 23 (note)
Mendelssohn Scholarship, won by Sullivan and renewed, 15, 26
Merchant of Venice, The, incidental music to, produced at Manchester, 273
Mercy and Truth (chorus adapted from Russian Church music), 275
Merry Wives of Windsor, incidental music to, 70, 74, 277
Messager's *Mirette,* failure of, 231
Metzler editions of *Pinafore,* rapid sale of, 93
Mikado, The, or The Town of Titipu (comic opera), 279
authorized version produced in New York, 151, 152
autograph score bequeathed to Royal Academy of Music, 265
completed music delivered, 149

Index

Mikado, The, or The Town of Titipu,
  first number of, composed, 148
  just retribution for a piratical theatrical
    manager, 151, 153
  last performance of, 164
  long run of, 156, 158
  revival of, 176, 235
  seven encores at first performance of,
    149
  toured in the provinces, 156
Millais, and Tennyson, 58
  at Sullivan's birthday party, 133
  first meeting with, 58 (note)
  his portrait of Sullivan left by will to
    National Portrait Gallery, 265
  illustration for Tennyson's delayed
    work, 58, 60
  paints Sullivan's portrait, 176
Mills sings in *Golden Legend*, 194
Milman, Dean, his religious drama *The
  Martyr of Antioch*, 110
Molesworth, Lady, Sullivan's stay with,
  125
Monte Carlo, earthquake at, 165
  Gilbert's luck at casino tables, 175-6
Montholon, Comte, exile of, 6
Montrose, Duchess of, sells her yearlings,
  229-30
Moon in silent brightness, The (song), 272
Morn, happy morn (trio in *Olivia* by
  W. G. Wills), 278
Moscheles, Ignez, as friend of young
  musicians of talent, 21
  becomes professor at Leipzig Conserva-
    toire, 22
  his adoration of Mendelssohn and
    Schumann, 21
  his pride in Sullivan, 56
  letter to Klingemann on curriculum at
    Leipzig Conservatoire, 22-3
  member of committee for publication
    of Mendelssohn MSS., 23
Mother's Dream, The (song), 272
"Mount Zion" (hymn tune), 271
Mozart, birthplace of, visited, 53
Mozart's Concerto in A, Cadenza to, 269
Musical Times, The, 11, 13
My Child and I (song), 282
My dear and only Love (song), 275
My dearest Heart (song), 278
"My God, I thank Thee" (hymn tune),
  278

My Heart is like a silent lute (song), 282
My Love beyond the sea (song), 271
"My Times are in Thy Hand" (hymn
  tune), 282

N

Naples, illness in, 167
Napoleon in exile, memories of, 5, 6, 66
National Portrait Gallery, Sullivan's
  bequest to, 265
National Training School of Music,
  Sullivan Principal of, 78
Nel ciel seren (serenata), 273
New York, a gala performance of *Mikado*
  in: Sullivan's speech, 154-5
  authorized version of *Pinafore* given
    in, 98 *et seq.*
  Carte's case against plagiarists fails, 151
  Iolanthe produced in, 131
  pirated versions of *Pinafore* in, 93-4
  Sullivan's diary entries *re* visit to,
    100-2
"Ney" or "Ni" (Arab musical instru-
  ment), 120
Niagara Falls, Sullivan visits, 107
None but I can say (song), 274
Norwich Festival (1866), Overture to *In
  Memoriam* produced at, 51, 270
Norwich Festival (1880), Sullivan con-
  ducts *Martyr of Antioch* at, 118
Norwich Festival (1886), *Golden Legend*
  at, 173
Nubar Pasha, 119

O

O fair Dove, O fond Dove (song), 60, 72,
  272
O God, Thou art worthy (anthem), 270
O hush thee, my Babie (part song), 60,
  270
O Israel (sacred song), 268
O King of Kings (Jubilee hymn), 281
O Love that wilt not let me go, tune for,
  282
O love the Lord (anthem), 270
O Mistress mine (song), 41, 269
O Swallow, Swallow (song), 282
O sweet and fair (song), 272
O taste and see (anthem), 270
Odes by Tennyson, set by Sullivan, 159,
  171-2, 280
"Of Thy Love" (hymn tune), 271

Index

Oh! bella mia (Italian version of *Oh! ma charmante*), 274

Oh! ma charmante (romance), 274

Old Jew, An (Grundy's play), a song for, 228

Old Love Letters (song), 279

O'Leary, Mr., 16

Olympic Theatre, unauthorized version of *Pinafore* at, 96

On Shore and Sea (cantata), 273

Once again (song), 41, 275

"Onward, Christian Soldiers" (hymn tune), 70, 273

Opera Comique Theatre, a raid on; litigation follows, 95, 96

  D'Oyly Carte and co-directors of, 88, 90, 92

  D'Oyly Carte manager of, 87

  lease to Comedy Opera Company expires, 94

  Patience at, 114

  Pirates of Penzance produced at, 107

Orpheus with his Lute (song), 41, 269

Osman Pasha, 119

Ottawa visited by Sullivan, 107

"Our blest Redeemer" (hymn tune), 277

Ouseley, Frederick, his *Martyrdom of St. Polycarp*, 14

"Out" (Arab musical instrument), 119

Over the Roof (song), 269, 270

Overture di Ballo, 273

Overture in C Minor, "Timon of Athens," 268

Overture in D Minor, 268

Owen, Sir Philip, calls on Sullivan with request from Prince of Wales, 159

P

Paignton, copyright performance of *Pirates* at, 102

Palmay, Mdme. von, *début* in London, 228

  her part in *The Grand Duke*, 234

"Paradise" (hymn tune), 276

Paris, Moscheles in, 22

  scandal regarding Gambetta's death in, 131–2

  scenes in, after Franco-German War, 66

Paris Exhibition, Sullivan chosen as Royal Commissioner of Music at, 109

Parsifal, first performance in London of, 147

  performed at Bayreuth, 242

Parting Gleams (part song), 272

Pasdeloup tentatively promises to produce *In Memoriam* in Paris, 61

Passmore, Walter, his part in *Rose of Persia*, 254

  succeeds Grossmith at the Savoy, 227

Patey, Mdme., sings in *Golden Legend*, 162

Patience or Bunthorne's Bride (æsthetic opera), 279

  enthusiastic reception of, 114

  last performance of, 128

  long run of, 118, 124

  newly constructed, 111

  revival of, 254, 262

  strenuous work on, 113–14

  Sullivan's bequest of autograph score of, 265 (and note)

  transferred to the Savoy, 117

Pattini sings in command performance of *Golden Legend* in Berlin, 168, 169

Payne, fellow-student at Conservatoire, 25, 26

Periola (*see* Iolanthe)

"Persian Opera," the (see *Rose of Persia*)

Peterhof Palace, primitive sanitary arrangements at, 116

Philadelphia, *Mikado* performed at, Sullivan's criticism of, 155

Philharmonic concerts, 13, 14

"Pilgrimage" (hymn tune), 276

Pinafore (see *H.M.S. Pinafore*)

Pinero, libretto of *The Beauty Stone* discussed with, 245

Pirates of Penzance, The, or Love and Duty (comic opera), 279

  alternative titles of, 100 (note)

  American interest in, entails extra companies for, 105

  attempted piracy of, in America, 104

  copyright performance at Paignton of, 102

  libretto of, received by Sullivan, 97

  music from *Thespis* used in, 69

  produced in New York, 101 *et seq.*

  revival of, 176, 254, 262

  score finished in New York, 99, 100–1

  Sullivan's bequest of autograph score of, 265 (and note)

Index

Plaidy, professor at Leipzig Conservatoire, 23, 31

Plees, William (Sullivan's schoolmaster at Bayswater), 8
accompanies Sullivan to see Sir George Smart, 9

Potter, Cipriani, advocacy of Schumann's music by, 35
at Chapel Royal, 34
Sullivan's description of, 35

Pounds, Courtice, 122

Prince Imperial, death in Zululand, 66

Princess Ida or Castle Adamant (comic opera), 279
first music to, 132
strenuous work on, 136
Sullivan, seriously ill, conducts first performance of, 137

Princess of Wales' March (orchestral work), 269

Procession March (orchestral work), 269

Procter, Adelaide, authoress of words of *The Lost Chord*, 83

Prodigal Son, The (oratorio), 272
composition of, 60
produced at Worcester Festival, 61

"Promissio Patris" (hymn tune), 277

"Proprior Deo" (hymn tune), 274

Psalm for Chorus and Orchestra (in German), 269

Pygmalion and Galatea, success of, 69

Q

Queen's Hall, *Golden Legend* given at, 163

R

Rainy Day, The (part song), 270

Randegger, 114, 146

Raquet, Clothilde (housekeeper), 263

Reed, German, at Gallery of Illustration, Regent Street, 64
emigrates to St. George's Hall, 64
tries, but fails, to make collaborators of Gilbert and Sullivan, 68

Reeves, Sims, characteristic letter to Sullivan after production of *Trial by Jury*, 76
confuses his dates and disappoints Sullivan, 61

Rehan, Ada, 214

Rejoice in the Lord (anthem), 271

Remington, C. K., and American piracy of *Pinafore*, 94

"Rest" (hymn tune), 274

"Resurrexit" (hymn tune), 276

Reverie in A, 269

Reyer, Ernest, *Salammbo* by, 199

Rheingold, Wagner's, Sullivan's criticism of, 243

Richter, appointed conductor of Birmingham Festival, 146
organ teacher at Conservatoire, 23

Rienzi, Wagner's, Sullivan's disappointment with, 57

Rietz, farewell celebrations to, 27
leaves Leipzig for Dresden, 26
Sullivan's affection for, 27
teacher of instrumentation and composition at Leipzig, 23

Righi, Italian family of, 3

River, The (song), 278

Romance for String Quartet, 269

Ronalds, Mrs. (*née* Carter), daily letters to, 84, 257
her influence in Sullivan's life, 83
manuscript copy of *The Lost Chord* buried with, 84
Sullivan's bequest to, 84, 265
Sunday *salons* of, 83

Ronalds, Pierre, 83

Rooseveld, Blanche, accompanies Gilbert and Sullivan to America, 97

Rosa, Carl, and Gilbert-Sullivan partnership, 77
at Leipzig with Sullivan, 43 (note)
plays at reception by Rossini, 43

Rosa, Mdme. Paripa, sudden death of, 76

Rosalind (song), 269

Rosamunde music, Groves's ambition to complete, 52
search for and discovery of, 52 *et seq.*

Rose of Persia, The (comic opera), 281
first performance of, 253

"Roseate Hues, The" (hymn tune), 282

Rossini, duets with Sullivan, 42
introduces Carl Rosa to Sullivan, 43

Rothschild, Alfred, dinner to the Prince of Wales, 132

Rothschild, Ferdinand, at Sullivan's birthday party, 133

Royal Academy of Music, Sullivan's bequests to, 265

Royal College of Music, 78

Index

Royal College of Music, Sullivan's bequest to, 265
  (see also National Training School of Music)
Royal English Opera House (now Palace Theatre), 185 (note)
  opened with Ivanhoe, 208
  sale of, 219
Royal Military College, Sullivan's father appointed bandmaster at, 4
Royalty Theatre, D'Oyly Carte manager of, 75
  La Fille de Madame Angot runs in double harness with Trial by Jury, 76
Rubinstein, attends and plays at Gewandhaus concert, 57
Sullivan's opinion of his playing at the Philharmonic, 13
Ruddigore or The Witch's Curse (comic opera), 280
  first production of, 164
  Gilbert submits idea of, to Sullivan, 158
  libretto of, delivered, 162
  part of libretto previously used in Ages Ago, 69
  run of, 165
  Sullivan's own opinion of, 163
Russell, Sir Charles (Lord Russell of Killowen), at Sullivan's birthday party, 229
  counsel in case against Comedy Opera Company, 112
  death of, 259

S

Sad Memories (song), 272
"Safe Home" (hymn tune), 274
Sailor's Grave, The (song), 274
St. Agnes' Eve (song), 279
"St. Ann's" (hymn tune), 272
"St. Edmund" (hymn tune), 274
"St. Francis" (hymn tune), 276
St. George's Hall, The Contrabandista produced at, 65
"St. Gertrude" (hymn tune), 273
St. James's Hall, Golden Legend rendered at, 163
"St. Kevin" (hymn tune), 274
"St. Lucian" (hymn tune), 271
"St. Luke" (hymn tune), 271

St. Mark's College, Sullivan sings at, 11–12
"St. Mary Magdalene" (hymn tune), 274
St. Michael's, Chester Square, Sullivan organist at, 38–9
"St. Millicent" (hymn tune), 276
"St. Nathaniel" (hymn tune), 271
"St. Patrick" (hymn tune), 276
St. Paul's Cathedral, burial of Sullivan in, 264–5
  vandalism after Sullivan's funeral, 265
"St. Theresa" (hymn tune), 276
"Saints of God" (hymn tune), 276
Salt Lake City, visit to, 151
Sandringham, stay with Prince and Princess of Wales at, 193
Sapphire Necklace, The (unfinished opera), 46, 269
"Saviour, when in dust to Thee" (hymn tune), 274
Savoy Theatre, opened with Patience, 118
Saxe-Coburg and Gotha, Duke of (see Edinburgh, Duke of)
Schlemitz, Mr., Director of Leipzig Conservatoire, 33
  tribute to Sullivan's Feast of Roses, 29
Schneider, Dr., Schubert discoveries at house of, 53, 54 (and note), 55
Schubert, body exhumed and reburied, 237
  cult of, in London, 52
  Döppler's reminiscences of, 54, 55
  Sullivan and Grove search for and discover Rosamunde music, 52 et seq.
Schumann, cult of, in London, 52
  Moscheles' adoration for, 21
  Sullivan's admiration of music of, 34
  Sullivan's lament of London's ignorance of, 29–30
Schumann, Mdme., visit to, 52
Seaside Thoughts (four-part song), 268
Sedie at Rossini's reception, 43
Seuff, David, 57
Seymour, Ernest Clay Ker, 229 (note)
Shadow, A (song), written for Madame Patey, 147, 280
Shakesperian songs, set by Sullivan, 41
She is not fair to outward view (song), 270
Siegfried, von, Döppler's reminiscences of, 54
Siegfried, Sullivan's opinion of, 243

Index

Sigh no more, Ladies (song), 269

Silva (valet to Sullivan), 89

Simpson, Palgrave, 113
  draws a prize in a raffle, 69
  suggests a version of *Le Palais de la Vérité* to Gilbert, 69

Sims, George R., Clay paralysed while walking with, 136

Sing, O Heavens (anthem), 272

Sing unto the Lord and praise His Name (anthem), 268

Sisters, The (duet), 278

Sleep, my Love, sleep (song), 275

Smart, Sir George (organist of Chapel Royal), 9
  acknowledges dedication of anthem by Sullivan, 26
  advises Sullivan to learn German, 19
  as Sullivan's musical sponsor, 18
  discourages idea of Sullivan's becoming conductor, 24
  finds Weber dead in bed, 37
  sends Sullivan to Mr. Helmore, 9
  Tempest music dedicated to, 38
  tests Sullivan's voice before Leipzig course, 20
  warns Sullivan that his voice is breaking, 17

Smith, Rt. Hon. W. H., supposed caricature of (in *Pinafore*), disclaimed, 90, 91

Smythe, Walter (Sullivan's secretary), 167, 233
  death of, 239 (note)

Snow lies white, The (song), 272

Solomon, Edward, parodies Sullivan's *Lost Chord*, 83

Sometimes (song), 278

Sonata for Piano (MS.), 268

Song of Peace (part song), from Cantata *On Shore and Sea*, 272

Songs and Part Songs (MS.), 268

Songs of Two Savoyards, words and illustrations by Gilbert, music by Sullivan, 281

Sorcerer, The (comic opera), 278
  produced at Opera Comique, 88
  revival of, 146, 147, 248–9
  run of, 88
  Sullivan commences music of, 85
  twenty-first anniversary of production of, 248–9

South African War (*see* Boer War)

Spark, F. R. (secretary to Leeds Festival), letters from Sullivan to, 246, 248
  records an amusing incident at rehearsal for Leeds Festival, 135

Spina, Herr, aids search for Schubert MSS., 52 *et seq.*

Stanford, Sir Charles V., as reserve conductor for Leeds Festival (1898), 246

Stradler, Döppler's recollections of, 54

Strahan, Mr., Tennyson's letter assenting to publication of his cycle of songs, 59

Sturgis, Julian, scenario of *Ivanhoe* by, 193

"Succour" (hymn tune), 273

Suffield, Lord, 254

Sullivan, Arthur Seymour, acclaims Coleridge-Taylor, 244
  acclaims Schumann, 29, 30, 35, 36
  admitted to Chapel Royal, 10
  adopts his nephew Herbert, 124
  ambitions to join Chapel Royal, 8, 9
  ambitious to become master of pianoforte, 23
  and Helmore's discipline, 12, 13
  anxiety as to second examination for Mendelssohn Scholarship, 17
  asks Gilbert's collaboration in grand opera, 185 *et seq.*
  at bedside of his brother, 81–2
  attacks American law permitting piracy and reproves American women in English Society, 94, 106
  attends Royal Academy, 16
  attends Wagner celebration at Bayreuth, 242–4
  bankruptcy of his brokers, 129
  baptism of, 4
  bibliography of standard works on, 284 *et seq.*
  birth at Bolwell Terrace, 4
  birthday dinners, 133–4, 229
  chorister at Duke of Albany's christening, 11
  collapses after first performance of *Princess Ida*, 137
  composition becomes his purpose in life, 44
  conductorship ambitions of, 23, 24
  conducts a Philharmonic Concert for first time, 148

Index

Sullivan, Arthur Seymour, conducts
Leeds Festival for last time, 247

congratulations on success of *Ivanhoe*
to, 209 *et seq.*

cosmopolitan tastes in music, 37

criticizes Rubinstein's piano-playing,
13–14

Dean of Chapel Royal and, 17 (note)

degree of Mus.Doc. conferred on, 80

describes visit to Sir G. Smart, 9

description of storm of Aug. 1860, 30–1

desires to buy a fifteen-and-sixpenny
piano, 8

determines to abandon comedy, 138
et seq., 174 *et seq.*

diary story of an earthquake, 165

differences with Gilbert, 140 *et. seq.*,
157, 172, 173, 180, 184 *et seq.*, 199
et seq.

directions for his burial, 264

displeased with his own work in
Utopia, composes a new Finale, 227

drinks waters at Bertrich, 126

Duke of Wellington's talk with and
present to, 10

encore of *Absent-Minded Beggar* conducted by, 252

end of the partnership, 235 *et seq.*

entertains idea of theatrical ownership,
256

fad for inventing novelties, 254–5

fad for "J" pens, 178

failing health induces mental malaise,
250–1, 253

final meeting with Gilbert, 249

first anthem (at age of eight), 8

first days in light opera, 63 *et seq.*

founds Civil Service Orchestral Society,
60

gifts on leaving Chapel Royal choir,
19

goes back to serious music, 66

his last Christmas, 255

holiday with Payne at Schandau, 25–6

hopes of again conducting Leeds
Festival frustrated by death, 248

how he tested Walter Browne's voice,
114

illness and death, 260 *et seq.*

impressed by *Martyrdom of St. Polycarp*, writes band parts from
memory, 14

Sullivan, Arthur Seymour, income of,
and his reckless generosity, 233

instance of his good nature, 130

involved in "a dangerous accident,"
256

Jubilee Medal sent to, 242

knighthood conferred on, 133

last weeks at Leipzig, 32

Legion of Honour for, 109

Lewis Carroll's request for collaboration with, 85–6

list of works in chronological order,
268 *et seq.*

love of the Turf and horses owned,
229–30, 232, 236, 257

lure of composition develops in, 27

method of work, 178

mistaken for boxer namesake, 152

moves into Queen's Mansions, Victoria
Street, 118

non-existent compositions by, 27

obituary notices and memoirs of, 286

on committee for relief of sufferers in
Franco-German War, 66

on the "expressiveness" of German
language, 19

opinion of his opera *Ivanhoe*, 206–7

organist at St. Michael's, Chester
Square, 38–9

origin of his first symphony, 46

ovation at Leeds Festival (1898), 247

partnership with Gilbert, 74

plays, by Royal command, at Duke of
Albany's wedding, 11 (note)

plays on great organ in Mormon
Tabernacle, 151

precautions against piracy of *Pirates* in
America, 104

Principal of National Training School
of Music, 78

professor of pianoforte and ballad
singing, 37

Promenade Concerts at Covent Garden
conducted by, 93

rapprochements with Gilbert, 145, 146,
203, 212, 213

reception in America, 98

re-elected Mendelssohn Scholar for
second year, 17, 19

refuses to engage foreign performers in
place of British, 78

rehearsal incidents recalled, 135

Index

Sullivan, Arthur Seymour, rewrites *Contrabandista* music with new songs, etc.; opera produced as *The Chieftain*, 232
round of visits during summer of 1884, 146
Royal Commissioner for Music at Paris Exhibition, 109
runs an unorthodox orcheſtra, 16
serenaded after Leeds Feſtival (1898), 247
sits to Millais for his portrait, 176
solo singing in Chapel Royal, 11
song-composition as a boy: a bishop's gratuity, 17
Spartan economy of, 24, 25
ſtudies grand opera at Covent Garden, 44–5
suffers from kidney trouble, 80, 91, 92, 106, 127, 137, 172–3, 214 *et seq.*, 236, 247
takes his phonograph to Sandringham, 192
teaches Chapel Royal boys, 37
Tennyson and, 57–60
terms on which copyrights of famous songs were sold, 41
three months in Egypt, 118 *et seq.*
thrilled by singing of Czar's Imperial Chapel Choir, 116
tireless energy of, 66–7, 70, 74, 79, 80, 106 (*and passim*)
two love affairs of, 71, 72
undergoes an operation, 95
views on preliminary expenses of *Gondoliers*: breach with Gilbert, 201 *et seq.*
visits Russia as gueſt of Duke of Edinburgh, 115 *et seq.*
voice-compass of, 10
will of, bequeſts in, 265
wins Mendelssohn Scholarship, 15
writes music for *Cox and Box* without fee, 63
Sullivan, Elizabeth (aunt), daily gifts from Napoleon to, 5
death at Bruges, 5 (note)
Sullivan, Frederic (brother), birth of, 3
and his father, 82
appears in Offenbach's *La Perichole*, 76
as Judge in *Trial by Jury*, 76, 81

Sullivan, Frederic (brother), criticizes *Messiah*, and Arthur's retort, 28
death of his widow, 148
his passion for children, 82
his widow marries again, 136
illness and death of, 81 *et seq.*
marriage of, 43
musical bent of, forsaken for drawing, 4
put out to nurse, 3
sends lines, for setting, to Sullivan, 27–8
violoncelliſt at firſt Handel Feſtival, 12
Sullivan, Herbert (nephew), adoption of, 124, 136
enters Polytechnic at Zurich, 147
Gilbert's kindness to, 266
Gilbert's letter of condolence on death of Sullivan, 265
part song written for, 60 (note)
telegraphed for on illness of his uncle, 216
Sullivan, John (uncle), birth of, 5
memories of return of his family from St. Helena, 6
Sullivan, Sergeant (grandfather), as Napoleon's guard at St. Helena, 5
becomes pensioner at Chelsea Hospital, 6
Sullivan, Mrs. (grandmother), firſt matron of Duke of York's School, 6
returns from St. Helena, 6
Sullivan, Thomas (father), affection for his wife, 3
appointed bandmaſter at Royal Military College, 4
at Kneller Hall, 7
at No. 8 Bolwell Terrace, 2, 3
birth of his sons, 3, 4
clarionette player at Surrey Theatre, 2
death of: Sullivan's grief, 50, 51
how he received news of Arthur's award of Mendelssohn Scholarship, 16
marriage of, 3
music-copying as means of supplementing income, 2, 3, 4
refuses Arthur's requeſt to join Chapel Royal, but, later, assents, 9
sacrifices for his children, 4, 32, 33
secures employment at Broadwoods, 32
tribute of colonel of Royal Military College to musical ability of, 5

Index

Sullivan, Thomas (father), visits Birmingham to hear *Kenilworth* cantata, 47

Sullivan, Mrs. Thomas (*née* Coghlan) (mother of Sir A. Sullivan), as governess, 3
apprised of success of *Pirates* in America, 102–4
Helmore's letters on Sullivan to, 13
her antipathy towards tobacco smoking, 82
illness and death of, 122–3
love-for her husband, 3
musical instincts of, 3

"Surprise March" re-named "Imperial March," 221

Surrey Theatre, 243 (note)
Sullivan's father as clarionette player at, 2, 3

Sutherland, Duchess of, 11

Swallow, Mr., 121

Sweet day, so cool (song), 270

Sweet Dreamer (English version of *Oh! ma charmante*), 274

Sweethearts (song), 41, 277

Symphony in E, the Irish (orchestral), 270

Symphony in E Flat, production of, 48

T

Taylor, John Franklin, shares apartments with Sullivan, 24–5

Tears, idle Tears (song), 282

Te Deum, Jubilate and Kyrie (in D), 270

Te Deum laudamus, a thanksgiving for victory, 257, 282

Te Deum laudamus and *Domine salvam fac Reginam*, 274

Te Deum laudamus, the Festival, 70

Tempest, The, music to, 269
first produced in Leipzig, 33
produced at Crystal Palace, 38, 40
re-scored by Sullivan, 36

Tender and true (song), 275

"Tender Shepherd" (hymn tune), 274

Tennyson, agreement with Sullivan to set cycle of songs, 57–8
and title of *The Foresters*, 214
desires cancellation of arrangement with Sullivan, 58
Odes by, set to music, 159, 171, 280
preface to his cycle of songs: Sullivan and, 59, 60
Sullivan's maid and, 58

"The Church has waited long" (hymn tune), 277

"The Son of God" (hymn tune), 272

"The Strain upraise" (hymn tune), 272

There is none like unto the God of Jeshurun (anthem), composed by Goss, completed by Sullivan, 279

There sits a Bird (song), 275

Thespis or The Gods Grown Old (comic opera), 273
music from, used in *Pirates of Penzance*, 69
short run of, 68

Thornton, Dr., Master at Cambridge University, 80

Thou art lost to me (song), 270

Thou art weary (song), 275

"Thou God of Love" (hymn tune), 271

Thou to Whom the sick and dying (tune to), 282

Thoughts (for Pianoforte), 269

Thou'rt passing hence (song), 77, 277

Through Sorrow's path (sacred part song), 273

Tigrane Bey, 119

Titiens, Mdlle., 61

"To mourn our Dead we gather here" (hymn tune), 282

To one in Paradise (song), 282

Toboganning in Canada, 107

Tosti, F. Paolo, praises *Ivanhoe*, 210

Tower of London, The, original title of *Yeomen of the Guard*, 173

Tower Warden, The, title changed to *Yeomen of the Guard*, 173

Trebelli, Mdme., 127

Tree, Mr. and Mrs. Beerbohm, 172, 229

Trial by Jury (dramatic cantata), 69, 277
composed in two weeks, 76
enthusiastic reception of, 76
revival of, 146

Trollope, Anthony, begs Sullivan to meet Miss Dalany, 79

Troubadour, The (song), 272

Turn Thee again (chorus adapted from Russian Church music), 275

Turn Thy Face (anthem), 278

Twilight (piano solo), 272

U

Ulmar, Miss Geraldine, her part in *Yeomen of the Guard*, 181

Index

"Ultor omnipotens" (hymn tune), 276
Upon the snow-clad Earth (carol), 278
Utopia Limited (comic opera), 281
  diary record of last stages of, 225–6
  double call for Gilbert and Sullivan at production of, 227
  fails in New York, 228
  preliminary expenses of, 221, 230
  produced at the Savoy, 227
  public rehearsal before production, 226
  run of, 228
  sketched plot submitted to Sullivan, 220
  withdrawal of, 228

V

"Valete" (hymn tune), 276
Venetian Serenade, 273
"Veni Creator" (hymn tune), 276
Venice visited by Sullivan, 193
"Venite" (hymn tune), 274
Viardot, Mdme., visit to, 42
"Victoria" (hymn tune), 282
Victoria and Merrie England (ballet), 236, 281
  national atmosphere of, 238
  produced at the Alhambra, 241
Victoria, Princess, poses as "Yum-Yum" in *Mikado*, 168
  Sullivan's birthday gift to, 170
Victoria, Queen, and obsequies of Sullivan, 264
  asks for complete set of Sullivan's works, 71
  commands Sullivan to play at wedding of Duke of Albany, 11 (note)
  concern at Sullivan's illness, 216
  condolences on death of Sullivan, 263
  confers knighthood on Sullivan, 133
  congratulations on success of *Ivanhoe*, 209
  Diamond Jubilee of, 239 *et seq.*
  hears *Golden Legend* and expresses her appreciation, 177
  her admiration of Mendelssohn's music, 36
  Jubilee of, 171
  requests copy of *Absent-Minded Beggar*, 252
  sends music by Prince Consort to Sullivan for correction, 71

Victoria, Queen, souvenir of an Easter Day service at Cimiez, 240
  tribute to *The Light of the World*, 74
  writes for music of *Mikado*, 158
Vienna, search for lost music of Schubert in, 52 *et seq.*
Village Chimes, The (song), 273
Violette, Paul, Gambetta's *valet-de-chambre*, 131–2

W

Wagner celebration at Bayreuth, 242–4
Walküre, Wagner's, Sullivan's opinion of, 243
Watchman, what of the Night? (sacred part song), 273
Way is long and drear, The (sacred part song), 273
We have heard with our ears (anthem dedicated to Smart), 26, 270
Weber, C. M. von, death in London, 37
"Welcome, happy Morning" (hymn tune), 274
Wellington, Duke of, a welcome gift from, 10
We've ploughed our land (song), 278
What does little Birdie say? (song), 271
When Love and Beauty (madrigal), 269
When thou art near (song), 278
White Plume, The (song), 274
Who is like unto Thee? (anthem), 132, 279
Will he come? (song), 41, 270
William I, German Emperor, 167–8
William of Prussia, Prince (afterwards Kaiser), a *Pinafore* air sung by, 117
  entertains Duke of Edinburgh and party, 117
  his telegram to Kruger, 257
  invited to express his opinion of *Mikado*, 156–7
Willow Song, The, 41, 269
Wilton, Lord, 11
Window, The: or the Songs of the Wrens (cycle of 12 songs), 273
Wreaths for our Graves (choral song), 281
Wyndham, Charles, at Sullivan's birthday dinner, 229

Y

Yeomen of the Guard or The Merryman and His Maid (comic opera), 280

Index

Yeomen of the Guard or The Merryman and His Maid, autograph score bequeathed to Royal College of Music, 265

discussion on a cut in, 180–1

enthusiastic reception of, 181

previous proposed titles of, 173

reconstruction of portion of, mars friendly relations between librettist and composer, 177

revival of, 228, 235

Sullivan at work on, 177 *et seq.*

York, Duchess of, Sullivan's fateful visit to, 260

York, Duke of (King George V), Sullivan's bequest to, 265

Yosemite Valley, a tour through, 151

You sleep (serenata), 280

Young Mother, The (songs), 275

Z

Zoo, The (comic opera), 277

music from, used in later operas, 79 (note)